3,500 GOOD QUOTES FOR SPEAKERS

An effective all-purpose reference book
for all those engaged in the art of speech-making.

3,500 GOOD QUOTES FOR SPEAKERS

by

Gerald F. Lieberman

THORSONS PUBLISHERS LIMITED
Wellingborough, Northamptonshire

First published in the United Kingdom 1984

Original American edition published by
Doubleday & Company, Inc., Garden City, New York.

© 1983 by GERALD F. LIEBERMAN

British Library Cataloguing in Publication Data

Lieberman, Gerald F.
  3,500 good quotes for speakers
  1. Quotations, English
  I. Title
  082   PN6081

ISBN 0-7225-0903-0

Printed and bound in Great Britain

To David and Jarrett

ACKNOWLEDGMENTS

I am indebted to many individuals and institutions for invaluable assistance in gathering much of the material that appears in this book. Special thanks go to the New York Public Library and its wonderful staff. I also owe a deep debt of gratitude to Bernard and Saul Miller for allowing me to use their private library, one of the finest repositories of specialized books and periodicals in the United States. I was the first person ever allowed unlimited access to this superb collection and the Miller brothers assured me that even though they are my landlords, their decision was based on my professionalism rather than any desire to collect the rent on time.

To Peter Kihss, my good friend and former colleague at the New York *Times,* goes a particular nod of gratitude; and to Dr. Murry Blum, Benjamin R. Katz of Baltimore, Leon S. Thiel, Laurie Jo Wojcik, and Lawrence J. Wojcik. I am also very grateful to my Doubleday editors—Gerard Helferich, Ferris Mack, and Peyton Moss—for listening patiently to my problems and offering first-rate suggestions when the going was rough.

And, finally, special credit goes to my wife, Sylvia, who never wavered from her wifely duties as the work progressed. She was a model of forbearance as I converted every room and article of furniture in our apartment to a work tool and archive, including closets, beds, and her vanity table. As these and other personal domains fell victim to the drive of annexation—such as the tops of the freezer, refrigerator, washing machine, dryer, and bathroom hamper—she remained patiently silent, muttering nary a word of protest. Well, hardly a word . . .

INTRODUCTION

The purpose of this book is to supply speakers, writers, students—and anyone else who feels the need—with pointed and often funny observations on the frailty of human behavior. I have also included enough general material to make this book an effective all-purpose tool for those whose requirements call for the less acerbic remark. But my cardinal aim was for a quote book of social criticism designed to comment on, and poke fun at, the human condition as it is today and will continue to be in the future—without overlooking the past.

To accomplish my purpose I searched through material from ancient to modern times for the cogent observations that may have served an identical purpose and now apply to contemporary society with equal, or perhaps greater, emphasis. Fame was not the criterion for inclusion here. I called on the well known, the little known, and the unknown; men and women who had something effective to say and proceeded to say it.

So you will find some entries that are subtle, sharp, volatile, and incisive, while others are blunt and hammerlike, eye-opening for the way they cut through evasiveness to tell more in a few sentences than entire books written on the same subjects. Because they are both substantive and spare, they will often evoke laughter and sometimes even tears.

This is also a book of ideas. While the quotations can stand on their own, they can also serve as the spark for more lengthy dissertations.

Public speaking and public speakers are a phenomenon of the times that all too often threatens to inundate us with a plethora of boredom and dullness—maybe because too many are doing it, but undoubtedly because so many are not doing it well. Aside from lack of preparation, the main reason for this ever-increasing rhetorical wasteland is the failure of the speaker to say things the audience would appreciate hearing, even if it means a temporary digression from the main topic. *The topic may be dull, but the speaker need not be.* And the speaker will avoid restiveness if he or she finds common ground with the audience.

Frankly stated, that most common of common ground is the hypocrisy of human behavior in everything we do, be it political, economic, or moral. It has been forced upon us by the atmosphere in which we live. And the speaker whose oratory skillfully acknowledges this, no matter the subject addressed, will fascinate and delight an audience. To assist in that direction is one of the key objectives of this book.

Gerald F. Lieberman

LIST OF SUBJECTS

Ability	23	Anatomy	31
Absence	23	Ancestry	32
Abstinence	23	Anger	32
Absurdity	24	Animals	32
Accent	24	Anniversary	33
Accident	24	Antiques	33
Achievement	24	Anti-Semitism	33
Action	24	Apology	33
Actor	24	Appearance	33
Actress	25	Applause	34
Address	25	Appointees	34
Ad lib	25	Argument	34
Admiration	25	Army	34
Adultery	26	Art	35
Advantages	26	Artist	35
Adventure	26	Assassination	36
Adversity	26	Atheist	36
Advertising	27	Author	36
Advice	27	Autobiography	36
Affair	28	Automobile	37
Affectation	28	Avarice	37
Affection	28	Awards	37
Age	28	Babies	37
Agnostic	30	Bachelor	38
Agree	30	Baldness	38
Alcohol	30	Banker	38
Alimony	30	Barber	38
Ambition	30	Bargain	39
America	31	Bastard	39

Beard	39	Character	49
Beauty	40	Charity	50
Bed	40	Charm	50
Behavior	40	Chastity	51
Belief	40	Children	51
Benefactor	41	Christian	52
Bible	41	Christmas	52
Bigamy	41	Church	52
Biography	41	College	52
Bi-sexual	41	Comedy	53
Blessing	41	Comfort	53
Blind	42	Common Sense	53
Boasting	42	Communication	53
Book	42	Communism	53
Bore	43	Company	54
Boredom	43	Complex	54
Boss's Son	43	Compliment	54
Brain	44	Conceit	54
Brevity	44	Conduct	55
Bribe	44	Conference	55
Broke	44	Confession	55
Broker	45	Confidence	55
Bureaucracy	45	Conformity	55
Bureaucrat	45	Confusion	56
Business	45	Congress	56
Cabinet (political)	46	Conquest	56
Candidate	46	Conscience	56
Cannibal	46	Conscription	57
Capital Punishment	47	Conservative	57
Career	48	Constitution	57
Caution	48	Contemptible	58
Celebrity	48	Contentment	58
Celibacy	48	Contract	58
Cemetery	48	Conversation	58
Censorship	48	Cook	58
Centerfold	49	Cooking	59
Ceremony	49	Corruption	59
Champagne	49	Cosmetics	59
Chance	49	Courage	60
Change	49	Court	60

13

CONTENTS

Courtship	61	Dogma	76
Coward	61	Doubt	76
Credit	61	Dream	76
Crime	62	Drink	76
Critic	63	Drugs	78
Criticism	64	Economics	78
Crowd	65	Economist	78
Culture	65	Economy	78
Curse	65	Editor	79
Custom	65	Education	79
Cynic	66	Egg	81
Dance	66	Ego	81
Death	66	Election	82
Debate	67	Eloquence	82
Debt	68	Emotion	82
Deception	68	Employment	82
Decision	68	Enemy	82
Decorator	68	Energy	83
Deed	69	England	83
Delinquent	69	Enterprise	84
Delusion	69	Entertainment	84
Demagogue	69	Environment	84
Democracy	69	Envy	84
Democrat	70	Epigram	84
Depression	70	Epitaph	85
Desire	70	Equality	86
Destiny	71	Escape	86
Devil	71	Ethics	86
Devotion	71	Eulogy	87
Diamond	71	Evidence	87
Diet	71	Evil	87
Different	72	Evolution	88
Dignity	73	Exaggeration	88
Diplomacy	73	Example	88
Disappointment	73	Excuse	88
Disease	73	Execution	88
Distance	74	Executive	89
Divorce	74	Exercise	89
Doctor	75	Expedience	89
Dog	75	Expense	89

Experience	89	Gold	106
Explanation	90	Golden Rule	107
Facts	90	Good	107
Failure	90	Gossip	107
Faith	90	Government	108
Fame	91	Government Spending	108
Familiarity	92	Grammar	108
Family	92	Gratitude	109
Fanaticism	92	Greatness	109
Fascism	93	Grief	110
Fashion	93	Hair	110
Fate	94	Happiness	110
Father	94	Hate	111
Favor	95	Health	111
Fear	95	Heaven	111
Fidelity	95	Heir	112
Fight	95	Hell	112
Finance	95	Help	112
Flattery	96	Hero	113
Flirtation	96	Hesitation	113
Folly	96	History	113
Food	96	Holiday	114
Fool	97	Hollywood	114
Foreign Aid	99	Home	115
Fortune	99	Honesty	115
France	99	Honeymoon	116
Freedom	99	Honor	116
Friendship	100	Hope	116
Funeral	101	Hospitality	117
Furniture	102	Hotel	117
Future	102	Humanity	117
Gallantry	102	Humility	117
Gambling	103	Humor	117
Game	103	Hunger	118
Genius	104	Hunting	118
Gentleman	104	Husband	118
German	105	Hypocrisy	118
Germany	105	Idea	119
Gift	105	Idealism	119
God	105	Ignorance	119

15

CONTENTS

Illness	120	Lawyer	133
Illusion	120	Leadership	135
Imagination	120	Liar	135
Immortality	121	Libel	135
Imperfection	121	Liberal	135
Impossible	121	Liberty	136
Income	121	Library	136
Indecision	121	Lie	136
Independence	121	Life	137
Inequality	122	Lips	138
Infidelity	122	Literature	139
Inflation	122	Living Together	139
Ingrate	123	Loan	139
Inheritance	123	Logic	139
Insanity	123	Loneliness	139
Inspiration	124	Looks	140
Insurance	124	Loser	140
Intelligence	124	Love	140
Invention	125	Love Letter	142
Investment	125	Lover	142
Ireland	125	Loyalty	142
Israel	126	Luck	143
Italy	126	Lying	143
Jealousy	126	Madness	144
Jew	126	Magic	144
Joke	127	Mail	144
Journalism	127	Majority	144
Journey	127	Man	144
Judge	127	Management	146
Judgment	128	Manners	146
Jury	128	Marriage	147
Justice	128	Masturbation	150
Kindness	129	Matchmaking	150
Kiss	129	Medication	150
Knowledge	130	Medicine	150
Lady	131	Mediocrity	151
Landlord	131	Membership	151
Language	131	Memory	151
Law	131	Mercy	152
Lawsuit	133	Metaphysics	152

Military	152	Nudity	167
Mind	153	Numbers	167
Minority	153	Nun	167
Miracle	153	Oath	167
Miser	154	Obituary	167
Misfortune	154	Obscenity	168
Mistake	154	Occupation	168
Mistress	155	Ocean	168
Mob	155	Odor	168
Moderation	155	Omen	168
Modesty	155	Opera	168
Monarchy	156	Opinion	169
Money	156	Opportunity	169
Monogamy	158	Opposition	170
Monopoly	158	Optimist	170
Monument	158	Orator	171
Morality	158	Originality	171
Mortgage	159	Orphan	171
Mother	159	Orthodoxy	171
Mother-in-law	159	Pain	172
Mouse	160	Parent	172
Movies	160	Paris	172
Murder	161	Partnership	172
Music	161	Passion	173
Mystery	162	Past	173
Mythology	162	Patience	173
Name	162	Patriotism	174
Nature	163	Peace	174
Necessity	163	Pedigree	175
Neighbor	163	People	175
Neutrality	164	Performance	176
News	164	Perseverance	176
Newspaper	164	Pessimist	176
New Year	165	Philadelphia	177
New York	165	Philanthropist	177
Noise	166	Philanthropy	177
Nomination	166	Philosopher	177
Non-Conformist	166	Philosophy	178
Nonsense	166	Physician	178
Nothing	166	Piety	178

Pilgrim	179	Prophet	193
Pioneer	179	Prosperity	193
Pity	179	Prostitution	194
Plagiarism	179	Protest	194
Plan	180	Proverb	194
Pleasure	181	Psychiatry	195
Poet	181	Psychoanalysis	195
Poetry	182	Publicity	195
Policy	182	Publishing	195
Politician	182	Punishment	196
Politics	183	Puritan	196
Pollution	185	Push	196
Polygamy	185	Quarrel	196
Popularity	185	Quotation	197
Posterity	185	Race	197
Poverty	186	Radical	198
Power	186	Railroad	198
Praise	187	Rascal	198
Prayer	187	Real Estate	199
Preaching	188	Reason	199
Preface	188	Rebellion	199
Prejudice	188	Recollection	200
President	189	Reform	200
Press	189	Reincarnation	200
Pride	189	Rejection	200
Principle	190	Religion	201
Prison	190	Remedy	202
Prize	190	Repentance	203
Problem	190	Report	203
Procrastination	190	Reporter	203
Producer	191	Republican	203
Profession	191	Reputation	204
Professor	191	Research	204
Profit	191	Resignation	205
Progress	191	Respect	205
Prohibition	192	Responsibility	205
Promise	192	Rest	205
Promptness	192	Restitution	205
Propaganda	193	Retirement	206
Property	193	Retreat	206

Retribution	206	Smoking	219
Retrospect	206	Snob	220
Revenge	206	Sobriety	221
Revolution	207	Socialism	222
Rich	208	Social Security	222
Rights	208	Society	222
Romance	208	Soldier	223
Rome	208	Song	223
Rumor	209	Soul	223
Russia	209	Soup	223
Sabbath	209	Space	224
Safety	210	Spain	224
Saint	210	Speaker	224
Salary	210	Specialist	224
Sanity	210	Speculation	224
Satire	211	Speech	225
Savage	211	Spelling	226
Scholar	211	Spinster	226
Scholarship	211	Sport	226
School	211	Spring	227
Science	211	Spy	227
Scotch	213	Stage	227
Secret	213	Statesman	228
Secretary	213	Statistics	228
Seduction	213	Status	228
Self-Control	214	Stock Market	230
Sensitive	214	Student	230
Sermon	214	Study	231
Servant	215	Stupidity	231
Sex	215	Style	232
Shakespeare	216	Subsidy	232
Shame	217	Substitute	232
Sight	217	Subway	232
Silence	217	Success	232
Silly	217	Suicide	235
Sin	217	Supermarket	235
Sincerity	218	Superiors	235
Slander	218	Superstition	236
Sleep	219	Surprise	236
Smile	219	Surrender	236

19

Survival	236	Truth	251
Suspicion	236	Tyranny	252
Swearing	237	Ugliness	253
Sympathy	237	Understanding	253
Tact	237	Undertaker	253
Talent	238	Unemployment	254
Tariff	238	Unhappiness	254
Taste	238	Union	254
Taxes	239	United Nations	255
Teacher	240	Universe	256
Tears	241	Unreliable	256
Television	241	Utilities	256
Temper	242	Vacation	256
Temperance	242	Valor	256
Temptation	242	Value	257
Texas	243	Vanity	257
Theater	243	Variety	258
Thief	243	Vegetarian	258
Think	243	Venereal Disease	258
Thought	244	Vice	258
Thrift	244	Vice-President (Corporate)	259
Time	245	Vice President (Political)	259
Timing	246	Victory	259
Title	246	Villain	260
Toast	246	Vindication	260
Togetherness	246	Violence	260
Tomorrow	246	Virgin	260
Tongue	247	Virtue	261
Town	247	Vote	262
Toy	247	Wages	262
Trade	247	War	263
Tradition	248	Washington, D.C.	264
Tragedy	248	Water	264
Transportation	248	Weakness	264
Travel	248	Wealth	265
Treason	249	Weapons	266
Trial	249	Weather	266
Triumph	250	Wedding	267
Trouble	250	Welfare	267
Trust	250	West	267

Whiskey	267	Witness	273
Whisper	267	Woe	273
Why	268	Woman	273
Wicked	268	Women's Lib	276
Widow	268	Word	278
Widower	268	Work	279
Wife	268	World	280
Will	269	Worry	280
Wind	270	Worship	281
Wine	270	Writer	281
Winning	270	Writing	282
Winter	270	Wrong	283
Wisdom	271	Yesterday	284
Wise	271	Youth	284
Wish	272	Zeal	285
Wit	272	Zoo	285

3,500
GOOD QUOTES
FOR SPEAKERS

ABILITY:

Ability is commonly found to consist mainly in a high degree of solemnity.

AMBROSE BIERCE

Ability is nothing without opportunity.

NAPOLEON

Some men have been worthy of a better century.

BALTASAR GRACIÁN

They are able because they think they are able.

VIRGIL

ABSENCE:

A short absence is safest.

OVID

Absence makes the heart grow fonder.

THOMAS HAYNES BAYLY

Absence, and a friendly neighbor, washeth away love.

ENGLISH PROVERB

Achilles absent was Achilles still.

HOMER

How like a winter hath my absence been
From thee, the pleasure of the fleeting year!
What freezings have I felt, what dark days seen!
What old December's bareness everywhere.

WILLIAM SHAKESPEARE

[See also Love, Man, Woman]

ABSTINENCE:

I can't drink a little, therefore I never touch it. Abstinence is as easy to me as temperance would be difficult.

SAMUEL JOHNSON

I went on a diet, swore off drinking and heavy eating, and in fourteen days I lost two weeks.

JOE E. LEWIS

[*See also* Diet, Drink, Manners]

ABSURDITY:

Every absurdity has a champion to defend it.

OLIVER GOLDSMITH

[*See also* Fool, Liar, Politician, Propaganda]

ACCENT:

To say "mither" instead of "mother" seems to many the acme of romance.

OSCAR WILDE

ACCIDENT:

Accidents will happen—that's why there are so many different kinds of croquettes.

Human life, its growth, its hopes, fears, loves, et cetera, are the result of accidents.

LORD RUSSELL

ACHIEVEMENT:

The world is divided into people who do things—and people who get the credit.

DWIGHT MORROW

Now landsmen all, whoever you
   may be,
If you want to rise to the top of
   the tree,
If your soul isn't fettered to an
   office stool,
Be careful to be guided by this
   golden rule—
   Stick close to your desks and
   never go to sea,
And you all may be Rulers of
   the Queen's Navee.

W. S. GILBERT

The only thing some people do is grow older.

ED HOWE

You aim for the palace and get drowned in the sewer.

MARK TWAIN

ACTION:

The beginning is the half of every action.

GREEK PROVERB

An act done against my will is not my act.

LATIN LAW MAXIM

ACTOR:

Some of the greatest love affairs

I've known involved one actor—unassisted.

WILSON MIZNER

When an actor has money he doesn't send letters, he sends telegrams.

ANTON CHEKHOV

In my last movie I played an unsympathetic character—myself.

OSCAR LEVANT

I'm now at the age where I've got to prove that I'm just as good as I never was.

REX HARRISON

I always wanted to be on the stage. I didn't want to do Hamlet so I did the next best thing, omelette. I laid eggs.

MAXEY ROSENBLOOM

I never said all actors are cattle, what I said was all actors should be treated like cattle.

ALFRED HITCHCOCK

An actor entering through the door, you've got nothing. But if he enters through the window, you've got a situation.

BILLY WILDER

The actor's tour was a great success. He outran every audience.

ACTRESS:

Actresses will happen in the best regulated families.

OLIVER HERFORD

Show me a great actor and I'll show you a lousy husband. Show me a great actress, and you've seen the devil.

W. C. FIELDS

ADDRESS:

A man without an address is a vagabond; a man with two addresses is a libertine.

GEORGE BERNARD SHAW

AD LIB:

His impromptus smell of the lamp.

PYTHEAS

It usually takes me more than three weeks to prepare a good impromptu speech.

MARK TWAIN

ADMIRATION:

Man's admiration for woman never flags. He will give her half his fortune. He will give her his whole heart. He appears willing to give her everything he possesses, except his seat on a streetcar.

HORACE PORTER

Americans adore me and will go on adoring me until I say something nice about them.

GEORGE BERNARD SHAW

We are all too ready to imitate the base and the depraved.

JUVENAL

ADULTERY:

In every affair consider what precedes and what follows.

EPICTETUS

You cannot tell your friend you've been cuckolded. Even if he doesn't laugh at you he may put the information to good use.

MICHEL DE MONTAIGNE

What men call gallantry, and gods adultery,
Is much more common where the climate's sultry.

LORD BYRON

You cannot pluck roses without fear of thorns,
Nor enjoy a fair wife without danger of horns.

BENJAMIN FRANKLIN

Some cheat by not cheating.

BALTASAR GRACIÁN

People say you mustn't love your friend's wife. But how are you to love your enemy's wife?

GEORGE MOORE

[See also Fidelity, Husband, Infidelity, Love, Man, Sex, Woman, Women's Lib]

ADVANTAGES:

Adam and Eve had many advantages, but the principal one was that they escaped teething.

MARK TWAIN

ADVENTURE:

Every man thinks meanly of himself for not having been a soldier, or not having been to sea.

SAMUEL JOHNSON

It is only adventurers that perform great actions, and not the sovereigns of large empires.

MONTESQUIEU

[See also Military, Soldier, War]

ADVERSITY:

Adversity has the effect of eliciting talents which, in prosperous circumstances, would have lain dormant.

HORACE

Adversity makes men think of God.

LIVY

Adversity is the trial of principle. Without it a man hardly knows whether he is honest or not.

HENRY FIELDING

By trying we can easily endure adversity. Another man's, I mean.

MARK TWAIN

In time of prosperity friends will
    be plenty;
In time of adversity not one in
    twenty.

ENGLISH PROVERB

[See also Charity, Friendship, Money]

ADVERTISING:

Advertising agency: eighty-five percent confusion and fifteen percent commission.

FRED ALLEN

Advertisement conquers all in our land, including the Stars and Stripes.

CHARLES MACARTHUR

The idea that you can merchandise candidates for high office like breakfast cereal is, I think, the ultimate indignity of the democratic process.

ADLAI E. STEVENSON

Commercial: The pause that depresses.

Doing business without advertising is like winking at a girl in the dark: You know what you are doing but nobody else does.

ED HOWE

[See also Propaganda]

ADVICE:

In giving advice I advise you, be short.

HORACE

One can give advice comfortably from a safe port.

JOHANN FRIEDRICH VON SCHILLER

To attempt to advise conceited people is like whistling against the wind.

THOMAS HOOD

Old men are fond of giving advice to console themselves for being no longer in a position to give bad examples.

FRANÇOIS DE LA ROCHEFOUCAULD

Don't give a woman advice; one should never give a woman anything she can't wear in the evening.

OSCAR WILDE

When a man comes to me for advice I find out the kind of advice he wants—and I give it to him.

JOSH BILLINGS

When a man seeks your advice he generally wants your praise.

LORD CHESTERFIELD

"Be yourself" is about the worst advice you can give to people.

TOM MASSON

A good scare is worth more to a man than good advice.

ED HOWE

It is always a silly thing to give advice, but to give good advice is fatal.

OSCAR WILDE

AFFAIR:

There are few people who are not ashamed of their love affairs when the infatuation is over.

FRANÇOIS DE LA ROCHEFOUCAULD

You may talk all you please about patriotism and religion, but a right good love affair moves a man more than anything else.

ED HOWE

[See also Adultery, Love]

AFFECTATION:

Almost every man wastes part of his life in attempts to display qualities which he does not possess.

SAMUEL JOHNSON

All affectation is the vain and ridiculous attempt of poverty to appear rich.

JOHANN CASPAR LAVATER

[See also Snob, Status]

AFFECTION:

All my life affection has been showered upon me, and every forward step I have made has been taken in spite of it.

GEORGE BERNARD SHAW

I could never learn to like her, except on a raft at sea with no other provisions in sight.

MARK TWAIN

[See also Love, Man, Woman]

AGE:

If youth had but the knowledge and old age the strength.

FRENCH PROVERB

When I was young I used to say good-natured things, and nobody listened to me. Now that I am old I say ill-natured things and everybody listens to me.

SAMUEL ROGERS

I am not young enough to know everything.

OSCAR WILDE

The longer thread of life we spin
The more occasion still to sin.
                    ROBERT HERRICK

In ancient times a woman was considered old at the age of forty. Today a woman of that age is only twenty-nine.

For the unlearned old age is winter; for the learned it is the season of the harvest.
                    THE TALMUD

A man of sixty has spent twenty years in bed and over three years in eating.
                    ARNOLD BENNETT

Middle age is the time when a man is always thinking that in a week or two he will feel as good as ever.
                    DON MARQUIS

The ten best years of a woman's life are between the ages of twenty-nine and thirty.
                    PETER WEISS

I refuse to admit that I am more than fifty-two, even if that does make my sons illegitimate.
                    LADY ASTOR

Grow old along with me!
The best is yet to be.
                    ROBERT BROWNING

The best years are the forties. After fifty a man begins to deterio-rate, but in the forties he is at the maximum of his villainy.
                    H. L. MENCKEN

Youth had been a habit of hers for so long that she could not part with it.
                    RUDYARD KIPLING

Whenever a man's friends begin to compliment him about looking young, he may be sure that they think he is growing old.
                    WASHINGTON IRVING

Forty is the old age of youth, fifty is the youth of old age.
                    VICTOR HUGO

Man fools himself. He prays for a long life, and he fears an old age.
                    CHINESE PROVERB

Old men are twice children.
                    GREEK PROVERB

No man is so old as to think he cannot live one more year.
                    CICERO

We look forward to a disorderly, vigorous, unhonored and disreputable old age.
                    DON MARQUIS

[*See also* Time, Youth]

AGNOSTIC:

I am an agnostic. I do not pretend to know what many ignorant men are sure of.

CLARENCE DARROW

[See also Faith, God, Religion]

AGREE:

My idea of an agreeable person is a person who agrees with me.

BENJAMIN DISRAELI

On one issue at least, men and women agree; they both distrust women.

H. L. MENCKEN

ALCOHOL:

Gasoline and alcohol don't mix—but try drinking them straight.

20TH CENTURY AMERICANA

[See also Drink, Sobriety]

ALIMONY:

You never realize how short a month is until you pay alimony.

JOHN BARRYMORE

She cried, and the judge wiped her tears with my checkbook.

TOMMY MANVILLE

Alimony is like buying oats for a dead horse.

ARTHUR "BUGS" BAER

Alimony: Bounty after the mutiny.

To whomsoever a man grants a thing (divorce), he grants that without which the thing cannot be enjoyed.

LATIN LAW MAXIM

Alimony: A gambling debt.

[See also Divorce, Man, Marriage, Woman]

AMBITION:

Every normal man must be tempted, at times, to spit on his hands, hoist the black flag, and begin slitting throats.

H. L. MENCKEN

Ours is a world where people don't know what they want and are willing to go through hell to get it.

DON MARQUIS

Everybody sets out to do something, and everybody does something, but no one does what he sets out to do.

GEORGE MOORE

Every French soldier carries the marshal's baton in his knapsack.

LOUIS XVIII

31

By working faithfully eight hours a day you may eventually get to be a boss and work twelve hours a day.
ROBERT FROST

One can never consent to creep when one feels an impulse to soar.
HELEN KELLER

There was a kid on the block who always wanted to be a pirate when he grew up. Today he is a doctor. He's lucky. Not every man realizes the ambitions of his youth.

[See also Opportunity]

AMERICA:

America is a large friendly dog in a small room. Every time it wags its tail it knocks over a chair.
ARNOLD TOYNBEE

America had often been discovered before Columbus, but it had always been hushed up.
OSCAR WILDE

The things that will destroy America are prosperity-at-any-price, safety-first instead of duty-first, the love of soft living, and the get-rich-quick theory of life.
THEODORE ROOSEVELT

Only Americans can hurt America.
DWIGHT D. EISENHOWER

America is the country where you buy a lifetime supply of aspirins and use it up in two weeks.
JOHN BARRYMORE

I don't know why vigor went out of America and why a con-man blandness replaced it.
BEN HECHT

Americans are like a rich father who wishes he knew how to give his sons the hardships that made him rich.
ROBERT FROST

A man who thinks of himself as belonging to a particular national group in America has not yet become an American.
WOODROW WILSON

It is rarely you see an American writer who is not hopelessly sane.
MARGARET ANDERSON

[See also Politics, Taxes]

ANATOMY:

We are all alike, on the inside.
MARK TWAIN

Anatomy is destiny.
SIGMUND FREUD

Between man and woman there is little difference, but *vive la différence.*
FRENCH PROVERB

[*See also* Man, Sex, Woman, Women's Lib]

ANCESTRY:

None of us can boast about the morality of our ancestors. The records do not show that Adam and Eve were married.

ED HOWE

She's descended from a long line her mother listened to.

GYPSY ROSE LEE

The sharp thorn often produces delicate roses.

OVID

Good wine needs no vine.

FRENCH PROVERB

He who boasts of his descent praises the deeds of another.

SENECA

Birth, ancestry, and that which you yourself have not achieved can hardly be called your own.

GREEK PROVERB

[*See also* Family, Snob, Status]

ANGER:

My liver swells with bile difficult to repress.

HORACE

A contest between relatives is usually conducted with more acrimony than a dispute with strangers.

LATIN PROVERB

When angry, count four; when very angry, swear.

MARK TWAIN

Never forget what a man has said to you when he was angry.

HENRY WARD BEECHER

ANIMALS:

Animals have these advantages over man: . . . they have no theologians to instruct them, . . . their funerals cost them nothing, and no one starts lawsuits over their wills.

VOLTAIRE

Mankind differs from the animals only by a little—and most people throw that away.

CONFUCIUS

I distrust camels, and anyone else who can go a week without a drink.

JOE E. LEWIS

Men are the only animals that devote themselves, day in and day out, to making one another unhappy.

H. L. MENCKEN

Animals are such agreeable friends, they ask no questions, they pass no criticisms.

GEORGE ELIOT

[*See also* Man, Woman]

ANNIVERSARY:

Most modern calendars mar the sweet simplicity of our lives by reminding us that each day that passes is the anniversary of some perfectly uninteresting event.

OSCAR WILDE

The very fact that we make such a to-do over golden weddings indicates our amazement at human endurance.

ILKA CHASE

ANTIQUES:

People do not become more valuable with age.

SAM LEVENSON

ANTI-SEMITISM:

If Christians were Christians there would be no anti-Semitism. Jesus was a Jew. There is nothing that the ordinary Christian so dislikes to remember as this awkward historical fact.

JOHN HAYNES HOLMES

[*See also* Christian, Jews]

APOLOGY:

To apologize is to lay the foundation for a future offense.

AMBROSE BIERCE

[*See also* Manners, Tact]

APPEARANCE:

Though patrician, he was also stupid.

GREEK PROVERB

Be careless in your dress if you must, but keep a tidy soul.

MARK TWAIN

Any man with a fine shock of hair, a good set of teeth, and a bewitching smile can park his brains, if he has any, and run for public office.

AMERICANA

Under a tattered cloak you will generally find a good drinker.

SPANISH PROVERB

First appearance deceives many.

PHAEDRUS

How holy people look when they are sea-sick!

SAMUEL BUTLER

Things are seldom what they seem.
Skim milk masquerades as cream.

W. S. GILBERT

An ape is an ape, a varlet's a varlet, though clothed in silk, or clothed in scarlet.

SPANISH PROVERB

[*See also* Beauty, Fashion]

APPLAUSE:

Excesses of applause never satisfy the sensible.

BALTASAR GRACIÁN

A yawn is a silent shout.

G. K. CHESTERTON

My advice to you concerning applause is this: enjoy it but never quite believe it.

ROBERT MONTGOMERY

[*See also* Actor, Actress, Ego, Flattery, Hollywood, Movies, Praise]

APPOINTEES:

Politics makes strange postmasters.

KIN HUBBARD

[*See also* Candidate, Politician, Politics]

ARGUMENT:

I always get the better when I argue alone.

OLIVER GOLDSMITH

You raise your voice when you should reinforce your argument.

SAMUEL JOHNSON

There is no sense in having an argument with a man so stupid he doesn't know you have the better of him.

JOHN RAPER

[*See also* Debate, Stupidity]

ARMY:

An army of sheep led by a lion would defeat an army of lions led by a sheep.

ARAB PROVERB

None but an armed nation can dispense with a standing army.

THOMAS JEFFERSON

A standing army is one of the greatest mischiefs that can possibly happen.

JAMES MADISON

Had we formed a permanent army in the beginning . . . we never should have had to retreat with a handful of men across the Delaware in '76.

GEORGE WASHINGTON

[*See also* Military, Soldier]

ART:

Art hath an enemy called ignorance.

BEN JONSON

Bad artists always admire each other's work.

OSCAR WILDE

Modern art is what happens when painters stop looking at girls and persuade themselves that they have a better idea.

JOHN CIARDI

It is not hard to understand modern art. If it hangs on a wall it's a painting, and if you can walk around it it's a sculpture.

The human face is my landscape.

JOSHUA REYNOLDS

Painting can illustrate, but it cannot inform.

SAMUEL JOHNSON

The English public, as a mass, takes no interest in a work of art until it is told that the work in question is immoral.

OSCAR WILDE

I may not understand, but I am willing to admire.

ANTHONY HOPE

A woman is fascinated not by art but by the noise made by those in the field.

ANTON CHEKHOV

Any authentic work of art must start an argument between the artist and his audience.

DAME REBECCA WEST

What garlic is to salad, insanity is to art.

AUGUSTUS SAINT-GAUDENS

If Botticelli were alive today he'd be working for *Vogue*.

PETER USTINOV

Good work rarely sells. I believe this of any art.

ARTHUR WING PINERO

The artistic atmosphere is everywhere. Even my cook cannot escape it. She came into the studio today and said: "About the potatoes for lunch, sir; will you have them in the jockets or in the nood?"

JAMES MONTGOMERY FLAGG

[*See also* Artist, Genius, Talent]

ARTIST:

What an artist the world is losing in me.

NERO

Every artist was first an amateur.

RALPH WALDO EMERSON

The great artists of the world are never Puritans, and seldom even ordinarily respectable.

H. L. MENCKEN

[*See also* Art, Genius, Talent]

ASSASSINATION:

Absolute monarchy: One in which the monarch does as he pleases as long as he pleases the assassins.

AMBROSE BIERCE

America is the place where you cannot kill your government by killing the men who conduct it.

WOODROW WILSON

[*See also* Crime, Criticism, Politics]

ATHEIST:

Irreligious men are often better suited for godly missions.

HASIDIC SAYING

[*See also* God, Religion]

AUTHOR:

A pin has as much head as some authors, and a good deal more point.

GEORGE D. PRENTICE

No author is a man of genius to his publisher.

HEINRICH HEINE

When I want to read a book, I write one.

BENJAMIN DISRAELI

Abuse is often of service. There is nothing so dangerous to an author as silence.

SAMUEL JOHNSON

The devil is the author of confusion.

ROBERT BURTON

The author who speaks about his own books is almost as bad as a mother who talks about her own children.

BENJAMIN DISRAELI

[*See also* Publishing, Writer, Writing]

AUTOBIOGRAPHY:

Autobiography at least saves a man or woman that the world is curious about from the publication of a string of mistakes called "Memoirs."

GEORGE ELIOT

An autobiography is the story of how a man thinks he lived.

HERBERT SAMUEL

If you don't advertise yourself you will be advertised by your loving enemies.

ELBERT HUBBARD

[Autobiographies are] recollections of gentlemen who tell us what they please, and amuse us, in their old age, with the follies of their youth.

GEORGE CRABBE

[*See also* Biography]

AUTOMOBILE:

If you drink like a fish, don't drive. Swim.

JOE E. LEWIS

He who looketh upon a woman loseth a fender.
SIGN IN AN AUTO COLLISION REPAIR SHOP

A careful driver is one who honks his horn when he goes through a red light.

HENRY MORGAN

A tree never hits an automobile except in self-defense.

AMERICAN PROVERB

In America the automobile has become a big hit—and they aim it pretty good in Europe too.

It seems to make an auto driver mad if he misses you.

KIN HUBBARD

An old-timer is one who remembers when it cost more to run a car than to park it.

Any car will last a lifetime, if you're careless enough.

[*See also* Transportation]

AVARICE:

Great abundance of riches cannot be gathered and kept by any man without sin.

ERASMUS

How much money is enough?
THE TALMUD

If money be not thy servant, it will be thy master. The covetous man cannot so properly be said to possess wealth, as that it may be said to possess him.

FRANCIS BACON

[*See also* Business, Love, Miser, Money]

AWARDS:

Shoot a few scenes out of focus. I want you to win the foreign film award.
BILLY WILDER to an American cameraman

[*See also* Hollywood, Movies]

BABIES:

There are no premature babies, only delayed weddings.

AMERICAN PROVERB

[*See also* Children, Family]

BACHELOR:

Call no man unhappy until he is married.

SOCRATES

By persistently remaining single a man converts himself into a permanent public temptation.

OSCAR WILDE

Bachelors know more about women than married men. If they didn't they'd be married, too.

H. L. MENCKEN

A bachelor never quite gets over the idea that he is a thing of beauty and a boy forever.

HELEN ROWLAND

[*See also* Man, Marriage, Sex, Woman]

BALDNESS:

A hair in the head is worth two in the brush.

OLIVER HERFORD

There's one thing about baldness, it's neat.

DON HEROLD

[*See also* Hair]

BANKER:

God knows I would willingly have become a banker, but I could never bring myself to that pass.

HEINRICH HEINE

The human species is composed of two distinct races: the men who borrow, and the men who lend.

CHARLES LAMB

Gentlemen, you are as fine a group of men as ever foreclosed a mortgage on a widow. I'm glad to be among you Shylocks.
WILL ROGERS (acknowledging an introduction at a bankers' convention)

Mark the blind folly of the usurer. If a man were to call him a scoundrel, he would fight him to the death. And yet he takes pen, ink, and paper, and in the presence of witnesses solemnly writes himself down as a rogue.

THE TALMUD

[*See also* Money]

BARBER:

What one experiences in a barber's shop the first time he enters one is what he always experiences in barbers' shops afterward till the end of his days.

MARK TWAIN

BARGAIN:

A woman will buy anything she thinks the store is losing money on.
KIN HUBBARD

One of the difficult tasks in this world is to convince a woman that even a bargain costs money.
ED HOWE

America's best buy for a nickel is a telephone call to the right man.
ILKA CHASE

People will buy anything that's one to a customer.
SINCLAIR LEWIS

Marriage is a bargain. And somebody has to get the worst of a bargain.
HELEN ROWLAND

What costs little is little worth.
BALTASAR GRACIÁN

BASTARD:

People are not born bastards, they have to work at it.
FRANK DANE

Everything worth having is either owned by bastards or the descendants of bastards.
GREGORY NUNN

Poor people send their children to school to be bastards. Rich people teach that at home.
GERALD BARZAN

Beware of bastards.
HINDU PROVERB

Money makes a bastard legitimate.
THE TALMUD

BEARD:

That ornamental excrement which groweth beneath the chin.
THOMAS FULLER

If Providence did beards devise
To prove the wearers of them wise,
A fulsome goat would then by nature
Excel each other human creature.
THOMAS D'URFEY

There was an old man with a beard,
Who said: "It is just as I feared—
Two owls and a hen,
Four larks and a wren,
Have all built their nests in my beard."
EDWARD LEAR

[See also Baldness]

BEAUTY:

In the eyes of a lover pockmarks are dimples.

JAPANESE PROVERB

The loveliest faces are to be seen by moonlight, when one sees half with the eye and half with the fancy.

PERSIAN PROVERB

Few girls are as well shaped as a good horse.

CHRISTOPHER MORLEY

I'm tired of all this nonsense about beauty being only skin deep. That's deep enough. What do you want, an adorable pancreas?

JEAN KERR

A beautiful woman is paradise for the eyes, hell for the soul, and purgatory for the purse.

SÉBASTIEN CHAMFORT

The only way to behave to a woman is to make love to her if she is pretty and to someone else if she is plain.

OSCAR WILDE

An ugly woman is a disease of the stomach, a handsome woman a disease of the head.

ITALIAN PROVERB

Love is a great beautifier.

LOUISA MAY ALCOTT

The beauty of most women is in-versely proportional to the distance of the observer.

The most beautiful things in the world are the most useless; peacocks and lilies, for instance.

JOHN RUSKIN

[See also Man, Sex, Woman]

BED:

No civilized person goes to bed the same day he gets up.

RICHARD HARDING DAVIS

No bed is big enough to hold three.

GERMAN PROVERB

[See also Sleep]

BEHAVIOR:

Few things are harder to put up with than the annoyance of a good example.

MARK TWAIN

[See also Manners, Tact]

BELIEF:

I can believe anything provided it is incredible.

OSCAR WILDE.

[See also Faith, Religion]

BENEFACTOR:

Take egotism out and you would castrate the benefactors.

RALPH WALDO EMERSON

[*See also* Charity, Philanthropist]

BIBLE:

When a politician swears on the Bible that a thing is so, and then immediately goes ahead and proves it, I know he's lying.

SAMUEL BONOM

BIGAMY:

Bigamy is one way of avoiding the painful publicity of divorce and the expense of alimony.

OLIVER HERFORD

[*See also* Alimony, Divorce, Monogamy]

BIOGRAPHY:

Biography is one of the new terrors of death.

JOHN ARBUTHNOT

Sinatra played my life in *The Joker Is Wild.* He had more fun playing it than I had living it.

JOE E. LEWIS

Biography is a region bounded on the north by history, on the south by fiction, on the east by obituary, and on the west by tedium.

PHILIP GUEDALLA

Every great man nowadays has his disciples, and it is always Judas who writes the biography.

OSCAR WILDE

It is, as I have long suspected, very difficult for a writer to write about anybody but himself.

H. L. MENCKEN

[*See also* Autobiography]

BI-SEXUAL:

There's nothing wrong with going to bed with somebody of your own sex. People should be very free with sex—they should draw the line at goats.

ELTON JOHN

Sensible persons enjoy alternating pleasures.

BALTASAR GRACIÁN

[*See also* Sex]

BLESSING:

No blessing lasts forever.

PLAUTUS

We mistake the gratuitous blessings of heaven for the fruits of our industry.

ROGER L'ESTRANGE

BLIND:

In the land of the blind those who are blessed with one eye are kings.

FRENCH PROVERB

Blessed are the blind, for they know not enough to ask why.

ERNEST RENAN

A good marriage would be between a blind wife and a deaf husband.

MICHEL DE MONTAIGNE

If the blind lead the blind, both shall fall into a ditch.

THE BIBLE

There's none so blind as they that won't see.

JONATHAN SWIFT

BOASTING:

Noise proves nothing. Often a hen who has merely laid an egg cackles as if she laid an asteroid.

MARK TWAIN

[See also Conceit, Ego, Egotist]

BOOK:

Everything comes to him who waits, except a loaned book.

KIN HUBBARD

I've given up reading books. I find it takes my mind off myself.

OSCAR LEVANT

The best thing in the famous novels at present is that one does not need to read them; one knows them already.

HENRY DAVID THOREAU

You can't tell a book by its movie.

HOLLYWOOD MAXIM

The drift of literary fiction is largely shown by the department store. The reader has gone slumming.

OPIE P. READ

Most contemporary books give the impression of having been manufactured in a day, out of books read the day before.

SÉBASTIEN CHAMFORT

I never read a book before reviewing it—it prejudices a man so!

SYDNEY SMITH

For a man who can't see an inch into human nature, give me a psychological novelist.

JOHN GALSWORTHY

The books that everybody admires are those that nobody reads.

ANATOLE FRANCE

Books have led some to learning and others to madness.

PETRARCH

'Tis pleasant, sure, to see one's
    name in print;
A book's a book, although there's
    nothing in't.

LORD BYRON

This book is dull, therefore it may be sold in Massachusetts.

ANONYMOUS REVIEW

There are two kinds of books: those that no one reads and those that no one ought to read.

H. L. MENCKEN

Never lend books, for no one ever returns them. The only books I have in my library are those that other folks have lent me.

ANATOLE FRANCE

Classic: A book which people praise and don't read.

MARK TWAIN

A room without books is a body without a soul.

CICERO

[*See also* Publishing, Writer, Writing]

BORE:

If you are a bore strive to be a rascal also, so that you may not discredit virtue.

GEORGE BERNARD SHAW

Somebody's boring me—I think it's me.

DYLAN THOMAS

A bore is a man who, when you ask him how he is, tells you.

FRANK DANE

BOREDOM:

Sometimes too much drink is barely enough.

MARK TWAIN

Like warmed-up cabbage served
    at each repast,
The repetition kills the wretch at
    last.

JUVENAL

BOSS'S SON:

An unlearned Prince is a crowned ass.

WILLIAM I

Pedantry carries a history of moral assertion no other field can boast, little of which is evident today. Gone is the attitude that knowledge is the preparation for experience; it is replaced by the pose that knowledge is a substitute for experience. The mark of the scholar is now only an embellishment to the status conscience, the key to a phenomenon known as boss's-sonism, a process whereby a young man newly academized starts at the top and works his say up.

GERALD F. LIEBERMAN

Beware of men who flourish with hereditary honors.

LATIN PROVERB

[*See also* Snob, Status]

BRAIN:

The brain is only one condition out of many on which intellectual manifestations depend.

THOMAS HENRY HUXLEY

We may thank Heaven that we have something better than our brains to depend on.

LORD CHESTERFIELD

What's on your mind? If you will forgive the overstatement.

FRED ALLEN

The brain is a wonderful organ. It starts working the moment you get up in the morning, and does not stop until you get into the office.

ROBERT FROST

BREVITY:

It is when I am struggling to be brief that I become unintelligible.

HORACE

In all pointed sentences some degree of accuracy must be sacrificed to conciseness.

OSCAR WILDE

BRIBE:

He fishes well who uses a golden hook.

LATIN PROVERB

A Triumph—when Temptation's Bribe
Be slowly handed back—
One eye upon the Heaven renounced—
And One—upon the Rack—

EMILY DICKINSON

Gold is more powerful than thunder. It forces a passage through the strongest barriers.

HORACE

[*See also* Politician]

BROKE:

No one ever went broke underestimating the taste of the American public.

H. L. MENCKEN

I was once so broke I forgot whether you cut steak with a knife or drank it with a spoon.

BOB HOPE

[*See also* Depression, Poverty]

BROKER:

With an evening coat and a white tie, anybody, even a stock broker, can gain a reputation for being civilized.

OSCAR WILDE

I do not regard a broker as a member of the human race.

HONORÉ DE BALZAC

Every time my broker advises me to buy stocks to go up they go down, every time he tells me to buy to go down they go up; it's lucky for him they can't go sideways.

GERALD F. LIEBERMAN

[*See also* Stock Market]

BUREAUCRACY:

If the first person who answers the phone cannot answer your question it's a bureaucracy. If the first person *can* answer your question, it's a miracle.

GERALD F. LIEBERMAN

BUREAUCRAT:

A bureaucrat is a Democrat who holds some office that a Republican wants.

ALBEN W. BARKLEY

BUSINESS:

The business of America is business.

CALVIN COOLIDGE

Where there is a sea there are pirates.

GREEK PROVERB

Unconscionableness, to define it, is a neglect of reputation for the pursuit of filthy lucre.

THEOPHRASTUS

One third of the people in the United States promote while the other two thirds provide.

WILL ROGERS

Business is so bad, even the accounts that don't intend to pay ain't buying.

GARMENT CENTER ADAGE

To get ten per cent out of some businessmen you have to be a fifty-fifty partner.

AMERICAN PROVERB

It is just as important that business keep out of government as that government keep out of business.

HERBERT HOOVER

For de little stealin' dey gits you in jail soon or late. For de big stealin' dey makes you emperor and puts you in de Hall o' Fame when you croaks.

EUGENE O'NEILL

He who has reaped the profits has committed the crime.

SENECA

Let the buyer beware.

LATIN MAXIM

There are very honest people who do not think they have had a bargain unless they have cheated a merchant.

ANATOLE FRANCE

It is well known what a middleman is; he is a man who bamboozles one party and plunders the others.

BENJAMIN DISRAELI

Business will get better, but we won't know it when it does.

HENRY FORD

Men with crooked fingers like Harpies seek from every stone an unholy gain. The sanctity of oaths has perished.

CERCIDAS

There is hardly anything in the world that some man cannot make a little worse, and sell a little cheaper.

JOHN RUSKIN

A little stealing is a dangerous part,
But stealing largely is a noble art;
'Tis mean to rob a hen-roost of a hen,
But stealing millions makes us gentlemen.

[See also Crime, Thief]

CABINET (POLITICAL):

My sayings are my own, my actions are my ministers'.

CHARLES II

[See also Appointees, Politics]

CANDIDATE:

The world is weary of statesmen whom democracy has degraded in politicians.

BENJAMIN DISRAELI

Never vote for the best candidate, vote for the one who will do the least harm.

FRANK DANE

[See also Democracy, Election, Politics]

CANNIBAL:

Whenever cannibals are on the brink of starvation Heaven, in its

47   CAPITAL PUNISHMENT

infinite mercy, sends them a nice plump missionary.

OSCAR WILDE

Albert Schweitzer's philosophy is that a sick, miserable African of today can be a strong healthy cannibal tomorrow.

JOE E. LEWIS

I have spoken of love. It is hard to go from people who kiss one another to people who eat one another.

VOLTAIRE

One Queen Artemisa, as old stories tell,
When depriv'd of her husband she loved so well,
In respect for the love and affection he'd show'd her,
She reduc'd him to dust and she drank the powd'r.
But Queen Netherplace, of a different complexion,
When call'd on to ord'r the fun'ral direction,
Would have eat h'r dead lor, on a slend'r pretense,
Not to show h'r respect, but to save the expense.

ROBERT BURNS

CAPITAL PUNISHMENT:

To reform a man is tedious and uncertain labor; hanging is the sure work of a minute.

DOUGLAS JERROLD

Gallows: A stage for the performance of miracle plays in which the leading actor is translated to heaven. In this country the gallows is chiefly remarkable for the number of persons who escape it.

AMBROSE BIERCE

In some states they no longer hang murderers. They kill them by elocution.

WILL ROGERS

It is sweet to dance to violins
    When love and life are fair:
To dance to flutes, to dance to lutes
    Is delicate and rare:
But it is not so sweet with nimble feet
    To dance upon the air.

OSCAR WILDE

Does the death sentence deter crime? It always deterred those who suffered from it.

It is no sin to kill a killer.

HINDU PROVERB

No man e'er felt the halter draw
With good opinion of the law.

JOHN TRUMBULL

Let the punishments of criminals be useful. A hanged man is good for nothing, but a man condemned to public works still serves the country, and is a living person.

VOLTAIRE

[*See also* Crime, Mercy, Punishment]

CAREER:

An endeavor to please elders is at the bottom of high marks and mediocre careers.

JOHN JAY CHAPMAN

There are only two ways of getting on in the world: by one's own industry, or by the stupidity of others.

JEAN DE LA BRUYÈRE

[*See also* Work]

CAUTION:

Put all your eggs in one basket and *watch that basket*.

MARK TWAIN

Be on your guard against a silent dog and still water.

LATIN PROVERB

There's always free cheese in a mousetrap.

CELEBRITY:

A celebrity is a person who works hard all his life to become well known, then wears dark glasses to avoid being recognized.

FRED ALLEN

Censure is the tax a man pays to the public for being eminent.

JONATHAN SWIFT

It is the usual ill-luck of all celebrities not to fulfill the expectations beforehand formed of them.

BALTASAR GRACIÁN

CELIBACY:

As to marriage or celibacy, let a man take which he will, he is sure to repent.

SOCRATES

Marriage has many pains, but celibacy has no pleasures.

SAMUEL JOHNSON

[*See also* Marriage, Sex]

CEMETERY:

The fence around a cemetery is foolish, for those inside can't get out and those outside don't want to get in.

ARTHUR BRISBANE

CENSORSHIP:

Censorship ends in logical completeness when nobody is allowed to read any books except the books nobody reads.

GEORGE BERNARD SHAW

CENTERFOLD:

The picture of a woman one knows is never so agreeable a companion as the picture of a woman one has never seen.

GEORGE MOORE

CEREMONY:

Nothing is more ridiculous or troublesome than mere ceremony.

FRENCH PROVERB

CHAMPAGNE:

If the aunt of the vicar
Has never touched liquor
Look out when she finds the champagne.

RUDYARD KIPLING

[See also Drink, Intoxication]

CHANCE:

A fool must now and then be right by chance.

WILLIAM COWPER

Even a clock that is not going is right twice a day.

POLISH PROVERB

CHANGE:

Change is not progress.

H. L. MENCKEN

It's hard for me to get used to these changing times. I can remember when the air was clean and sex was dirty.

GEORGE BURNS

There is no reason why the same man should like the same book at eighteen and at forty-eight.

EZRA POUND

If you want to make enemies, try to change something.

WOODROW WILSON

[See also Progress]

CHARACTER:

A rich man has no need of character.

HEBREW PROVERB

If a man's character is to be abused there's nobody like a relative to do the business.

WILLIAM MAKEPEACE THACKERAY

Underneath this flabby exterior is an enormous lack of character.

OSCAR LEVANT

The universe seems bankrupt as soon as we begin to discuss the characters of individuals.

HENRY DAVID THOREAU

CHARITY:

It is more blessed to give than to receive.

THE BIBLE

'Tis more blessed to give than to receive; for example, wedding presents.

H. L. MENCKEN

I have no faith, very little hope, and as much charity as I can afford.

THOMAS HENRY HUXLEY

In the United States doing good has come to be, like patriotism, a favorite device of persons with something to sell.

H. L. MENCKEN

The greatest pleasure I know is to do a good action by stealth and have it found out by accident.

CHARLES LAMB

Charity is the sterilized milk of human kindness.

OLIVER HERFORD

A man who spends ten thousand a year will do more good than a man who spends two thousand and gives away eight.

SAMUEL JOHNSON

Posthumous charities are the very essence of selfishness when bequeathed by those who, when alive, would part with nothing.

C. C. COLTON

Simple rules for saving money. To save half, when you are fired by an eager impulse to contribute to a charity, wait and count forty. To save three-quarters, count sixty. To save it all, count sixty-five.

MARK TWAIN

Who depends upon another man's table often dines late.

ITALIAN PROVERB

People will try anything if the price is right. A charity bazaar in New York once raffled off a traffic ticket.

[See also Philanthropist, Philanthropy]

CHARM:

If you have [charm], you don't need to have anything else; and if you don't have it, it doesn't much matter what else you have.

JAMES M. BARRIE

Everything that deceives may be said to enchant.

PLATO

The greatest mistake is trying to be more agreeable than you can be.

WALTER BAGEHOT

To captivate the masses is to ensnare the vulgar.

LATIN PROVERB

CHASTITY:

Of all sexual aberrations perhaps the most peculiar is chastity.
REMY DE GOURMONT

Chastity is curable, if detected early.
MOTTO ON A PUBLIC SCHOOL BOOK COVER

Give me chastity and self-restraint, but do not give it yet.
ST. AUGUSTINE

Coal that wrought swords for the Crusaders also heated casts of a family defender, the chastity belt.
GERALD F. LIEBERMAN

Chastity: the most unnatural of sexual perversions.
ALDOUS HUXLEY

[See also Virtue]

CHILDREN:

Wealth and children are the adornment of life.
THE KORAN

To the ass, or the sow, their own offspring appears the fairest in creation.
LATIN PROVERB

A child, when newly born.
But grown up, a thorn.
MALAY PROVERB

God help me, my own children have forsaken me!
JAMES II when told that his daughter Anne, as well as Mary, sided with William of Orange.

How sharper than a serpent's tooth it is
To have a thankless child!
WILLIAM SHAKESPEARE

The best way to keep children at home is to make the home atmosphere pleasant, and let the air out of the tires.
DOROTHY PARKER

The thorns which I have reaped are of the tree I planted.
LORD BYRON

Oh, what a tangled web we weave
When first we practice to conceive.
DON HEROLD

There is a mythological place where the population has remained constant some sixty years. Every time a baby is born somebody gets out of town.

Children begin by loving their parents; as they grow older they judge them; sometimes they forgive them.
OSCAR WILDE

Kids used to ask where they came from, now they tell you where to go.

Before I got married I had six theories about bringing up children; now I have six children, and no theories.

LORD ROCHESTER

[See also Family]

CHRISTIAN:

Christians are rare people on earth.

MARTIN LUTHER

Christendom has done away with Christianity without being quite aware of it.

SØREN KIERKEGAARD

If Christian nations were nations of Christians there would be no wars.

SOAME JENYNS

The Christian ideal has not been tried and found wanting, it has been found difficult and left untried.

G. K. CHESTERTON

Christianity is completed Judaism, or it is nothing.

BENJAMIN DISRAELI

Christianity, with its doctrine of humility, of forgiveness, of love, is incompatible with the state, with its haughtiness, its violence, its punishment, its wars.

LEO TOLSTOY

[See also Church, Faith, Religion]

CHRISTMAS:

Mail your packages early, so the post office can lose them in time for Christmas.

JOHNNY CARSON

It was always said of him, that he knew how to keep Christmas well.

CHARLES DICKENS

Christmas comes, but once a year is enough.

AMERICAN PROVERB

CHURCH:

Where God has his church, the Devil will have his chapel.

SPANISH PROVERB

A church is a place in which gentlemen who have never been to heaven brag about it to persons who will never get there.

H. L. MENCKEN

[See also Christian, Faith, Religion]

COLLEGE:

You've got to educate him first. You can't expect a boy to be vicious till he's been to a good school.

H. H. MUNRO

A set o' dull conceited hashes
Confuse their brains in college
    classes;
They gang in stirks, and come out
    asses.

ROBERT BURNS

Hamlet is the tragedy of tackling
a family problem too soon after college.

TOM MASSON

Colleges don't make fools, they
only develop them.

GEORGE HORACE LORIMER

The boastful blockhead ignorantly
    read,
With loads of learned lumber in
    his head.

ALEXANDER POPE

Knowledge without sense is doubly folly.

BALTASAR GRACIÁN

A university is an institution that
has two thousand seats in the class-
rooms and eighty thousand in the
stadium.

You don't get fired for cheating,
you get fired for losing.
DARRYL ROGERS, head football
coach, Arizona State

You can always tell a Harvard
man—but you can't tell him much.

You can lead a boy to college but
you cannot make him think.

ELBERT HUBBARD

[*See also* Education, School]

COMEDY:

Life is a tragedy for those who
feel, and a comedy for those who
think.

JEAN DE LA BRUYÈRE

[*See also* Jokes, Life]

COMFORT:

Give us the luxuries of life and
we will dispense with the necessities.
OLIVER WENDELL HOLMES

COMMON SENSE:

Common sense makes men, the
rest is all rubbish.

PETRONIUS

Common sense could prevent
most divorces. Also most marriages.

COMMUNICATION:

The world ain't getting no worse,
we've only got better facilities.

KIN HUBBARD

COMMUNISM:

Communism is in conflict with
human nature.

ERNEST RENAN

If you are not a Marxist when you are twenty you are not too bright. If you are still a Marxist at forty you're still not too bright.

ANONYMOUS ANGOLAN GUERRILLA

Communism is the death of the soul . . . it is committed to making tyranny universal.

ADLAI E. STEVENSON

COMPANY:

Every man is like the company he is wont to keep.

EURIPIDES

In our society a man is known by the company he owns.

GERALD F. LIEBERMAN

A man should not so much respect what he eats as with whom he eats.

MICHEL DE MONTAIGNE

Nothing annoys a woman more than to have company drop in unexpectedly and find the house looking as it usually does.

FRANK DANE

[See also Friendship]

COMPLEX:

No man can ever end with being superior who will not begin with being inferior.

SYDNEY SMITH

If you think the world is against you, it doesn't necessarily mean that it isn't.

COMPLIMENT:

Some people pay a compliment as if they expected a receipt.

KIN HUBBARD

When you cannot get a compliment in any other way, pay yourself one.

MARK TWAIN

I can live for two months on a good compliment.

MARK TWAIN

CONCEIT:

I think mankind by thee would be
    less bored
If only thou wert not thine own
    reward.

JOHN KENDRICK BANGS

He was like a cock who thought the sun had risen to hear him crow.

GEORGE ELIOT

There is nothing you and I make so many blunders about, and the world so few, as the actual amount of our importance.

JOSH BILLINGS

Conceit is incompatible with understanding.

LEO TOLSTOY

[*See also* Ego]

CONDUCT:

It's no use growing older if you only learn new ways of misbehaving yourself.

H. H. MUNRO

Anybody can be good in the country.

OSCAR WILDE

Almost all absurdity of conduct arises from the imitation of those we cannot resemble.

SAMUEL JOHNSON

CONFERENCE:

A conference is a gathering of important people who singly can do nothing but together can decide that nothing can be done.

FRED ALLEN

Conference: Hot air on a high level.

GERALD BARZAN

[*See also* United Nations]

CONFESSION:

Confession may be good for the soul but it is bad for the reputation.

THOMAS R. DEWAR

The more sins you confess, the more books you will sell.

AMERICAN PROVERB

Religious people spend so much time with their confessors because they like to talk about themselves.

MARQUISE DE SÉVIGNÉ

CONFIDENCE:

You have noticed that the less I know about a subject the more confidence I have; and the more light I throw on it.

MARK TWAIN

Confidence is the thing you had before you knew better.

[*See also* Ego, Success]

CONFORMITY:

To rebel in season is not to rebel.

GREEK PROVERB

There is no conversation more boring than one where everybody agrees.

MICHEL DE MONTAIGNE

Lots of times you have to pretend to join a parade in which you are really not interested in order to get where you're going.

CHRISTOPHER MORLEY

We know what happens to people who stay in the middle of the road. They get run over.

ANEURIN BEVAN

[*See also* Non-Conformist]

CONFUSION:

Pandemonium did not reign; it poured.

JOHN KENDRICK BANGS

Expert: Someone who brings confusion to simplicity.

GREGORY NUNN

CONGRESS:

It could probably be shown by facts and figures that there is no distinctly native criminal class except Congress.

MARK TWAIN

Reader, suppose you were an idiot. And suppose you were a member of Congress. But I repeat myself.

MARK TWAIN

There are two enemies to every bill proposed in Congress—the fools who favor it and the lunatics who oppose it.

With Congress, every time they make a joke it's a law, and every time they make a law it's a joke.

WILL ROGERS

Representative: In national politics, a member of the Lower House in this world, and without discernible hope of promotion in the next.

AMBROSE BIERCE

[*See also* Lies, Politician, Politics]

CONQUEST:

I am the man who has given you more kingdoms than you had towns before.

CORTEZ, to Charles V, who asked who Cortez was

He conquers twice who conquers himself in victory.

PUBLIUS SYRUS

[*See also* War]

CONSCIENCE:

Conscience and cowardice are really the same things.

OSCAR WILDE

Conscience: The inner voice that warns us that someone may be looking.

H. L. MENCKEN

God may forgive your sins but your nervous system won't.

CONSCRIPTION:

I have already given two cousins to the war and I stand ready to sacrifice my wife's brother.

ARTEMUS WARD

We must train and classify the whole of our male citizens, and make military instruction a regular part of collegiate education. We can never be safe till this is done.

THOMAS JEFFERSON

CONSERVATIVE:

A conservative is a fellow who thinks a rich man should have a square deal.

FRANK DANE

A conservative is a man who wants the rules changed so no one can make a pile the way he did.

GREGORY NUNN

[A Conservative is] a statesman who is enamored of existing evils, as distinguished from the Liberal, who wishes to replace them with others.

AMBROSE BIERCE

A conservative is a man with two perfectly good legs, who has never learned to walk.

FRANKLIN D. ROOSEVELT

Some fellows get credit for being conservative when they are only stupid.

KIN HUBBARD

Men who are orthodox when they are young are in danger of being middle-aged all their lives.

WALTER LIPPMANN

Conservatism, being an upper-class characteristic, is decorous; and conversely innovation, being a lower-class phenomenon, is vulgar.

THORSTEIN VEBLEN

Loyalty to petrified opinion never yet broke a chain or freed a human soul.

MARK TWAIN

A conservative is a man who will not look at the new moon, out of respect for that ancient institution, the old one.

DOUGLAS JERROLD

[See also Liberal]

CONSTITUTION:

My constitution grows worse, even worse than the constitution of Prussia.

HEINRICH HEINE

The American Constitution is the most wonderful work ever struck off at a given time by the brain and purpose of man.

WILLIAM GLADSTONE

The American Constitution is not really a constitution but a Charter of Anarchism. . . . It was a guarantee to the whole American nation that it never should be governed at all.

GEORGE BERNARD SHAW

[*See also* Democracy]

CONTEMPTIBLE:

There is no being so poor and contemptible, who does not think there is somebody still poorer and still more contemptible.

SAMUEL JOHNSON

[*See also* Bastard]

CONTENTMENT:

Strange how little a while a person can be contented.

MARK TWAIN

Never be content with your lot, try for a lot more.

AMERICAN PROVERB

CONTRACT:

An agreement that is binding only on the weaker party.

The large print giveth and the small print taketh away.

CONVERSATION:

A single conversation with a wise man is better than ten years of study.

CHINESE PROVERB

Conversation is a serious matter. There are men with whom an hour's talk would weaken one more than a week's fasting.

19TH CENTURY ENGLISH, uncredited

[*See also* Speech]

COOK:

There is one thing more exasperating than a wife who can cook and won't and that's a wife who can't cook and will.

ROBERT FROST

The only good thing about him is his cook. The world visits his dinners, not him.

MOLIÈRE

God sends meat—the Devil sends cooks.

CHARLES VI

We may live without friends; we may live without books;
But civilized man cannot live without cooks.

OWEN MEREDITH

[*See also* Cooking, Food]

COOKING:

There is death in the pot.
THE BIBLE

Do not overdo what has already been overdone.
TERENCE

A practical cookbook is one that has a blank page in the back—where you list the numbers of the nearest delicatessen.

Homemade dishes drive one from home.
THOMAS HOOD

The only premarital thing girls don't do these days is cooking.
OMAR SHARIF

[See also Cook, Food]

CORRUPTION:

The more corrupt the state, the more numerous the laws.
TACITUS

If you steal something small you are a petty thief, but if you steal millions you are a gentleman of society.
GREEK PROVERB

Shall a few designing men, for their own aggrandizement, and to gratify their own avarice, overset the goodly fabric we have been rearing at the expense of so much time,

blood, and treasure? And shall we at last become victims of our own lust of gain?
GEORGE WASHINGTON

I think I can say, and say with pride, that we have some legislatures that bring higher prices than any in the world.
MARK TWAIN

All great calamities on land and sea have been traced to inspectors who did not inspect.
KIN HUBBARD

When it comes to corruption, nothing succeeds like money.
AMERICAN PROVERB

[See also Congress, Crime, Law, Lawyer, Philanthropist, Philanthropy, Politician, Politics]

COSMETICS:

Money is the best cosmetic.
INTERNATIONAL PROVERB

[Be it resolved] that all women, of whatever age, rank, profession, or degree; whether virgin maids or widows; that shall after the passing of this act, impose upon and betray into matrimony any of His Majesty's male subjects, by scents, paints, cosmetics, washes, artificial teeth, false hair, Spanish wool, iron stays, hoops, high-heeled shoes, or bolstered hips, shall incur the penalty of the laws now in force against witchcraft, sorcery, and such like misdemeanors, and that the marriage, upon conviction, shall stand null and void.

BY ACT OF PARLIAMENT, 1670

Nature scarcely ever gives us the very best; for that we must have recourse to art.

BALTASAR GRACIÁN

Perfume: Any smell that is used to drown a worse one.

ELBERT HUBBARD

[*See also* Beauty, Ugliness]

COURAGE:

He was a bold man who first swallowed an oyster.

JAMES I

Name me an emperor who was ever struck by a cannon-ball.

CHARLES V

Fortune favors the bold.

JUVENAL

If men knew all that women think, they'd be twenty times more daring.

ALPHONSE KARR

I never thought much of the courage of a lion-tamer. Inside the cage he is at least safe from people.

GEORGE BERNARD SHAW

Muster your wits; stand in your own defence;
Or hide your heads like cowards, and fly hence.

WILLIAM SHAKESPEARE

No man in the world has more courage than the man who can stop after eating one peanut.

CHANNING POLLOCK

One of our American wits said that it took only half as long to train an American army as any other, because you had only to train them to go one way.

WOODROW WILSON

To bear other people's afflictions, everyone has courage and enough to spare.

BENJAMIN FRANKLIN

If you stand up to be counted, someone will take your seat.

[*See also* Coward]

COURT:

A court is an assembly of noble and distinguished beggars.

CHARLES MAURICE DE TALLEYRAND

In America a court is an assembly of noble and distinguished grafters.

GREGORY NUNN

A receiver is appointed by the court to take what's left.

ROBERT FROST

[*See also* Jury, Justice, Law, Lawyer]

COURTSHIP:

It is assumed that the woman must wait, motionless, until she is wooed. That is how the spider waits for the fly.

GEORGE BERNARD SHAW

I found the ideal girl. Her father is a bookmaker and her brother owns a liquor store.

JOE E. LEWIS

The days just prior to marriage are like a snappy introduction to a tedious book.

WILSON MIZNER

A fool and her money are soon courted.

HELEN ROWLAND

Nothing upsets a woman like somebody getting married she didn't even know had a beau.

KIN HUBBARD

COWARD:

The human race is a race of cowards; and I am not only marching in that procession but carrying a banner.

MARK TWAIN

It's better to be killed than frightened to death.

ROBERT SMITH SURTEES

Cowards die many times before their deaths;
The valiant never taste of death but once.

WILLIAM SHAKESPEARE

To know what is right and not do it is the worst cowardice.

CONFUCIUS

There are several good protections against temptations but the surest is cowardice.

MARK TWAIN

[*See also* Courage]

CREDIT:

Credit is a system whereby a person who can't pay gets another person who can't pay to guarantee that he can pay.

CHARLES DICKENS

Let us all be happy and live within our means, even if we have to borrow to do it.

ARTEMUS WARD

You can take a chance with any man who pays his bills on time.

TERENCE

Who recalls when folks got along without something if it cost too much?

KIN HUBBARD

The creditor hath a better memory than the debtor.

JAMES HOWELL

Some people use one half their ingenuity to get into debt, and the other half to avoid paying it.

GEORGE D. PRENTICE

A bank is a place where they lend you an umbrella in fair weather and ask for it back again when it begins to rain.

ROBERT FROST

No man's credit is as good as his money.

ED HOWE

[See also Debt]

CRIME:

Save a thief from the gallows and he will be the first to cut your throat.

ITALIAN PROVERB

Most people fancy themselves innocent of those crimes of which they cannot be convicted.

SENECA

When a man commits the same crime twice, and is not punished, it seems to him permissible.

THE TALMUD

In the twenties there were persistent rumors of young doctors being tried in medical society star chamber proceedings, their crime being that of treating patients for indigestion when they could well have afforded appendicitis.

In France we leave unmolested those who set fire to the house and persecute those who sound the alarm.

SÉBASTIEN CHAMFORT

It is to their crimes that most great men are indebted for their gardens, their palaces, their tables, their fine old plate—their love.

LATIN PROVERB

Of all tasks of government the most basic is to protect its citizens against violence.

JOHN FOSTER DULLES

He's a good boy; everything he steals he brings right home to mother.

FRED ALLEN

Crime expands according to our willingness to put up with it.

BARRY FARBER

Many commit the same crime with very different results. One bears a cross for his crime, the other a crown.

JUVENAL

If you do big things they print your face, and if you do little things they only print your thumbs.

ARTHUR "BUGS" BAER

Every once in a while some feller without a single bad habit gets caught.

KIN HUBBARD

The punishment of the criminal is measured by the degree of astonishment of the judge who finds his crime incomprehensible.

FRIEDRICH NIETZSCHE

[See also Corruption, Politician, Thief]

CRITIC:

A drama critic is a person who surprises the playwright by informing him what he meant.

WILSON MIZNER

Those who have free seats at a play hiss first.

CHINESE PROVERB

A critic is a legless man who teaches running.

CHANNING POLLOCK

What a blessed thing it is that nature, when she invented, manufac-
tured and patented her authors, contrived to make critics out of the chips that were left.

OLIVER WENDELL HOLMES

They condemn what they do not understand.

CICERO

I always get the heaves in the presence of critics.

GENE FOWLER

Critics! . . . Those cut-throat bandits in the paths of fame.

ROBERT BURNS

It is easier to pull down than to build up.

LATIN PROVERB

As soon
Seek roses in December—ice in June;
Hope constancy in wind, or corn in chaff;
Believe a woman or an epitaph, Or any other thing that's false, before
You trust in critics.

LORD BYRON

When a book and a head come into contact and one of them sounds hollow, is it always the book?

ARTHUR SCHOPENHAUER

I look upon reviews as a kind of children's disease which more or less attacks newborn books. There are cases on record where the healthiest have succumbed to them, and the puniest have often survived them.

G. C. LICHTENBERG

They get excited about the sort of stuff I could get shooting through a piece of Kleenex.

BILLY WILDER, on critics who praise foreign cinematography

Has anybody ever seen a dramatic critic in the daytime? Of course not. They come out after dark, up to no good.

P. G. WODEHOUSE

Don't abuse your friends and expect them to consider it criticism.

ED HOWE

CRITICISM (BY CRITICS):

Chuang Tzu was born in the fourth century before Christ. The publication of his book in English, two thousand years after his death, is obviously premature.

OSCAR WILDE

Excellent, were it not for its length.

SÉBASTIEN CHAMFORT, on a couplet

Corneille is to Shakespeare as a clipped hedge is to a forest.

SAMUEL JOHNSON

A vast improvement can be made in the third act. Instead of the hero dying on the scaffold he should be shot by a firing squad. It would not only wake up the audience but it would let them know the show is over.

ANON

He isn't the kind of performer who stops a show; he is content to merely slow it up.

ANON

They couldn't find the artist, so they hung the picture.

ANON

A man shot himself to death in a movie house. We believe we saw that picture.

ANON

You can stay away anytime because it's continuous.

ANON

The House Beautiful is the play lousy.

DOROTHY PARKER

The dogs were poorly supported by the rest of the cast.

DON HEROLD, review of *Uncle Tom's Cabin*

In the film version of *Kiss the Boys Goodbye* the producers have kept the boys and kissed the script goodbye.

NEW YORK *Times,* uncredited

It was one of those plays in which the actors unfortunately enunciated very clearly.

ROBERT BENCHLEY

The rattlings of the milk-cans of human kindness.
PHILIP GUEDALLA, on the writing of James M. Barrie

The covers of this book are too far apart.

AMBROSE BIERCE

March came in like a lion and went out like a ham.
FRANK NUGENT, of Fredric March in *The Buccaneer*

The title of *Wake Up and Live* ought to be changed to *Wake Up and Leave*.

WALTER WINCHELL

CROWD:

Far from the madding crowd's ignoble strife.

THOMAS GRAY

The thing which in the subway is called congestion is highly esteemed in the night spots as intimacy.

[*See also* Subway]

CULTURE:

There is a difference between culture and taste.

QUINTILIAN

The test of a man or woman's breeding is how they behave in a quarrel.

GEORGE BERNARD SHAW

Training is everything. The peach was once a bitter almond; cauliflower is nothing but cabbage with a college education.

MARK TWAIN

[*See also* Manners, Snob, Status]

CURSE:

Work is the curse of the drinking class.

OSCAR WILDE

Let us be grateful to Adam: He cut us out of the blessing of idleness and won for us the curse of labor.

MARK TWAIN

CUSTOM:

It is a custom
More honoured in the breach than the observance.

WILLIAM SHAKESPEARE

When thou enter a city abide by its customs.

THE TALMUD

[*See also* Tradition]

CYNIC:

A cynic is a man who, when he smells flowers, looks around for a coffin.

H. L. MENCKEN

Cynicism is intellectual dandyism.

GEORGE MEREDITH

DANCE:

Since the dubious dawn of human history dancing has been one of the more adroit female ruses for the sexual stimulation of the male. A young woman who embraces a man while he is being assailed by primitive drum beats and bacchanalian horn tootings may pretend she is interested only in the technique of dancing. I wonder if the same woman, naked in bed with a man, would insist that she is only testing the mattress.

MAXWELL BODENHEIM

I don't think much of a dance step where the girl looks like she was being carried out of a burning building.

KIN HUBBARD

DEATH:

A person who can break wind is not dead.

JEAN-JACQUES ROUSSEAU

If your time ain't come not even a doctor can kill you.

AMERICAN PROVERB

We are but tenants and shortly the great Landlord will give us notice that our lease has expired.

JOSEPH JEFFERSON

My idea of walking into the jaws of death is marrying some woman who's lost three husbands.

KIN HUBBARD

Live your life, do your work, then take your hat.

HENRY DAVID THOREAU

I am dying beyond my means.

OSCAR WILDE

Strange, is it not, that of the myriads who
Before us pass'd the door of darkness through,
Not one returns to tell us of the road
Which to discover we must travel too.

OMAR KHAYYÁM

Into the darkness they go, the wise and the lovely.

EDNA ST. VINCENT MILLAY

Whom the gods favor die young.
                              PLAUTUS

For he who lives more lives than
    one
More deaths than one must die.
                         OSCAR WILDE

Except for the young or very
happy, I can't say I am sorry for
anyone who dies.
WILLIAM MAKEPEACE THACKERAY

I am going to seek a great perhaps.
FRANÇOIS RABELAIS, his dying words

Do not weep, my friend. If I want
anything up there, I'll ring for you.
DUMAS THE ELDER, on his death-
bed, to a weeping servant

His death, which happened in his
    berth,
    At forty-odd befell:
They went and told the sexton,
    and
The sexton tolled the bell.
                        THOMAS HOOD

Farewell, my good master, home-
ward I fly:
One day thou shall gain the same
    freedom as I.
              JELALEDDIN OF PERSIA

You cannot live without lawyers,
and certainly you cannot die without
them.
            JOSEPH HODGES CHOATE

Men have a much better time of it
than women; for one thing they
marry later; for another thing they
die earlier.
                      H. L. MENCKEN

I didn't know he was dead, I
thought he was British.

There is no cure for death, save to
enjoy the interval.
                 GEORGE SANTAYANA

It matters not how a man dies, but
how he lives.
                   SAMUEL JOHNSON

It is not death that alarms me, but
dying.
             MICHEL DE MONTAIGNE

There's a thing that keeps surpris-
ing you about stormy old friends
after they die: their silence.
                        BEN HECHT

It's all the same in the end.
                       TITUS OATES

If death did not exist . . . it
would be necessary to invent it.
                    J. B. MILHAUD

DEBATE:

It is not necessary to understand
things in order to argue about them.
          PIERRE DE BEAUMARCHAIS

Never argue with a fool, people might not know the difference.

[*See also* Eloquence, Speech]

DEBT:

Never run into debt, not if you can find anything else to run into.
JOSH BILLINGS

When I was born I owed twelve dollars.
GEORGE S. KAUFMAN

Blessed are the young, for they shall inherit the national debt.
HERBERT HOOVER

The Lord forbid that I should be out of debt, as if, indeed, I could not be trusted.
FRANÇOIS RABELAIS

If it isn't the sheriff it's the finance company. I've got more attachments on me than a vacuum cleaner.
JOHN BARRYMORE

Do not take payment in politeness.
BALTASAR GRACIÁN

In the midst of life we are in debt.
ETHEL W. MUMFORD

No matter how a dun is addressed, it always reaches you.
KIN HUBBARD

Debts increase by arrears of interest.
LIVY

[*See also* Credit]

DECEPTION:

It is in the ability to deceive oneself that the greatest talent is shown.
ANATOLE FRANCE

Every individual may deceive and be deceived, but no person has deceived the whole world, nor has the whole world deceived any person.
DOMINIQUE BOUHOURS

[*See also* Fool]

DECISION:

Decide promptly, but never give any reasons. Your decisions may be right, but your reasons are sure to be wrong.
LORD MANSFIELD

DECORATOR:

It's a good thing that when God created the rainbow He didn't consult a decorator or He would still be picking colors.
SAM LEVENSON

DEED:

Don't take the will for the deed.
Get the deed.

AMERICAN LEGAL MAXIM

[See also Property]

DELINQUENT:

Children are said to be delinquent
when they reach the stage where
they want to do what their parents
are doing.

DELUSION:

The people never give up their
liberties but under some delusion.

EDMUND BURKE

Love is the delusion that one
woman differs from another.

H. L. MENCKEN

DEMAGOGUE:

A demagogue is a person with
whom we disagree as to which gang
should mismanage the country.

DON MARQUIS

A good trumpeter has the power
to rouse fools into making slaughter.

VIRGIL

DEMOCRACY:

I hold it to be the inalienable right
of anybody to go to hell in his own
way.

ROBERT FROST

Because in the administration it
hath respect not to the few but to
the many, our form of government
is called a democracy.

THUCYDIDES

Democracy substitutes election by
the incompetent many for appointment by the corrupt few.

GEORGE BERNARD SHAW

If there were a people consisting
of gods, they would be governed
democratically. So perfect a government is not suitable to men.

JEAN-JACQUES ROUSSEAU

Democracy means simply the
bludgeoning of the people by the
people for the people.

OSCAR WILDE

Democracy breeds the germs of
its own destruction.

V. I. LENIN

It is by the goodness of God that
in our country we have those three
unspeakably precious things: freedom of speech, freedom of conscience, and the prudence never to
practice either of them.

MARK TWAIN

Democracy gives every man the right to be his own oppressor.

JAMES RUSSELL LOWELL

The ship of Democracy, which has weathered all storms, may sink through the mutiny of those aboard.

GROVER CLEVELAND

Democracy is the art of running the circus from the monkey cage.

H. L. MENCKEN

Democracy becomes a government of bullies tempered by editors.

RALPH WALDO EMERSON

[See also Freedom]

DEMOCRAT:

I never said all Democrats were saloonkeepers; what I said was all saloonkeepers were Democrats.

HORACE GREELEY

Any well-established village . . . could afford a town drunkard, a town atheist, and a few Democrats.

DENIS W. BROGAN

[See also Liberal, Politician, Republican]

DEPRESSION:

Most of today's families are broke. It will just take a depression to make it official.

GREGORY NUNN

These dark days will be worth all they cost us if they teach us that our true destiny is not to be ministered unto but to minister to ourselves and to our fellow men.

FRANKLIN D. ROOSEVELT

No matter how bad things get you got to go on living, even if it kills you.

SHOLOM ALEICHEM

What if my trousers are shabby and worn, they cover a warm heart.

TOM MASSON

A recession is a period in which you tighten up your belt. In a depression you have no belt to tighten up. And when you have no pants to hold up, it's a panic.

[See also Poverty]

DESIRE:

If the desire to kill and the opportunity to kill came always together, who would escape hanging?

MARK TWAIN

Life contains but two tragedies. One is not to get your heart's desire; the other is to get it.

SOCRATES

DESTINY:

It's all luck. The cotton packing in a pill bottle could just as easily have plugged the earache of a millionaire or eased the menstrual pains of a queen.

YIDDISH SAYING

The Dodo never had a chance. He seems to have been invented for the sole purpose of becoming extinct, and that was all he was good for.

WILL CUPPY

Thy fate is the common fate of all;
Into each life some rain must fall.

HENRY WADSWORTH LONGFELLOW

Destiny is a Paris driver pushing a taxicab with my name on it.

FRANK DANE

[See also Fate, Luck]

DEVIL:

Why should the Devil have all the good tunes?

ROWLAND HILL

One sees more devils than vast Hell can hold.

WILLIAM SHAKESPEARE

The devil can cite Scripture for his purpose.

WILLIAM SHAKESPEARE

Speak of the Devil and he appears.

ITALIAN PROVERB

[See also Heaven, Hell, Religion]

DEVOTION:

There is nothing in the world like the devotion of a married woman. It's a thing no married man knows anything about.

OSCAR WILDE

No humor is more easily counterfeited, than devotion.

MICHEL DE MONTAIGNE

[See also Fidelity]

DIAMOND:

Next to good judgment, diamonds and pearls are the rarest things in the world.

JEAN DE LA BRUYÈRE

It is better to have old secondhand diamonds than none at all.

MARK TWAIN

DIET:

Eat a third, drink a third, and then leave the remaining third of your stomach empty. Then, if anger overtakes you, there will be room in it for gas.

THE TALMUD

As a child my family's menu consisted of two choices: take it, or leave it.

BUDDY HACKETT

An ancient tablet, c. 4000 B.C., tells of a mystic who vowed to learn the secret of life-without-food. Just as he was learning to live without food, he died.

Tell me what you eat and I'll tell you what you are.

ANTHELME BRILLAT-SAVARIN

He dreamed he was eating shredded wheat and woke up to find the mattress half gone.

FRED ALLEN

All the things I really like to do are either immoral, illegal, or fattening.

ALEXANDER WOOLLCOTT

I told my doctor I get very tired when I go on a diet, so he gave me pep pills. Know what happened? I ate faster.

JOE E. LEWIS

It isn't so much what's on the table that matters, as what's on the chairs.

W. S. GILBERT

Jack Sprat could eat no fat,
His wife could eat no lean,
And so between the two of them
They licked the platter clean.

MOTHER GOOSE

The chief excitement in a woman's life is spotting women who are fatter than she is.

HELEN ROWLAND

I can reason down or deny everything except this perpetual belly: feed he must and will, and I cannot make him respectable.

RALPH WALDO EMERSON

He who does not mind his belly will hardly mind anything else.

SAMUEL JOHNSON

Indigestion is charged by God with enforcing morality on the stomach.

VICTOR HUGO

Part of the secret of success in life is to eat what you like and let the food fight it out inside.

MARK TWAIN

[See also Cook, Cooking, Food]

DIFFERENT:

If a man does not keep pace with his companions, perhaps it is because he hears a different drummer.

HENRY DAVID THOREAU

Strange all this difference should be 'Twixt Tweedledum and Tweedledee.

JOHN BYROM

[See also Conformity]

DIGNITY:

Dignity is the quality that enables a man who says nothing and knows nothing, to command a great deal of respect.

JOHN RAPER

[See also Manners]

DIPLOMACY:

Diplomacy: Lying in state.

OLIVER HERFORD

To deceive a diplomat speak the truth, he has no experience with it.

GREEK PROVERB

An ambassador has no need of spies; his character is always sacred.

GEORGE WASHINGTON

A man-of-war is the best ambassador.

OLIVER CROMWELL

A diplomat is a man who thinks twice before he says nothing.

The trouble with history is its dependence upon diplomats.

GERALD F. LIEBERMAN

I have discovered the art of fooling diplomats. I speak the truth, and they never believe me.

CAMILLO DI CAVOUR

An appeaser is one who feeds a crocodile hoping it will eat him last.

WINSTON CHURCHILL

A diplomat is a person who is appointed to avert situations that would never occur if there were no diplomats.

A diplomat is someone who can tell you to go to hell in such a way that you look forward to the trip.

A diplomat is one who can cut his neighbor's throat without his neighbor noticing it.

CARLOS ROMULO

A diplomatist is a man who always remembers a woman's birthday, but never remembers her age.

ROBERT FROST

[See also United Nations]

DISAPPOINTMENT:

Blessed be he who expects nothing, for he shall never be disappointed.

JONATHAN SWIFT

DISEASE:

The doctor is to be feared more than the disease.

LATIN PROVERB

Sickness soaks the purse.

INTERNATIONAL PROVERB

Fate favors the physician by inventing lingering disease for which there is no cure, and the sanitariums by inventing lingering cures for which there is no disease.

[*See also* Doctor, Illness, Medicine]

DISTANCE:

'Tis distance lends enchantment to the view.
THOMAS CAMPBELL

'Tis ever common
That men are merriest when they are from home.
WILLIAM SHAKESPEARE

My living in Yorkshire was so far out of the way, that it was actually twelve miles from a lemon.
SYDNEY SMITH

DIVORCE:

Marriage is grounds for divorce.
AMERICAN LAW MAXIM

Do not lengthen the quarrel while there is an opportunity of escaping.
LATIN PROVERB

The mind which renounces, once and forever, a futile hope, has its compensation in ever-growing calm.
GEORGE ROBERT GISSING

He that loseth his wife and a farthing, hath a great loss of a farthing.
ITALIAN PROVERB

How many a thing which we cast to the ground,
When others pick it up becomes a gem!
GEORGE MEREDITH

Acrimony: What a divorced man gives his wife.

Free of her lips, free of her hips.
ENGLISH PROVERB

Divorce: A Declaration of Independence with only two signers.
GERALD F. LIEBERMAN

It's well to be off with the Old Woman before you're on with the New.
GEORGE BERNARD SHAW

Love the quest; marriage the conquest; divorce the inquest.
HELEN ROWLAND

Take back the freedom thou cravest,
Leaving the fetters to me.
CHARLOTTE BARNARD

After living with the bum for fifteen years, why should I make him happy now?
COURT PROCEEDING; woman explaining why she would not agree to an uncontested divorce

[*See also* Alimony, Marriage]

DOCTOR:

Doctors are men who prescribe medicines of which they know little, to cure diseases of which they know less, in human beings of whom they know nothing.

VOLTAIRE

There are worse occupations in this world than feeling a woman's pulse.

LAURENCE STERNE

That patient's ear remorseless he assails,
Murders with jargon when his medicine fails.

JOHN GAY

Doctors will have more lives to answer for in the next world than even we generals.

NAPOLEON

A young doctor makes a humpy graveyard.

ENGLISH PROVERB

God heals and the doctor takes the fee.

BENJAMIN FRANKLIN

Doctors think a lot of patients are cured who have simply quit in disgust.

DON HEROLD

He has been a doctor a year now and has had two patients, no, three, I think—yes, it was three; I attended their funerals.

MARK TWAIN

The threat of a neglected cold is for doctors what the threat of purgatory is for priests—a gold mine.

SÉBASTIEN CHAMFORT

"Is there no hope?" the sick man said,
The silent doctor shook his head,
And took his leave with signs of sorrow,
Despairing of his fee tomorrow.

JOHN GAY

Ignorance is not so damnable as humbug, but when it prescribes pills it may happen to do more harm.

GEORGE ELIOT

[*See also* Disease, Illness, Medicine]

DOG:

If you pick up a starving dog and make him prosperous, he will not bite you. This is the principal difference between a man and a dog.

MARK TWAIN

The great pleasure of a dog is that you may make a fool of yourself with him and not only will he not scold you, but he will make a fool of himself too.

SAMUEL BUTLER

The poor dog, in life the firmest friend,
The first to welcome, foremost to defend.

LORD BYRON

A dog is the only thing on earth that loves you more than you love yourself.

JOSH BILLINGS

DOGMA:

The objection to Puritans is not that they try to make us think as they do, but that they try to make us do as they think.

H. L. MENCKEN

Loyalty to petrified opinion never yet broke a chain or freed a human soul.

MARK TWAIN

[See also Faith, Religion]

DOUBT:

He who knows nothing doubts nothing.

ITALIAN PROVERB

I wish I could be half as sure of anything as some people are of everything.

GERALD BARZAN

When in doubt, tell the truth.

MARK TWAIN

O thou of little faith, wherefore didst thou doubt?

THE BIBLE

DREAM:

My life's dream has been a perpetual nightmare.

VOLTAIRE

If you want your dreams to come true, don't sleep.

YIDDISH PROVERB

While sleep o'erwhelms the tired limbs, the mind plays with wantons unconfined.

PETRONIUS

[See also Hope]

DRINK:

Leave off all thin potations and addict thyself to sack.

WILLIAM SHAKESPEARE

I always wake up at the crack of ice.

JOE E. LEWIS

I have taken more out of alcohol than alcohol has taken out of me.

WINSTON CHURCHILL

Once, during Prohibition, I was forced to live for days on nothing but food and water.

W. C. FIELDS

I drink to forget I drink.
JOE E. LEWIS

When neebors angry at a plea,
An' just as wud as wud can be,
How easy can the barley-bree
Cement the quarrel.
It's aye the cheapest lawyer's fee
To taste the barrel.
ROBERT BURNS

It pays to get drunk with the best people.
JOE E. LEWIS

Drink! for you know not whence you came, nor why:
Drink! for you know not why you go, nor where.
OMAR KHAYYÁM

The worst thing about some men is that when they are not drunk they are sober.
WILLIAM BUTLER YEATS

I don't drink any more than the man next to me, and the man next to me is Dean Martin.
JOE E. LEWIS

Men, Englishmen too, have been heard of, who do not know the taste of porter. This cannot be credited; though it may be readily believed that many are quite ignorant of the taste of water.
WESTMINSTER REVIEW, 1846

In wine there is truth.
PLINY THE ELDER

A mixture of brandy and water spoils two good things.
CHARLES LAMB

Some men are like musical glasses; to produce their finest tones you must keep them wet.
SAMUEL TAYLOR COLERIDGE

Fill all the glasses there, for why
Should every creature drink but I,
Why, man of morals, tell me why?
ABRAHAM COWLEY

When the clergyman's daughter
Drinks nothing but water
She's certain to finish on gin.
RUDYARD KIPLING

Liquor talks mighty loud when it gets loose from the jug.
JOEL CHANDLER HARRIS

Drinking makes such fools of people, and people are such fools to begin with, that it's compounding a felony.
ROBERT BENCHLEY

Of all vices, drinking is the most incompatible with greatness.
SIR WALTER SCOTT

The best audience is one that is intelligent, well-educated, and a little drunk.
ALBEN W. BARKLEY

Absinthe makes the heart grow fonder.
ADDISON MIZNER

Absinthe makes the jag last longer.

A man is never drunk if he can lay on the floor without holding on.
JOE E. LEWIS

I'd take a bromo, but I can't stand the noise.
JOE E. LEWIS

[See also Water]

DRUGS:

There is no flying without wings.
FRENCH PROVERB

I'm dating a guy who flies, and he's not a pilot.
VOICE ON A CALL-IN RADIO SHOW

A drug is that substance which, when injected into a rat, will produce a scientific report.

ECONOMICS:

If you're not confused you're not paying attention.
WALL STREET WEEK

Tax cut: The kindest cut of all.

I learned more about economics from one South Dakota dust storm than I did in all my years in college.
HUBERT HUMPHREY

Among the propensities of humans which almost exceed understanding come the parsimony of the rich and the extravagance of the poor.
19TH CENTURY AMERICANA

[See also Economist, Money]

ECONOMIST:

The reason we do not have inflation or unemployment in Austria is, we've exported all our economists to the United States and Canada.
ANONYMOUS AUSTRIAN DIPLOMAT

If all economists were laid end to end, they would not reach a conclusion.
GEORGE BERNARD SHAW

The instability of our economy matches the instability of our economists.
AMERICAN PROVERB

If all economists were laid end to end—it wouldn't be a bad idea.

ECONOMY:

Economy is going without something you do want in case, perhaps, you should someday want something you probably won't want.
ANTHONY HOPE

EDITOR:

An editor should have a pimp for a brother, so he'd have somebody to look up to.

GENE FOWLER

An editor is a person employed on a newspaper, whose business it is to separate the wheat from the chaff, and to see that the chaff is printed.

ELBERT HUBBARD

There are just two people entitled to refer to themselves as "we"; one is a newspaper editor and the other is a fellow with a tapeworm.

BILL NYE

The unsigned articles appearing in this newspaper sometimes represent the view of the editors, and frequently of no one else.

DISCLAIMER

[See also Newspaper]

EDUCATION:

A man who has never gone to school may steal from a freight car; but if he has a university education, he may steal the whole railroad.

THEODORE ROOSEVELT

It is better to speak wisdom foolishly like the saints than to speak folly wisely like the deans.

G. K. CHESTERTON

By trimming fools about the gill,
A barber's 'prentice learns his skill.

FRENCH PROVERB

As for primitive society, it regarded education as the transmission of skills and the training of character. The apprentice-to-master way of life was encouraged. It was a hard existence, with learning primarily aimed at the preparation for war and the responsibility of marriage; the two were not yet synonymous. Only males attended school, and graduation consisted of tests of strength and playful scourging. The highlight of commencement came when the senior class lined up for their diplomas and were circumcised by the dean. There were no school songs, and students who yelled the loudest were graduated *cum laude*.

GERALD F. LIEBERMAN

In the first place God made idiots. This was for practice. Then He made school boards.

MARK TWAIN

It don't make much difference what you study, so long as you don't like it.

FINLEY PETER DUNNE

Let's not burn the universities yet. After all, the damage they do might be worse.

H. L. MENCKEN

All these books about sex education are a waste. All you have to
know about sex is that you enjoy it.

LARRY LEVENSON

They teach anything in universities today. You can major in mud
pies.

ORSON WELLES

I was a modest, good-humored
boy; it is Oxford that has made me
insufferable.

MAX BEERBOHM

An education obtained with
money is worse than no education at
all.

SOCRATES

He mastered whatever was not
worth the knowing.

JAMES RUSSELL LOWELL

I once knew a student who
boasted that he had graduated from
college without taking any course
that was offered above the first floor.

ROBERT HUTCHINS

Men can acquire knowledge but
not wisdom. Some of the greatest
fools ever known were learned men.

SPANISH PROVERB

If nobody dropped out at the
eighth grade, who would hire the
college graduates?

Our American professors like
their literature clear, cold, pure, and
dead.

SINCLAIR LEWIS

Stand firm in your refusal to remain conscious during algebra. In
real life, I assure you, there is no
such thing as algebra.

FRAN LEBOWITZ

There is now less flogging in our
great schools than formerly, but then
less is learned there; so that what the
boys get at one end they lose at the
other.

SAMUEL JOHNSON

When a subject becomes totally
obsolete we make it a required
course.

PETER DRUCKER

A learned blockhead is a greater
blockhead than an ignorant one.

BENJAMIN FRANKLIN

A mugwump is a person educated
beyond his intellect.

HORACE PORTER

Education is the ability to listen to
almost anything without losing your
temper or your self-confidence.

ROBERT FROST

There are lessons to be learned
from a stupid man.

HORACE

The ridiculous is more easily re-
tained than the admirable.

HORACE

[*See also* College, Scholar, Teacher]

EGG:

A hen is only an egg's way of
making another egg.

SAMUEL BUTLER

EGO:

To love oneself is the beginning
of a lifelong romance.

OSCAR WILDE

The way Shaw believes in himself
is very refreshing in these atheistic
days when so many people believe in
no God at all.

ISRAEL ZANGWILL; on George Bernard Shaw

Ego: The fallacy whereby a goose
thinks he's a swan.

There are two sides to every question: my side and the wrong side.

OSCAR LEVANT

I have lived long enough to satisfy
both nature and glory.

JULIUS CAESAR

I should not talk so much about
myself if there were anybody else
whom I knew as well.

HENRY DAVID THOREAU

The last time I saw him he was
walking down Lover's Lane holding
his own hand.

FRED ALLEN

There is nothing will kill a man so
soon as having nobody to find fault
with but himself.

GEORGE ELIOT

You have no idea what a poor
opinion I have of myself and how
little I deserve it.

W. S. GILBERT

What the world needs is more
geniuses with humility, there are so
few of us left.

OSCAR LEVANT

H. L. Mencken suffers from the
hallucination that he is H. L.
Mencken. There is no cure for a disease of that magnitude.

MAXWELL BODENHEIM

When a man is wrapped up in
himself he makes a pretty small
package.

JOHN RUSKIN

The cemeteries are filled with people who thought the world couldn't
get along without them.

AMERICAN PROVERB

He that falls in love with himself
will have no rivals.

BENJAMIN FRANKLIN

A self-made man? Yes. And worships his creator.

WILLIAM COWPER

Egotist: A person of low taste, more interested in himself than in me.

AMBROSE BIERCE

ELECTION:

Elections are held to delude the populace into believing that they are participating in government.

GERALD F. LIEBERMAN

The election isn't very far off when a candidate can recognize you across the street.

KIN HUBBARD

The only thing we learn from new elections is we learned nothing from the old.

AMERICAN PROVERB

Did you too, O friend, suppose democracy was only for elections, for politics, for a party name?

WALT WHITMAN

[See also Politician, Politics, Vote]

ELOQUENCE:

Money will say more in one moment than the most eloquent lover can in years.

HENRY FIELDING

No speech can be so poor that the newspapers will not describe it as able and eloquent, these being the lowest terms to which friendly reporters could reduce even a worthless discourse.

WILLIAM M. EVARTS

[See also Debate, Speech]

EMOTION:

There is always something ridiculous about the emotions of people whom one has ceased to love.

OSCAR WILDE

EMPLOYMENT:

Few great men could pass Personnel.

PAUL GOODMAN

It is a novel kind of supremacy, the best that life can offer, to have as servants by skill those who by nature are our masters.

BALTASAR GRACIÁN

[See also Work]

ENEMY:

We have met the enemy and they is us.

POGO

It is difficult to say who do you the most mischief: enemies with the worst intentions or friends with the best.

E. R. BULWER-LYTTON

Love your enemies, bless them that curse you, do good to them that hate you, and pray for them which despitefully use you, and persecute you.

THE BIBLE

Instead of loving your enemies treat your friends a little better.

ED HOWE

Scratch a lover and find a foe.

DOROTHY PARKER

It is not necessary to have enemies if you go out of your way to make friends hate you.

FRANK DANE

A friend is one who has the same enemies you have.

ABRAHAM LINCOLN

To make an enemy, do someone a favor.

If you have no enemies you are apt to be in the same predicament in regard to friends.

ELBERT HUBBARD

ENERGY:

One minute gives invention to destroy

What to rebuild will a whole age employ.

WILLIAM CONGREVE

Lack of pep is often mistaken for patience.

KIN HUBBARD

ENGLAND:

The world is a bundle of hay,
Mankind are the asses who pull;
Each tugs it a different way,
And the greatest of all is John Bull.

LORD BYRON

The English instinctively admire any man who has no talent and is modest about it.

JAMES AGEE

The British have a remarkable talent for keeping calm, even when there is no crisis.

FRANKLIN P. JONES

The English have better sense than any other nation; and they are fools.

PRINCE VON METTERNICH

England can never be ruined except by a Parliament.

LORD BURLEIGH

An Englishman thinks he is moral when he is only uncomfortable.

GEORGE BERNARD SHAW

84

ENTERPRISE

If you want to eat well in England, eat three breakfasts.

SOMERSET MAUGHAM

In dealing with Englishmen you can be sure of one thing only, that the logical solution will not be adopted.

WILLIAM RALPH INGE

ENTERPRISE:

Beware of all enterprises that require new clothes.

HENRY DAVID THOREAU

ENTERTAINMENT:

Americans don't spend billions for entertainment. They spend it in search of entertainment.

I am a great friend of public amusements, they keep people from vice.

SAMUEL JOHNSON

Night club: A place where people who have nothing to remember go to forget.

ENVIRONMENT:

The mind unlearns with difficulty what it has long learned.

SENECA

A maggot must be in the rotten cheese to like it.

GEORGE ELIOT

ENVY:

Oh, what a bitter thing it is to look into happiness through another man's eyes.

WILLIAM SHAKESPEARE

Man will do many things to get himself loved; he will do all things to get himself envied.

MARK TWAIN

Envy is the companion of glory.

LATIN PROVERB

All the world is competent to judge my pictures except those who are of my profession.

WILLIAM HOGARTH

To all my foes, dear fortune, send
Thy gifts! but never to my friend:
I tamely can endure the first;
But this with envy makes me burst.

JONATHAN SWIFT

[*See also* Jealousy]

EPIGRAM:

Epigrams succeed where epics fail.

PERSIAN PROVERB

85

An epigram of two lines has every merit, and if you exceed three lines it is a rhapsody.

CYRILLUS

An epigram is a half-truth so stated as to irritate the person who believes the other half.

SHAILER MATHEWS

An epigram is only a wisecrack that's played Carnegie Hall.

OSCAR LEVANT

The qualities rare in a bee that we meet
    In an epigram never should fail;
The body should always be little and sweet,
    And a sting should be left in the tail.

The weightiest writer of maxims in our language is Bacon, who attempted to combine a career of affairs and of thought, and spoilt both by so doing.

JOSEPH JACOBS

EPITAPH:

If men could see the epitaphs their friends write they would believe they had got into the wrong grave.

AMERICAN PROVERB

In lapidary inscriptions a man is not upon oath.

SAMUEL JOHNSON

The most touching epitaph I ever encountered was on the tombstone of the printer of Edinburgh. It said simply: "He kept down the cost and set the type right."

GREGORY NUNN

Reading the epitaphs, our only salvation lies in ressurecting the dead and burying the living.

PAUL ELDRIDGE

Epitaph: A belated advertisement for a line of goods that has been discontinued.

IRVIN S. COBB

Posterity will ne'er survey
    A nobler grave than this:
Here lies the bones of Castlereagh:
    Stop, traveler—(do not piss).

LORD BYRON

In a cemetery outside of Paris the memory of a nineteenth-century wizard was kept alive by the symbol of his inventive genius: a lamp, which burned perpetually over his grave. On the headstone was this inscription:

"Here lies Pierre Fournier, inventor of the everlast lamp, which consumes only one centime's worth of oil an hour. He was a good father, a devoted son, and a cherished husband. His eternally mourning widow continues his business on the Rue Aux Trois. Goods sent to all parts of the city. Do not mistake the opposite shop for this."

GERALD F. LIEBERMAN

[*See also* Biography]

EQUALITY:

Democracy is a charming form of government, full of confusion and variety and dispensing a sort of equality to equals.

PLATO

Subordination tends greatly to human happiness. Were we all upon an equality, we should have no other enjoyment than mere animal pleasure.

SAMUEL JOHNSON

We haven't all had the good fortune to be ladies, we haven't all been generals or poets or statesmen; but when the toast works down to babies, we stand on common ground.

MARK TWAIN

His lordship may compel us to be equal upstairs but there will never be equality in the servants' hall.

JAMES M. BARRIE

Equality is what does not exist among mortals.

E E CUMMINGS

I died for Beauty—but was scarce Adjusted in the Tomb

When One who died for Truth, was lain
In an adjoining room—

EMILY DICKINSON

That all men are equal is a proposition to which, at ordinary times, no sane individual has ever given his assent.

ALDOUS HUXLEY

Inferiors revolt in order that they may be equal, and equals that they may be superior.

ARISTOTLE

[*See also* Democracy, Women's Lib]

ESCAPE:

If at first you don't escape, try try again.

GULAG MOTTO; according to Herbert V. Evatt, Australian Minister of External Affairs

ETHICS:

A set of rules laid out by professionals to show the way they would like to act if it was profitable.

FRANK DANE

That business ethics are on the upswing, however, is illustrated by this recent event. A sales executive for a large corporation used devious tactics in an effort to secure a lucrative contract. To obtain his goal he bribed an official, acted as a procurer, seduced and blackmailed a secretary, conspired to inflict bodily harm on the representative of a competitor and organized a bacchanalian orgy. When the directors of his company were made aware of the tactics used they fired the executive—and shipped the merchandise. It's a beginning.

GERALD F. LIEBERMAN

The legal profession, like the medical profession, has a Canon of Ethics. And, as in the latter instance, it is generally ignored.

GERALD F. LIEBERMAN

EULOGY:

If I thought that people would eulogize me this much I'd have done the decent thing and died first.

JOE E. LEWIS, at a testimonial dinner in his honor

Satire lies about literary men while they live, and eulogy lies about them when they die.

VOLTAIRE

His books did not balance, but his heart always beat warmly for his native land.

EULOGY FOR A TEXAS LEGISLATOR

[See also Epitaph]

EVIDENCE:

Some circumstantial evidence is very strong, as when you find a trout in the milk.

HENRY DAVID THOREAU

Give me a few lines of a man's handwriting; that will be sufficient for me to get him hanged.

CARDINAL RICHELIEU

Whenever a husband and wife begin to discuss their marriage, they are giving evidence at an inquest.

H. L. MENCKEN

EVIL:

The evil that men do lives after them,
The good is oft interred with their bones.

WILLIAM SHAKESPEARE

Between two evils, I always pick the one I never tried before.

MAE WEST

He who accepts evil without protesting against it is really cooperating with it.

HENRY DAVID THOREAU

The love of evil is the root of all money.

AMERICAN PROVERB

We often do good in order that we may do evil with impunity.

FRANÇOIS DE LA ROCHEFOUCAULD

The evil men do survives them. They murder after their death by the sentiments they propagated and by the laws they have made.

LATIN PROVERB

Money is the fruit of evil, as often as the root of it.

HENRY FIELDING

Of two evils, it is always best to vote for the least hypocritical.

AMERICAN PROVERB

[See also Politician, Politics, Sin]

EVOLUTION:

The question is this: Is man an ape or an angel? I am on the side of the angels.

BENJAMIN DISRAELI

Two million years from now the scientists can start a row by claiming that the creatures of that period descended from us.

It is hard for the ape to believe he descended from man.

H. L. MENCKEN

EXAGGERATION:

There are some people so addicted to exaggeration that they can't tell the truth without lying.

JOSH BILLINGS

Gross exaggeration is 144 more times worse than ordinary exaggeration.

STUDENT ANSWER ON SCHOOL EXAM

[See also Lie, Lying, Politician, Politics]

EXAMPLE:

We are all too quick to imitate depraved examples.

JUVENAL

It is of the highest advantage to be able to derive instruction from the madness of another.

LATIN PROVERB

Few things are harder to put up with than the annoyance of a good example.

MARK TWAIN

EXCUSE:

If you don't want to do something, one excuse is as good as another.

YIDDISH SAYING

EXECUTION:

The executioner is, I hear, very expert; and my neck is very slender.

ANNE BOLEYN

If a woman were about to proceed to her execution she would demand a little time to perfect her toilet.

SÉBASTIEN CHAMFORT

[See also Capital Punishment]

EXECUTIVE:

It is ridiculous to suppose that the great head of things, whatever it be, pays any regard to human affairs.

PLINY THE ELDER

Blessed is he who talks in circles, for he shall become a big wheel.

FRANK DANE

Don't say yes until I've finished talking.

ATTRIBUTED TO MANY HOLLYWOOD EXECUTIVES

[See also Vice-President]

EXERCISE:

I get my exercise acting as a pallbearer to my friends who exercise.

CHAUNCEY DEPEW

I like long walks, especially when they are taken by people who annoy me.

FRED ALLEN

Whenever I feel like exercise I lie down until the feeling passes.

ROBERT MAYNARD HUTCHINS

EXPEDIENCE:

When you have got an elephant by the hind leg, and he is trying to run away, it's best to let him run.

ABRAHAM LINCOLN

Men resort to expedience when honor gets a little risky.

AMERICAN PROVERB

EXPENSE:

Love: An ocean of emotions entirely surrounded by expenses.

THOMAS R. DEWAR

If your outgo exceeds your income, your upkeep will be your downfall.

EXPERIENCE:

One must pass through the circumference of time before arriving at the center of opportunity.

BALTASAR GRACIÁN

The difference between an experienced person and an educated person is: an educated person recognizes his mistakes, then he makes them again.

Experience is what you get when you didn't get what you wanted.

The scalded dog fears hot water, and afterwards, cold.

ITALIAN PROVERB

I have never let my schooling interfere with my education.

MARK TWAIN

You don't learn to hold your own in the world by standing on guard, but by attacking and getting well hammered yourself.

GEORGE BERNARD SHAW

Experience . . . is simply the name we give our mistakes.

OSCAR WILDE

[See also Education, Life]

EXPLANATION:

I wish he would explain his explanation.

LORD BYRON

FACTS:

Get your facts first, then you can distort 'em as you please.

MARK TWAIN

The universal regard for money is the one hopeful fact in our civilization.

GEORGE BERNARD SHAW

Facts do not cease to exist because they are ignored.

ALDOUS HUXLEY

Practical politics consists in ignoring facts.

HENRY ADAMS

[See also Truth]

FAILURE:

Nothing fails like success.

G. K. CHESTERTON

There is no use in your walking five miles to fish when you can be just as unsuccessful near home.

MARK TWAIN

He has spent all his life in letting down buckets into empty wells; and he is frittering away his age in trying to draw them up again.

SYDNEY SMITH

We are all failures—at least the best of us are.

JAMES M. BARRIE

You don't die in the United States, you underachieve.

JERZY KOSINSKI

Stately towers tumble down with a heavier crash than more lowly buildings.

HORACE

[See also Money, Success]

FAITH:

I respect faith, but doubt is what gets you an education.

WILSON MIZNER

If there was no faith there would be no living in this world. We couldn't even eat hash with any safety.

JOSH BILLINGS

Faith: Belief without evidence is what is told by one who speaks without knowledge, of things without parallel.

AMBROSE BIERCE

There lives more faith in honest doubt,
Believe me, than in half the creeds.

ALFRED, LORD TENNYSON

If you have any faith, give me, for heaven's sake, a share of it! Your doubts you may keep to yourself, I have plenty of my own.

JOHANN WOLFGANG VON GOETHE

"Faith" is a fine invention
When gentlemen can *see*—
But *Microscopes* are prudent
In an Emergency.

EMILY DICKINSON

The greatest act of faith is when man decides that he is not God.

OLIVER WENDELL HOLMES

[*See also* God, Religion]

FAME:

Fame is proof that the people are gullible.

RALPH WALDO EMERSON

How great are the dangers I face to win a good name in Athens.

ALEXANDER THE GREAT

The fame of great men ought always to be estimated by the means used to acquire it.

FRANÇOIS DE LA ROCHEFOUCAULD

How many people live on the reputation of the reputation they might have made.

OLIVER WENDELL HOLMES

What rage for fame attends both great and small!
Better be damned than mentioned not at all.

PETER PINDAR

Fame: The advantage of being known to those who do not know us.

SÉBASTIEN CHAMFORT

How dreary—to be—Somebody!
How public—like a Frog—
To tell one's name—the livelong June—
To an admiring Bog!

EMILY DICKINSON

I would rather that men ask . . . why I have no statue than why I have one.

CATO THE ELDER

I was the only one there I never heard of.

BARRY FARBER

If you would not be forgotten as soon as you are dead, either write things worth reading or do things worth writing.

BENJAMIN FRANKLIN

FAMILIARITY:

Familiarity breeds contempt.

PUBLILIUS SYRUS

Familiarity breeds contempt—and children.

MARK TWAIN

Familiarity breeds attempt.

The first Rotarian was the first man to call John the Baptist "Jack."

H. L. MENCKEN

[See also Love, Manners]

FAMILY:

God gives us relatives; thank God we can choose our friends.

ETHEL W. MUMFORD

The hatred of relatives is the most violent.

TACITUS

All people are your relatives, therefore expect only trouble from them.

CHINESE PROVERB

A friend who is near and dear may in time become as useless as a relative.

GEORGE ADE

The rich never have to seek out their relatives.

ITALIAN PROVERB

The greater the kindred, the less the kindness.

JOHN LYLY

An advantage of poverty, your relatives gain nothing by your death.

HEBREW PROVERB

For the Colonel's Lady an' Judy O'Grady
Are sisters under their skins!

RUDYARD KIPLING

There is only one good substitute for the endearments of a sister, and that is the endearments of some other fellow's sister.

JOSH BILLINGS

The hardest thing is to disguise your feelings when you put a lot of relatives on the train for home.

KIN HUBBARD

[See also Children, Mother]

FANATICISM:

Fanaticism consists of redoubling your effort when you have forgotten your aim.

GEORGE SANTAYANA

FASCISM:

If Fascism came to America it would be on a program of Americanism.

HUEY P. LONG

FASHION:

However I am dressed, I shall still be Sancho Panza.

MIGUEL DE CERVANTES

The fashion of this world passeth away.

THE BIBLE

Any girl can be glamorous. All you have to do is stand still and look stupid.

HEDY LAMARR

Fine clothes are good only as they supply the want of other means of procuring respect.

SAMUEL JOHNSON

Her hat is a creation that will never go out of style. It will look just as ridiculous year after year.

FRED ALLEN

An ape is an ape, a varlet's a varlet
Though clothed in silk or clothed in scarlet.

SPANISH PROVERB

Change in fashion is the tax which the industry of the poor levies on the vanity of the rich.

SÉBASTIEN CHAMFORT

Woman's first duty in life is to her dressmaker. What the second duty is no one has yet discovered.

OSCAR WILDE

You couldn't tell if she was dressed for an opera or an operation.

IRVIN S. COBB

Judge not a man by his clothes, but by his wife's clothes.

THOMAS R. DEWAR

Fashion is gentility running away from vulgarity, and afraid of being overtaken.

WILLIAM HAZLITT

Fashion is a form of ugliness so intolerable that we have to alter it every six months.

OSCAR WILDE

Every generation laughs at the old fashions but religiously follows the new.

HENRY DAVID THOREAU

All women's dresses are merely variations on the eternal struggle between the admitted desire to dress and the unadmitted desire to undress.

LIN YUTANG

You must have women dressed, if it is only for the pleasure of imagining them Venuses.
GEORGE MOORE

Only men who are not interested in women are interested in women's clothes. Men who like women never notice what they wear.
ANATOLE FRANCE

The time he can spare from the adornment of his person he devotes to the neglect of his duties.
BENJAMIN JOWETT

A girl with cotton stockings never sees a mouse.
AMERICAN PROVERB

[See also Style]

FATE:

Lots of folks confuse bad management with destiny.
KIN HUBBARD

Persons who are born too soon, or born too late, seldom achieve the eminence of those who are born at the right time.
KATHARINE ANTHONY

Granting our wish is one of Fate's saddest jokes.
JAMES RUSSELL LOWELL

Why must the honest and the talented come to grief while the swag-

gering idiot lolls on the couches of fortune and stinks with smug comfort?
HEINRICH HEINE

The fate of a nation has often depended upon the good or bad digestion of a prime minister.
VOLTAIRE

Thou seest two bricks baked together, from the same clay and furnace; one shall be laid on top of a minaret, and the other at the bottom of an outhouse.
MOASI, king of the poets of Persia, 11th century

A good bone does not always come to a good dog.
FRENCH PROVERB

The Moving Finger writes; and having writ,
Moves on; nor all your Piety nor Wit
Shall lure it back to cancel half a Line,
Nor all your tears wash out a Word of it.
OMAR KHAYYÁM

[See also Destiny, Fortune, Sport]

FATHER:

Father's Day is like Mother's Day, except the gift is cheaper.

One father is more than a hundred school-masters.
GEORGE HERBERT

No more like my father
Than I to Hercules.
WILLIAM SHAKESPEARE

[See also Family, Mother]

FAVOR:

Most people return small favors, acknowledge medium ones and repay great ones—with ingratitude.
BENJAMIN FRANKLIN

[See also Gratitude, Ingrate]

FEAR:

Fear of becoming a has-been keeps some people from becoming anything.
ERIC HOFFER

'Twas only fear first in the world made gods.
BEN JONSON

Early and provident fear is the mother of safety.
EDMUND BURKE

[See also Courage]

FIDELITY:

To be constant in love to one is good; to be constant to many is great.
JAMES JEFFREY ROCHE

The worst revenge of a woman is to remain faithful to a man.
JACQUES BOSSUET

Fidelity bought with money can be overcome by money.
SENECA

A wit should be no more sincere than a woman constant.
WILLIAM CONGREVE

[See also Adultery, Faith, Infidelity]

FIGHT:

Thrusting my nose firmly between his teeth, I threw him heavily to the ground on top of me.
MARK TWAIN

FINANCE:

Just think how happy you would be if you lost everything you have right now, and then got it back again.
FRANCES RODMAN

Whether you wind up with a nest egg or a goose egg depends on the kind of chick you married.
Wall Street Journal

[*See also* Bank, Investment, Money, Stock Market]

FLATTERY:

'Tis an old maxim in the schools
That flattery's the food of fools;
Yet now and then your men of wit
Will condescend to take a bit.

JONATHAN SWIFT

He that loves to be flattered is worthy of the flatterer.

WILLIAM SHAKESPEARE

He that flatters you more than you desire either has deceived you or wishes to deceive.

ITALIAN PROVERB

He soft-soaped her until she couldn't see for the suds.

MARY ROBERTS RINEHART

[*See also* Applause, Praise]

FLIRTATION:

She learned to say things with her eyes that others waste time putting into words.

COREY FORD

God created the flirt as soon as He made the fool.

VICTOR HUGO

FOLLY:

Shoot folly as it flies.

ALEXANDER POPE

Every age has its folly, and the folly of the twentieth century is probably a desire to educate.

GEORGE MOORE

[*See also* Ignorance, Stupidity]

FOOD:

Abstain from beans.

PLUTARCH

I want every laborer in my realm to be able to put a fowl in the pot on Sunday.

HENRI IV

That all-softening, over-powering knell,
The tocsin of the soul—the dinner bell.

LORD BYRON

When one has tasted it [watermelon] he knows what the angels eat.

MARK TWAIN

No man is lonely while eating spaghetti; it requires so much attention.

CHRISTOPHER MORLEY

There is no love sincerer than the love of food.

GEORGE BERNARD SHAW

He that eats till he is sick must
fast till he is well.

HEBREW PROVERB

Mealtime: When youngsters sit
down to continue eating.

He may live without books—what
    is knowledge but grieving?
He may live without hope—what
    is hope but deceiving?
He may live without love—what
    is passion but pining?
But where is the man that can live
    without dining?

OWEN MEREDITH

Fishes live in the sea as men do
a-land; the big ones eat the little
ones.

PERICLES

The most dangerous food a man
can eat is wedding cake.

AMERICAN PROVERB

Serenely full, the epicure would
    say,
Fate cannot harm me—I have
    dined today.

SYDNEY SMITH

I would like to find a stew that
will give me heartburn immediately,
instead of at three o'clock in the
morning.

JOHN BARRYMORE

One would risk disgust if one saw
politics, justice, and one's dinner in
the making.

SÉBASTIEN CHAMFORT

For its merit I will knight it, and
then it will be Sir-loin.

CHARLES II, to a fine cut of beef

He that would live for aye, must
eat sage in May.

LATIN PROVERB

God preserve you from one who
eats without drinking.

ITALIAN PROVERB

Other men lived to eat, while he
ate to live.

SOCRATES

To eat is human, to digest, divine.

MARK TWAIN

[See also Cook, Cooking, Soup]

FOOL:

He is a fool that kisseth the maid
when he may kiss the mistress.

ENGLISH PROVERB

Fortune, seeing that she could not
make fools wise, has made them
lucky.

MICHEL DE MONTAIGNE

A learned fool is more foolish
than an ignorant one.

MOLIÈRE

How many fools does it take to
make up a public?

SÉBASTIEN CHAMFORT

No man was more foolish when he had not a pen in his hand, or more wise when he had.

SAMUEL JOHNSON

Who loves not women, wine and song
Remains a fool his whole life long.

MARTIN LUTHER

A fool there was and he made his prayer
(Even as you and I!)
To a rag and a bone and a hank of hair
(We called her the woman who did not care)
But the fool he called her his lady fair—
(Even as you and I!)

RUDYARD KIPLING

Let us be thankful for the fools. But for them the rest of us could not succeed.

MARK TWAIN

This fellow is wise enough to play the fool;
And to do that well craves a kind of wit.

WILLIAM SHAKESPEARE

Get the fools on your side and you can be elected to anything.

FRANK DANE

A mother takes twenty years to make a man of her boy, and another woman makes a fool of him in twenty minutes.

ROBERT FROST

You can educate a fool, but you cannot make him think.

THE TALMUD

A fool must now and then be right, by chance.

WILLIAM COWPER

Take all the fools out of this world and there wouldn't be any fun living in it, or profit.

JOSH BILLINGS

You don't show a fool a job half done.

HEBREW PROVERB

A fool and his father's money— can go places.

For fools rush in where angels fear to tread.

ALEXANDER POPE

Fools rush in where fools have been before.

The best way to convince a fool that he is wrong is to let him have his way.

JOSH BILLINGS

[See also Folly, Politician, Stupidity]

FOREIGN AID:

We have to be careful cutting back foreign aid to third world nations. They need the money, to buy Soviet weapons.

JOEY ADAMS

[See also United Nations]

FORTUNE:

The successful men of action are not sufficiently self-observant to know exactly on what their success depends.

JOSEPH JACOBS

Good fortune and evil fortune come to all things alike in this world of time.
MOASI, king of the poets of Persia, 11th century

Luck affects everything. Let your hook always be cast; in the stream where you least expect it there will be a fish.

OVID

Fortune favors the bold but abandons the timid.

LATIN PROVERB

[See also Fate, Luck]

FRANCE:

If it were not for the government,

we should have nothing to laugh at in France.

SÉBASTIEN CHAMFORT

He was a Frenchman, and that makes him a little dirty to begin with.

SHELLEY BERMAN, on André Gide

France . . . a despotism tempered by epigrams.

THOMAS CARLYLE

France is a place where the money falls apart in your hands but you can't tear the toilet paper.

BILLY WILDER

FREEDOM:

We are all of us the worse for too much liberty.

TERENCE

They want to be free and they do not know how to be just.

ABBÉ SIEYÈS

We are living in the excesses of freedom. Just take a look at 42nd Street and Broadway.

WILL DURANT

O Liberty! O Liberty! What crimes are committed in thy name!
MME. ROLAND, on her way to the guillotine

Mankind has a free will; but it is free to milk cows and to build houses, nothing more.

MARTIN LUTHER

American freedom consists largely in talking nonsense.

ED HOWE

Many politicians are in the habit of laying it down as a self-evident proposition that no people ought to be free until they are fit to use their freedom. The maxim is worthy of the fool in the old story who resolved not to go into the water until he had learned to swim.

THOMAS BABINGTON MACAULAY

A nation may lose its liberties in a day and not miss them for a century.

BARON DE LA BRÈDE ET DE MONTESQUIEU

[*See also* Democracy, Liberty]

FRIENDSHIP:

Nothing is there more friendly to a man than a friend in need.

PLAUTUS

Show me a friend in need and I'll show you a pest.

JOE E. LEWIS

Don't jump on a man unless he's down.

FINLEY PETER DUNNE

In all distresses of our friends
We first consult our private ends.

JONATHAN SWIFT

Those friends thou hast, and their adoption tried,
Grapple them to thy soul with hoops of steel,
But do not dull thy palm with entertainment
Of each new-hatch'd, unfledg'd comrade.

WILLIAM SHAKESPEARE

Ascend a step to choose a friend, descend a step to choose a wife.

THE TALMUD

The Holy Passion of Friendship is of so sweet and steady and loyal and enduring a nature that it will last through a whole lifetime, if not asked to lend money.

MARK TWAIN

Friend: One who knows all about you and loves you just the same.

ELBERT HUBBARD

Before borrowing money from a friend decide which you need most.

AMERICAN PROVERB

Show me your friends and I'll show you your ends.

PORTUGUESE PROVERB

You will always have the countenance of friends whilst fortune favors you.

OVID

A true friend is one who likes you despite your achievements.

It is well, when one is judging a friend, to remember that he is judging you with the same godlike and superior impartiality.

ARNOLD BENNETT

Friendship among women is only a suspension of hostilities.

COMTE DE RIVAROL

Never speak ill of yourself. Your friends will always say enough on that subject.

CHARLES MAURICE DE TALLEYRAND

Friendship may, and often does, grow into love; but love never subsides into friendship.

LORD BYRON

There are three faithful friends— an old wife, an old dog, and ready money.

BENJAMIN FRANKLIN

A man has confidence in untried friends, he remembers the many offers of service so freely made by boon companions when he wanted them not; he has hope—the hope of happy inexperience.

CHARLES DICKENS

Acquaintance: A degree of friendship called slight when its object is poor or obscure, and intimate when he is rich and famous.

AMBROSE BIERCE

The fellow that calls you "brother" usually wants something that doesn't belong to him.

KIN HUBBARD

If all persons knew what they said of each other there would not be four friends in the world.

BLAISE PASCAL

He makes no friend who never made a foe.

ALFRED, LORD TENNYSON

An acquaintance that begins with a compliment is sure to develop into a real friendship.

OSCAR WILDE

[See also Dog, Enemy]

FUNERAL:

Funeral: A pageant whereby we attest our respect for the dead by enriching the undertaker.

AMBROSE BIERCE

In the city a funeral is just an interruption of traffic; in the country it is a form of popular entertainment.

GEORGE ADE

What men prize most is a privilege, even if it be that of chief mourner at a funeral.

JAMES RUSSELL LOWELL

The pomp of funerals is more interesting to the vanity of the living than to the memory of the dead.

FRANÇOIS DE LA ROCHEFOUCAULD

Anything awful makes me laugh. I misbehaved once at a funeral.

CHARLES LAMB

[See also Undertaker]

FURNITURE:

No furniture so charming as books, even if you never open them, or read a single word.

SYDNEY SMITH

Desk: A wastebasket with drawers.

[See also Decorator]

FUTURE:

Who knows whether the gods will add tomorrow to the days already passed?

HORACE

I like men who have a future and women who have a past.

OSCAR WILDE

When the insects take over the world we hope they will remember, with gratitude, how we took them along on all our picnics.

BILL VAUGHN

I never think of the future. It comes soon enough.

ALBERT EINSTEIN

An optimist is someone who thinks the future is uncertain.

The future is no more uncertain than the present.

WALT WHITMAN

The future not being born, my friend, we will abstain from baptizing it.

GEORGE MEREDITH

There was the Door to which I
  found no key;
There was the Veil through which
  I might not see.

OMAR KHAYYÁM

The future lies ahead.

POLITICAL PROMISE

[See also Past]

GALLANTRY:

Gallantry was never overlooked in the olden days. When your great-great-great-grandmother was waiting to be burned at the stake, the executioner wrapped a blanket around her to keep her warm—until they got the fire started.

[See also Gentleman, Manners]

GAMBLING:

One should always play fairly when one has the winning cards.

OSCAR WILDE

If you play bridge badly you make your partner suffer; but if you play poker badly you make everybody happy.

JOE LAURIE, JR.

I'm on such a losing streak that if I had been around I would have taken General Custer and given points.

JOE E. LEWIS

No wife can endure a gambling husband—unless he is a steady winner.

THOMAS R. DEWAR

A Smith & Wesson beats four aces.

AMERICAN PROVERB

There are two times in a man's life when he should not speculate: when he can't afford it, and when he can.

MARK TWAIN

The gambling known as business looks with severe disfavor upon the business known as gambling.

AMBROSE BIERCE

Gaming, that direst felon of the breast,

Steals more than fortune from its wretched thrall,
Spreads o'er the soul the inert devouring pest
And gnaws, and rots, and taints, and ruins all.

PETRONIUS

I met with an accident on the way to the track. I arrived safely.

JOE E. LEWIS

Never do card tricks for the boys you play poker with.

AMERICAN PROVERB

Gambling promises the poor what property performs for the rich—something for nothing.

GEORGE BERNARD SHAW

The race is not always to the swift, nor the battle to the strong—but that's the way to bet.

DAMON RUNYON

The only man who makes money following the races is one who does it with a broom and shovel.

ELBERT HUBBARD

[See also Game, Stock Market]

GAME:

To play billiards well is a sign of ill-spent youth.

CHARLES ROUPELL

It doesn't matter whether you win or lose, but how you play the game.
GRANTLAND RICE

He played the King in the game of life
But someone played the ace.
GERALD BARZAN

[*See also* Gambling, Life]

GENIUS:

I have nothing to declare but my genius.
OSCAR WILDE, to a U.S. Customs officer

The public is wonderfully tolerant, it forgives everything except genius.
OSCAR WILDE

There is no great genius without a mixture of madness.
ARISTOTLE

Genius borrows nobly.
RALPH WALDO EMERSON

When a true genius appears in the world you know him by this sign, that the dunces are all in confederacy against him.
JONATHAN SWIFT

I do not think America is a good place in which to be a genius.
SAMUEL BUTLER

Great God! What a genius I had when I wrote that book.
JONATHAN SWIFT

[*See also* Ego]

GENTLEMAN:

A gentleman is one who never strikes a woman without provocation.
H. L. MENCKEN

One of the embarrassments of being a gentleman is that you are not permitted to be violent in asserting your rights.
NICHOLAS MURRAY BUTLER

Gentlemen who prefer blondes usually marry brunettes.

A gentleman may love like a lunatic but not like a beast.
FRANÇOIS DE LA ROCHEFOUCAULD

Gentleman: One who pronounces "to-may-to" "to-mah-to."

A gentleman never strikes a lady with his hat on.
FRED ALLEN

This is the final test of a gentleman: his respect for those who can be of no possible service to him.
WILLIAM LYON PHELPS

[*See also* Gallantry, Manners]

GERMAN:

When one is polite in German, one lies.

JOHANN WOLFGANG VON GOETHE

[The German] possesses in a superlative degree the art of being original by imitation.

G. C. LICHTENBERG

GERMANY:

They are a fine people but quick to catch the disease of anti-humanity. I think it's because of their poor elimination. Germany is a headquarters for constipation.

GEORGE GROSZ

We may never produce another Goethe but we may produce another Caesar.

OSWALD SPENGLER

GIFT:

Those gifts are ever the most acceptable which the giver has made precious.

OVID

Confound all presents that eat.

ROBERT SMITH SURTEES

Rich gifts wax poor when givers prove unkind.

WILLIAM SHAKESPEARE

He that parts with his property before his death prepares himself for much suffering.

FRENCH PROVERB

God gives nuts to them what has no teeth.

AMERICAN PROVERB

[See also Charity, Philanthropist, Philanthropy]

GOD:

They say that kings are made in the image of God. If that's what He looks like, I feel sorry for God.

FREDERICK THE GREAT

How gracious are the gods in bestowing high positions, and how reluctant are they to insure them when given.

LUCIAN

If I owe Smith ten dollars and God forgives me, that doesn't pay Smith.

ROBERT GREEN INGERSOLL

Every man for himself and God for us all.

SPANISH PROVERB

God will forgive me. That's His business.

HEINRICH HEINE

The Bible says that the last thing God made was woman. He must

have made her on Saturday night—
it shows fatigue.
                    ALEXANDRE DUMAS

Everyone is as God made him,
and often a great deal worse.
                    MIGUEL DE CERVANTES

God, if there is a God, take my
soul, if I have a soul.
                    ERNEST RENAN

Is man one of God's blunders or
is God one of man's blunders?
                    FRIEDRICH NIETZSCHE

An honest man's the noblest work
of God.
                    ALEXANDER POPE

An honest God is the noblest
work of man.
                    ROBERT GREEN INGERSOLL

God help those who do not help
themselves.
                    ADDISON MIZNER

God is always on the side of the
heaviest battalions.
                    VOLTAIRE

For where God built a church
there the Devil would build a
chapel. . . . The Devil is ever God's
ape.
                    MARTIN LUTHER

And almost everyone when age,
Disease, or sorrows strike him,

Inclines to think there is a God,
Or something very like Him.
                    ARTHUR HUGH CLOUGH

Ask God for what man can give,
and you may get it.
                    EUROPEAN PROVERB

Man is stark mad; he cannot
make a flea, and yet he will be making gods by the dozens.
                    MICHEL DE MONTAIGNE

If triangles made a God, they
would give Him three sides.
                    BARON DE LA BRÈDE ET DE MONTES-
                    QUIEU

If God did not exist, it would be
necessary to invent Him.
                    VOLTAIRE

There is no reason that the sense-
less Temples of God should abound
in riches, and the living Temples of
the Holy Ghost starve for hunger.
                    ETHELWOLD, Bishop of Winchester

[See also Faith, Religion]

GOLD:

An ass laden with gold overtakes
everything.
                    THOMAS FULLER

Gold makes the ugly beautiful.
                    MOLIÈRE

Accursed be he who first of yore
Discovered the pernicious ore.
This sets a brother's heart on fire
And arms the son against the sire.
ANACREON

[*See also* Love, Money]

GOLDEN RULE:

All things whatsoever ye would
that men should do to you, do ye
even so to them: for this is the law
and the prophets.
THE BIBLE

Do not do unto others as you
would that they should do unto you.
Their tastes may not be the same.
GEORGE BERNARD SHAW

The Golden Rule has no place in
a political campaign.
JOHN JAMES INGALLS

Every creature alive lives by the
Golden Rule, which they take to
mean, get all the gold you can.

[*See also* Avarice]

GOOD:

Only the young die good.
OLIVER HERFORD

GOSSIP:

It is perfectly monstrous the way
people go about nowadays saying
things against one, behind one's
back, that are absolutely and entirely
true.
OSCAR WILDE

If we all said to each other's faces
what we say behind each other's
backs, society would be impossible.
HONORÉ DE BALZAC

Gossip is what no one claims to
like, but everybody enjoys.
JOSEPH CONRAD

It is easier for a woman to defend
her virtue against men than her reputation against women.
FRENCH PROVERB

Women do not believe everything
they hear—but this doesn't prevent
them from repeating it.

I cannot tell how the truth may
be;
I say the tale as 'twas said to me.
SIR WALTER SCOTT

The things most people want to
know about are usually none of their
business.
GEORGE BERNARD SHAW

She poured a little social sewage
into his ears.
GEORGE MEREDITH

Love and scandal are the best sweeteners of tea.

HENRY FIELDING

Hear no evil, see no evil, speak no evil—and you'll never be invited to a party.

There is only one thing in the world worse than being talked about, and that is not being talked about.

OSCAR WILDE

A malignant sore throat is a danger, a malignant throat not sore is worse.

AMERICAN PROVERB

I don't care what is written about me so long as it isn't true.

KATHARINE HEPBURN

If you your lips would save from slips,
    Five things observe with care;
Of whom you speak, to whom you speak,
    And how—and when—and where.

[See also Slander]

GOVERNMENT:

Sure now, ivery child knows what's guvermint. It's half a dozen gintlemen an' the loike maybe, that meets an' thinks what's best fer thimsilves, an' thin says that's best fer us—an' that's guvermint.

AN ILLITERATE CIVIL WAR WIDOW

There's no trick to being a humorist when you have the whole government working for you.

WILL ROGERS

No man undertakes a trade he has not learned, even the meanest; yet everyone thinks himself sufficiently qualified for the hardest of all trades, that of government.

SOCRATES

You cannot extend the mastery of government over the daily working life of a people without at the same time making it the master of the people's souls and thoughts.

HERBERT HOOVER

Once businessmen are appointed to public office they run the government like nobody's business.

[See also Politician, Politics]

GOVERNMENT SPENDING:

It's a billion here and a billion there; the first thing you know it adds up to real money.

EVERETT DIRKSEN

GRAMMAR:

I am the King of Rome, and above grammar.

SIGISMUND

As to the adjective, when in doubt strike it out.

MARK TWAIN

I have heard, indeed, that two negatives make an affirmative; but I never heard that two nothings ever made anything.

GEORGE VILLIERS, THE SECOND DUKE OF BUCKINGHAM

A synonym is a word you use when you can't spell the other one.

GRATITUDE:

He that has satisfied his thirst turns his back on the well.

BALTASAR GRACIÁN

Hope has a good memory, gratitude a bad one.

BALTASAR GRACIÁN

He, all whose wants you have, when asked,
Supplied:
Will learn to take as soon as he's Denied.

PUBLILIUS SYRUS

Gratitude is a useless word. You will find it in a dictionary but not in life.

FRANÇOIS DE LA ROCHEFOUCAULD

Next to ingratitude, the most painful thing . . . is gratitude.

HENRY WARD BEECHER

[*See also* Ingrate]

GREATNESS:

Traditionally the great men of our country have sprung from poor environments; that being so, it would appear we have long suffered from a severe lack of poverty.

GERALD F. LIEBERMAN

He's the greatest man who ever came out of Plymouth, Vermont.

CLARENCE DARROW, on Calvin Coolidge

He was dull in a new way, and that made many think him great.

SAMUEL JOHNSON

What monster have we here?
A great Deed at this hour of day?
A great just Deed—and not for pay?
Absurd—or insincere.

ELIZABETH BARRETT BROWNING

Some are born great, some achieve greatness, and some have greatness thrust upon them.

WILLIAM SHAKESPEARE

Some have greatness thrust upon them—but not lately.

FRANK DANE

Formerly we used to canonize our great men; now we vulgarize them.

OSCAR WILDE

Ezra Pound wrote a book in which he called me a great artist, and almost everybody I knew started trying to borrow money from me.

GEORGE ANTHEIL

[See also Leadership]

GRIEF:

Where grief is fresh, any attempt to divert it only irritates.

SAMUEL JOHNSON

Grief may be joy misunderstood.

ELIZABETH BARRETT BROWNING

Grief, and an estate, is joy understood.

GREGORY NUNN

We weep to avoid the shame of not weeping.

FRANÇOIS DE LA ROCHEFOUCAULD

The woman was so grief stricken the day of her husband's funeral, she almost missed her beauty parlor appointment.

It is foolish to tear one's hair in grief, as though sorrow would be made less with baldness.

CICERO

. . . of all sad words of book or pen,
The saddest are these: "It might have been!"

JOHN GREENLEAF WHITTIER

[See also Tears]

HAIR:

Long on hair, short on brains.

FRENCH PROVERB

There's no time for a man to recover his hair that grows bald by nature.

WILLIAM SHAKESPEARE

The lovely hair that Galla wears
Is hers—who could have thought it?
She swears 'tis hers; and true she swears,
For I know where she bought it!

MARTIAL

[See also Baldness]

HAPPINESS:

No man is happy; he is at best fortunate.

SOLON

One kind of happiness is to know exactly at what point to be miserable.

FRANÇOIS DE LA ROCHEFOUCAULD

There is nothing which has yet been contrived by man, by which so much happiness is produced as by a good tavern.

SAMUEL JOHNSON

A lifetime of happiness? No man alive could bear it: it would be hell on earth.

GEORGE BERNARD SHAW

[Happiness] is a perpetual possession of being well deceived.

JONATHAN SWIFT

Happiness: An agreeable sensation, arising from contemplating the misery of others.

AMBROSE BIERCE

[See also Grief]

HATE:

Whom they have injured they also hate.

SENECA

Great hate follows great love.

IRISH PROVERB

The hatred of those who are near to us is the most violent.

TACITUS

Hatred is by far the longest pleasure;
Men love in haste, but they detest at leisure.

LORD BYRON

[See also Love]

HEALTH:

The healthy die first.

ITALIAN PROVERB

The art of medicine consists of amusing the patient while nature cures the disease.

VOLTAIRE

There's lots of people who spend so much time watching their health, they haven't got time to enjoy it.

JOSH BILLINGS

[See also Doctor, Medicine]

HEAVEN:

Heaven goes by favor; if it went by merit, you would stay out and your dog would go in.

MARK TWAIN

What a man misses most in heaven is company.

MARK TWAIN

Parting is all we know of heaven,
And all we need of hell.

EMILY DICKINSON

Heaven without good society cannot be heaven.

THOMAS FULLER

Good Americans, when they die, go to Paris.

THOMAS G. APPLETON

. . . when bad Americans die, they go to America.

OSCAR WILDE

What they do in heaven we are ignorant of; what they do not do we are told expressly.

JONATHAN SWIFT

Many might go to Heaven with half the labor they go to hell.

RALPH WALDO EMERSON

[See also Faith, Religion]

HEIR:

Never say you know a man until you have divided an inheritance with him.

JOHANN CASPAR LAVATER

It's going to be fun to watch and see how long the meek can keep the earth after they inherit it.

KIN HUBBARD

He who is anxious for the death of another has a long rope to pull.

FRENCH PROVERB

[See also Grief, Inheritance]

HELL:

If you want to study the social and political history of modern nations, study hell.

THOMAS MERTON

The road to hell is paved with good intentions.

KARL MARX

He did not think it was necessary to make a hell of this world to enjoy paradise in the next.

WILLIAM BECKFORD

I never did give anybody hell. I just told the truth and they thought it was hell.

HARRY TRUMAN

The only people I know who still believe in hell are the ones who had the proper kind of upbringing.

The trouble with you Chicago people is that you think you are the best people down here, whereas you are merely the most numerous.

MARK TWAIN

If I had a ticket to Heaven and
    you didn't have one too,
I'd give up my ticket to Heaven,
    and go to hell with you!

RONALD REAGAN, toast to House Speaker Thomas P. O'Neill, Jr.

[See also Heaven]

HELP:

If you ever need a helping hand you'll find one at the end of your arm.

YIDDISH PROVERB

It was as helpful as throwing a drowning man both ends of a rope.

ARTHUR "BUGS" BAER

HERO:

When, to evade Destruction's
  hand,
To hide they all proceeded,
No soldier in this gallant band
  Hid half as well as he did.
He lay concealed throughout the
  war,
  And so preserved his gore, O!
  That unaffected,
  Undetected,
  Well-connected Warrior
The Duke of Plaza-Toro.

W. S. GILBERT

We can't all be heroes because someone has to sit on the curb and clap as they go by.

WILL ROGERS

In war the heroes always outnumber the soldiers ten to one.

H. L. MENCKEN

I still think the movie heroes are in the audience.

WILSON MIZNER

[See also Courage, Coward, War]

HESITATION:

He who hesitates is last.

MAE WEST

HISTORY:

History says that whenever a weak and ignorant people possess a thing which a strong and enlightened people want, it must be yielded up peaceably.

MARK TWAIN

How many pens are broken, how many ink bottles consumed, to write about things that have never happened.

THE TALMUD

History books that contain no lies are extremely dull.

ANATOLE FRANCE

Very few things happen at the right time, and the rest do not happen at all. The conscientious historian will correct these defects.

HERODOTUS

We will hereafter believe less history than ever, now that we have seen how it is made.

DON HEROLD

History: An account mostly false, of events unimportant, which are brought about by rulers mostly knaves, and soldiers mostly fools.

AMBROSE BIERCE

History belongs to the winner.

God cannot alter the past, but historians can.

SAMUEL BUTLER

To give an accurate and exhaustive account of that period would need a far less brilliant pen than mine.

MAX BEERBOHM

To give an accurate description of what never happened is the proper occupation of the historian.

OSCAR WILDE

Only a fool would try to compress a hundred centuries into a hundred pages of hazardous conclusions. We proceed.

WILL AND ARIEL DURANT

History repeats itself; historians repeat each other.

PHILIP GUEDALLA

The main thing is . . . to make history, not to write it.

OTTO VON BISMARCK

We learn nothing from history except that we learn nothing from history.

The causes of events are ever more interesting than the events themselves.

CICERO

History is indeed little more than the register of the crimes, follies, and misfortunes of mankind.

EDWARD GIBBON

Throughout history females have picked providers. Males have picked anything.

MARGARET MEAD

[See also Conquest, Hell]

HOLIDAY:

A perpetual holiday is a good working definition of hell.

GEORGE BERNARD SHAW

April 1. This is the day upon which we are reminded of what we are on the other three hundred sixty-four.

MARK TWAIN

[See also Vacation]

HOLLYWOOD:

Strip away the phony tinsel of Hollywood and you will find the real tinsel underneath.

OSCAR LEVANT

In Hollywood blood is thicker than talent.

JOE LAURIE, JR.

Whenever a man wants to learn the truth [in Hollywood] let him ask thieves and whores. They're the only decent folk left in this welter.

GENE FOWLER

Hollywood Drink: Marriage on the rocks.

[See also Movies, Producer, Television]

HOME:

The fellow that owns his own home is always just coming out of a hardware store.

KIN HUBBARD

A man's home may seem to be his castle on the outside; inside, it is more often his nursery.

CLARE BOOTHE LUCE

There's no place like home, after the other places close.

Home is home, though it be homely.

ENGLISH PROVERB

I suppose I passed it a hundred times,
But I always stop for a minute
And look at the house, the tragic house,
The house with nobody in it.

JOYCE KILMER

HONESTY:

To be honest, as this world goes, is to be one man picked out of ten thousand.

WILLIAM SHAKESPEARE

An honest man is one who's never been caught.

AMERICAN PROVERB

Make yourself an honest man and then you may be sure there is one rascal less in the world.

THOMAS CARLYLE

All the honesty in the world ain't legal tender for a loaf of bread.

JOSH BILLINGS

Occasionally, when honesty was the best policy, he was honest.

GREGORY NUNN

I thought I was an honest guy, and just doing what everyone else was doing—bending the rules.
MANNY GOLDSTEIN, basketball recruiter for the University of New Mexico

There are no such things as honest people, there are only people less crooked.

GERALD F. LIEBERMAN

I do not know what the heart of a rascal may be, but I know what is in the heart of an honest man; it is horrible.

JOSEPH DE MAISTRE

[See also Honor, Truth]

HONEYMOON:

Niagara Falls must be one of the earliest, and keenest, disappointments in American married life.

OSCAR WILDE

HONOR:

The difference between a moral man and a man of honor is that the latter regrets a discreditable act, even when it has worked. . . .

H. L. MENCKEN

Honor before profit; where practical.

GERALD BARZAN

The louder he talked of his honor, the faster we counted our spoons.

RALPH WALDO EMERSON

What is honor? A word. What is that word honor? Air.

WILLIAM SHAKESPEARE

If you can't give me your word of honor, give me your promise.

SAM GOLDWYN

What is commonly called friendship is only a little more honor among rogues.

HENRY DAVID THOREAU

A man of honor should never forget what he is because he sees what others are.

BALTASAR GRACIÁN

There are people who observe the rules of honor as we observe the stars: from a distance.

VICTOR HUGO

But without money, honor is nothing but a malady.

JEAN RACINE

[See also Air, Morality]

HOPE:

"Hope" is the thing with feathers—
That perches in the soul—
And sings the tune without the words—
And never stops—at all—

EMILY DICKINSON

We are all in the gutter, but some of us are looking at the stars.

OSCAR WILDE

He that waits for a dead man's shoes may long go barefoot.

FRENCH PROVERB

Hope is the dream of a waking man.

ARISTOTLE

The miserable have no other medicine
But only hope.

WILLIAM SHAKESPEARE

Hope: Disappointment deferred.

Second marriage: The triumph of hope over experience.

SAMUEL JOHNSON

[*See also* Dreams, Optimist]

HOSPITALITY:

Hospitality: the virtue which induces us to feed and lodge certain persons who are in no need of food and lodging.

AMBROSE BIERCE

HOTEL:

The great advantage of a hotel is that it's a refuge from home life.

GEORGE BERNARD SHAW

Have you left anything? Have you anything left?

SIGN IN A CASINO-GAMBLING HOTEL

[*See also* Travel]

HUMANITY:

The so-called human race.

MARK TWAIN

Of mankind in general, the parts are greater than the whole.

ARISTOTLE

[*See also* Man, Woman]

HUMILITY:

He that shall humble himself shall be exalted.

THE BIBLE

He that makes himself a sheep shall be eaten by a wolf.

ITALIAN PROVERB

The more humble a man is before God the more he will be exalted; the more humble he is before man, the more he will get rode roughshod.

JOSH BILLINGS

HUMOR:

There are many humorous things in the world, among them the white man's notion that he is less savage than the other savages.

MARK TWAIN

We must laugh at man to avoid crying for him.

NAPOLEON

Even the gods love jokes.

PLATO

It's hard to be funny when you have to be clean.

MAE WEST

Fear not a jest. If one throws salt at thee thou wilt receive no harm unless thou hast sore places.

LATIN PROVERB

[See also Joke]

HUNGER:

A hungry dog will eat dirty pud-
dings.

LATIN PROVERB

If the people have no bread, let
them eat cake.

MARIE ANTOINETTE

[See also Poverty]

HUNTING:

[Fox hunting is] the unspeakable
in full pursuit of the uneatable.

OSCAR WILDE

The Prince is going to shoot wild
animals as fast as they come out of
their cages.
WILL ROGERS, on the Prince of
Wales's proposed hunting trip

HUSBAND:

God give me a rich husband,
though he be an ass.

THOMAS FULLER

A husband without faults is a dangerous observer.

SIR GEORGE SAVILE

Do married men make the best
husbands?

JAMES HUNEKER

Husbands, love your wives, and
be not bitter against them.

THE BIBLE

One can always recognize women
who trust their husbands. They look
so thoroughly unhappy.

OSCAR WILDE

It's a sad house where the hen
crows louder than the cock.

SCOTTISH PROVERB

When the American husband gets
as much appreciative fuss made over
him for providing food, shelter,
clothes, and education for the family
as dogs get for bringing in the morning newspaper, there will be fewer
divorces.

[See also Marriage, Wife]

HYPOCRISY:

Is it not possible to eat me without insisting that I sing the praises of
my devourer?

FYODOR DOSTOEVSKY

I despise the pleasure of pleasing
people whom I despise.

LADY MARY WORTLEY MONTAGU

In nine cases out of ten a woman
had better show more affection than
she feels.

JANE AUSTEN

The value of an idea has nothing whatever to do with the sincerity of the man who expresses it.

OSCAR WILDE

With people of limited ability modesty is merely honesty. But with those who possess great talent it is hypocrisy.

ARTHUR SCHOPENHAUER

The wicked work harder to preach hell than the righteous do to get to heaven.

AMERICAN PROVERB

Clean your finger before you point at my spots.

BENJAMIN FRANKLIN

We prefer the old-fashioned alarm clock to the kind that awakens you with music or a gentle whisper. If there's one thing we can't stand early in the morning it's hypocrisy.

BILL VAUGHN

[See also Lie, Politician, Politics, United Nations]

IDEA:

There are well-dressed foolish ideas, just as there are well-dressed fools.

SÉBASTIEN CHAMFORT

An idea that is not dangerous is unworthy of being called an idea at all.

DON MARQUIS

He was distinguished for ignorance; for he had only one idea, and that was wrong.

BENJAMIN DISRAELI

No army can withstand the strength of an idea whose time has come.

VICTOR HUGO

[See also Religion]

IDEALISM:

Idealism increases in direct proportion to one's distance from the problem.

JOHN GALSWORTHY

If you wish to find the most unromantic set of ideals nowadays you must go among the Romance nations.

JOSEPH JACOBS

[See also Liberal]

IGNORANCE:

Ignorance is not privileged by titular degrees.

LATIN PROVERB

To be ignorant of one's ignorance is the malady of the ignorant.

AMOS BRONSON ALCOTT

Oh, the ignorance of us upon whom Providence did not sufficiently smile to permit us to be born in New England.

HORACE PORTER

Where ignorance is bliss,
'Tis folly to be wise.

THOMAS GRAY

Mankind have a great aversion to intellectual labour; but, even supposing knowledge to be easily attainable, more people would be content to be ignorant than would take a little trouble to acquire it.

SAMUEL JOHNSON

Ignorance of the law must not prevent the losing lawyer from collecting his fee.

LEGAL MAXIM

I would rather have my ignorance than another man's knowledge, because I have so much of it.

MARK TWAIN

[See also Education, Knowledge, Stupidity]

ILLNESS:

People who take cold baths never have rheumatism, but they have cold baths.

AMERICAN PROVERB

She was dangerously ill, now she's dangerously well.

A person seldom falls sick, but the bystanders are animated with a faint hope that he will die.

RALPH WALDO EMERSON

I've just learned about his illness. Let's hope it's nothing trivial.

IRVIN S. COBB

[See also Health]

ILLUSION:

There are three species of creatures who when they seem coming are going,
When they seem going they come: Diplomats, women, and crabs.

JOHN HAY

It is respectable to have no illusions—and safe—and profitable, and dull.

JOSEPH CONRAD

Inflation: Everyone's illusion of wealth.

[See also Dream]

IMAGINATION:

Were it not for imagination, a man would be as happy in the arms of a chambermaid as of a duchess.

SAMUEL JOHNSON

Imagination is more important than knowledge.

ALBERT EINSTEIN

IMMORTALITY:

Men long for an afterlife in which there apparently is nothing to do but delight in heaven's wonders.
LOUIS D. BRANDEIS

Millions long for immortality who barely know how to scratch themselves on a rainy Sunday afternoon.
AMERICAN PROVERB

[See also Heaven, Hell]

IMPERFECTION:

She abounds with luscious faults.
QUINTILIAN

Stupidity is too often beauty's imperfection.
FRENCH PROVERB

IMPOSSIBLE:

It is impossible to overdo luxury.
FRENCH PROVERB

The difficult we do immediately, the impossible takes a little longer.
WORLD WAR II MILITARY SLOGAN

[See also Vice-President (Corporate)]

INCOME:

There is nothing more demoraliz-
ing than a small but adequate income.
EDMUND WILSON

I'm living so far beyond my income that we may almost be said to be living apart.
E E CUMMINGS

There are few sorrows, however poignant, in which a good income is of no avail.
ROBERT FROST

A miser is a person who lives within his income. He is also called a magician.

[See also Money]

INDECISION:

Once he makes up his mind, he's full of indecision.
OSCAR LEVANT, on Dwight D. Eisenhower

Don't stand shivering upon the bank; plunge in at once, and have it over.
SAM SLICK

INDEPENDENCE:

The only point in making money is, you can tell some big shot where to go.
HUMPHREY BOGART

When I was a boy I used to do what my father wanted. Now I have to do what my boy wants. My problem is: When am I going to do what I want?

SAM LEVENSON

I once worked as a salesman and was very independent. I took orders from no one.

GERALD BARZAN

INEQUALITY:

An earthly kingdom cannot exist without inequality of persons. Some must be free, some serfs, some rulers, some subjects.

MARTIN LUTHER

You can't have all chiefs; you gotta have indians too.

AMERICAN PROVERB

[See also Equality, Women's Lib]

INFIDELITY:

Cuckoldry is getting to be so frequent, it will soon become the customary thing.

MICHEL DE MONTAIGNE

When Eve saw her reflection in a pool, she sought Adam and accused him of infidelity.

AMBROSE BIERCE

When love becomes labored we welcome an act of infidelity towards ourselves, to free us from fidelity.

FRANÇOIS DE LA ROCHEFOUCAULD

The fickleness of the women I love is only equaled by the infernal constancy of the women who love me.

GEORGE BERNARD SHAW

To cast away honesty upon a foul slut, were to put meat into an unclean dish.

WILLIAM SHAKESPEARE

[See also Adultery]

INFLATION:

How is the human race going to survive now that the cost of living has gone up two dollars a quart?

W. C. FIELDS

[Bankers] know that history is inflationary and that money is the last thing a wise man will hoard.

WILL AND ARIEL DURANT

I wasn't affected by inflation—I had nothing to inflate.

GERALD BARZAN

The nation is prosperous on the whole, but how much prosperity is there in a hole?

WILL ·ROGERS

Try to save money. Someday it may be valuable again.

We have had two chickens in every pot, two cars in every garage, and now we have two headaches for every aspirin.

FIORELLO LA GUARDIA

Law of Inflation: Whatever goes up will go up some more.

If inflation continues the two-car garage will be replaced by the two-family garage.

Only one fellow in ten thousand understands the currency question, and we meet him every day.

KIN HUBBARD

[See also Economist]

INGRATE:

I have made ten people discontented and one ungrateful.
LOUIS XIV, after making an appointment

We seldom find people ungrateful so long as we are in a condition to render them service.
FRANÇOIS DE LA ROCHEFOUCAULD

[See also Children, Friendship]

INHERITANCE:

To kill a relative of whom you are tired is something. But to inherit his property afterwards, that is genuine pleasure.

HONORÉ DE BALZAC

The virtue of parents is in itself a great legacy.

ITALIAN PROVERB

If you want to really know what your friends and family think of you die broke, and then see who shows up for the funeral.

GREGORY NUNN

[See also Heir, Will]

INSANITY:

The whole religious complexion of the modern world is due to the absence from Jerusalem of a lunatic asylum.

HAVELOCK ELLIS

Insanity: Grounds for divorce in some states, grounds for marriage in all.

One half of the nation is mad—and the other half not very sound.

TOBIAS SMOLLETT

A little Madness in the Spring
Is wholesome even for the King . . .

EMILY DICKINSON

There is no need to visit a madhouse to find lunatics.

JOHANN WOLFGANG VON GOETHE

The way it is now, the asylums
can hold the sane people but if we
tried to shut up the insane we should
run out of building materials.

MARK TWAIN

Insanity in individuals is something rare, but in groups, parties, nations and epochs it is the rule.

FRIEDRICH NIETZSCHE

I sometimes wonder whether our
planet is the asylum of the universe
for disordered minds.

JOHANN WOLFGANG VON GOETHE

Insanity is hereditary. You can get
it from your kids.

SAM LEVENSON

[See also Madness]

INSPIRATION:

Inspiration at its best means
breath, and only too frequently
means wind.

G. K. CHESTERTON

A writer is rarely so well inspired
as when he talks about himself.

ANATOLE FRANCE

INSURANCE:

Down went the owners, greedy
    men whom hope of gain
    allured:

Oh, dry the starting tear, for they
were heavily insured.

W. S. GILBERT

Religion: Insurance in this world
against fire in the next.

Buy an annuity cheap, and make
your life interesting to yourself and
everybody else that watches the
speculation.

CHARLES DICKENS

Insurance: An ingenious modern
game of chance in which the player
is permitted to enjoy the comfortable conviction that he is beating the
man who keeps the table.

AMBROSE BIERCE

INTELLIGENCE:

At a certain age some people's
minds close up. They live on their
intellectual fat.

WILLIAM LYON PHELPS

There is nothing so irritating as
somebody with less intelligence and
more sense than we have.

DON HEROLD

She was short on intellect but long
on shape.

GEORGE ADE

One of the first conditions of
learning in a woman is to keep the
fact a profound secret.

HONORÉ DE BALZAC

A foolish consistency is the hobgoblin of little minds.

RALPH WALDO EMERSON

It is impossible to underrate human intelligence.

HENRY ADAMS

Merely having an open mind is nothing; the object of opening the mind, as of opening the mouth, is to shut it again on something solid.

G. K. CHESTERTON

You cannot gauge the intelligence of an American by talking with him.

ERIC HOFFER

[See also Brain]

INVENTION:

Edison did not invent the first talking machine. He invented the first one that could be turned off.

If you build a better mousetrap, you will catch better mice.

GEORGE GOBEL

If a man can write a better book, or preach a better sermon, or build a better mousetrap than his neighbor, though he builds his house in the woods, the world will make a beaten path to his door.

ATTRIBUTED TO RALPH WALDO EMERSON

If you build a better mousetrap,

the world will beat you out of the patent.

[See also Genius, Science]

INVESTMENT:

I was shipwrecked before I got aboard.

SENECA

Hard work is the soundest investment. It provides a neat security for your widow's next husband.

[See also Broker, Stock Market]

IRELAND:

It is the plain duty of every Irishman to disassociate himself from all memories of Ireland—Ireland being a fatal disease, fatal to Englishmen and doubly fatal to Irishmen.

GEORGE MOORE

In Ireland there is so little sense of compromise that a girl has to choose between perpetual adoration and perpetual pregnancy.

GEORGE MOORE

Had you English not persecuted the Catholics in Ireland . . . the greatest number of them would before now have become Protestants.

NAPOLEON

ISRAEL:

In Israel in order to be a realist you must believe in miracles.

DAVID BEN-GURION

The only thing chicken about Israel is their soup.

BOB HOPE

Your name shall be called Israel, for you have striven with God and with men, and have prevailed.

THE BIBLE

[See also Jew]

ITALY:

The Creator made Italy from designs by Michelangelo.

MARK TWAIN

A man who has not been to Italy is always conscious of his inferiority.

SAMUEL JOHNSON

JEALOUSY:

It is matrimonial suicide to be jealous when you have a really good reason.

CLARE BOOTHE LUCE

Yet he was jealous, though he did not show it,
For jealousy dislikes the world to know it.

LORD BYRON

Plain women are always jealous of their husbands. Beautiful women never are. They are always so occupied with being jealous of other women's husbands.

OSCAR WILDE

[See also Man, Marriage, Woman]

JEW:

We Jews have a secret weapon in our struggle with the Arabs; we have no place to go.

GOLDA MEIR

The Jews are a frightened people. Nineteen centuries of Christian love have broken their nerves.

ISRAEL ZANGWILL

The world is divided into two groups of nations—those which want to expel the Jews and those which do not want to receive them.

CHAIM WEIZMANN

The Jews are among the aristocracy of every land; if a literature is called rich in the possession of a few classic tragedies, what shall we say to a national tragedy lasting for fifteen hundred years, in which the poets and actors were also the heroes.

GEORGE ELIOT

[See also Israel]

JOKE:

I don't know jokes; I just watch the government and report the facts.
WILL ROGERS

Jesters do oft prove prophets.
WILLIAM SHAKESPEARE

My way of joking is telling the truth; that is the funniest joke in the world.
GEORGE BERNARD SHAW

A difference of taste in jokes is a great strain on the affections.
GEORGE ELIOT

[See also Congress, Humor, Life, Politician, Politics, United Nations]

JOURNALISM:

Journalism largely consists in saying "Lord Jones is dead" to people who never knew Lord Jones was alive.
G. K. CHESTERTON

Journalism is unreadable and literature is unread.
OSCAR WILDE

There was a press club meeting which had all the grace notes of our heyday, together with the almost forgotten noises of reporters falling into spittoons.
GENE FOWLER

[See also Newspaper]

JOURNEY:

I am going on a journey; they have greased my boots already.
SIR SAMUEL GARTH, after receiving extreme unction.

Journeys end in lovers' meeting,
Every wise man's son doth know.
WILLIAM SHAKESPEARE

[See also Travel]

JUDGE:

Judges, like the criminal classes, have their lighter moments.
OSCAR WILDE

The duty of a judge is to administer justice, but his practice is to delay it.
JEAN DE LA BRUYÈRE

The hungry judges soon the sentence sign,
And wretches hang that jury-men may dine.
ALEXANDER POPE

A judge is a law student who marks his own examination papers.
H. L. MENCKEN

[See also Crime, Justice, Law, Lawsuit, Lawyer]

JUDGMENT:

My salad days.
When I was green in judgment.
WILLIAM SHAKESPEARE

Good judgment comes from experience; and experience, well, that comes from bad judgment.

JURY:

Whom the juries would acquit they first make mad.

A jury is composed of twelve men of average ignorance.
HERBERT SPENCER

The stupidity of one brain multiplied by twelve.
ELBERT HUBBARD

The penalty for laughing in the courtroom is six months in jail. If it were not for this penalty, the jury would never hear the evidence.
H. L. MENCKEN

Despite the arguments of his attorney, we the jury find the defendant not guilty.
DECISION IN A MISSOURI MURDER TRIAL

A jury consists of twelve persons chosen to decide who has the better lawyer.
ROBERT FROST

[See also Judge, Justice, Law, Lawyer]

JUSTICE:

They acquit the vultures but condemn the doves.
JUVENAL

There is no such thing as justice—in or out of court.
CLARENCE DARROW

American judicial procedure's great difficulty seems to be how to proceed.

Thrice is he arm'd that hath his quarrel just.
WILLIAM SHAKESPEARE

Thrice is he armed that hath his quarrel just:
And four times he who gets his fist in fust.
JOSH BILLINGS

The efficiency of our criminal jury system is only marred by the difficulty of finding twelve men every day who don't know anything and can't read.
MARK TWAIN

Should vice expect to 'scape rebuke
Because its owner is a duke?
JONATHAN SWIFT

Thieves for their robbery have authority
When judges steal themselves.

WILLIAM SHAKESPEARE

He who spares the bad injures the good.

PUBLILIUS SYRUS

We leave unmolested those who set the fire to the house, and prosecute those who sound the alarm.

SÉBASTIEN CHAMFORT

Every unpunished delinquency has a family of delinquencies.

HERBERT SPENCER

Injustice is relatively easy to bear; what stings is justice.

H. L. MENCKEN

[See also Judge, Jury, Law, Lawyer, Mercy, Punishment]

KINDNESS:

Had we never loved sae kindly,
Had we never loved sae blindly,
Never met—or never parted—
We had ne'er been brokenhearted.

ROBERT BURNS

Kindness begets kindness.

GREEK PROVERB

He was so benevolent, so merciful a man that, in his mistaken passion,

he would have held an umbrella over a duck in a shower of rain.

DOUGLAS JERROLD

You can get more with a kind word and a gun than you can get with a kind word alone.

JOHNNY CARSON

[See also Charity]

KISS:

He who kisses ugly Philaenis sins against nature.

MARTIAL

Who would refuse to kiss a lapdog, if it were preliminary to the lips of his lady?

WILLIAM CONGREVE

When women kiss it always reminds me of prize fighters shaking hands.

H. L. MENCKEN

Some men kiss and tell. George Moore tells—but he does not kiss.

REVIEW OF THE MEMOIRS OF GEORGE MOORE

Give me a kiss, and to that kiss a score;
Then to that twenty, add a hundred more;
A thousand to that hundred; so kiss on,
To make that thousand up a million.

Treble that million, and when that
is done,
Let's kiss afresh, as when we first
begun.
                        ROBERT HERRICK

Kissing don't last; cookery do!
                        GEORGE MEREDITH

Do thou snatch treasures from my
lips, and I'll take kingdoms back
from thine.
            RICHARD BRINSLEY SHERIDAN

We have kiss'd away
Kingdoms and provinces.
                    WILLIAM SHAKESPEARE

What of soul was left, I wonder,
when the kissing had to stop?
                        ROBERT BROWNING

What lies lurk in kisses.
                        HEINRICH HEINE

If you are ever in doubt as to
whether or not you should kiss a
pretty girl, always give her the
benefit of the doubt.
                        THOMAS CARLYLE

Marriage is the miracle that trans-
forms a kiss from a pleasure into a
duty.
                        HELEN ROWLAND

Soul meets soul on lovers' lips.
                    PERCY BYSSHE SHELLEY

If you kiss enough asses you'll get
kicked in the teeth.
                        GERALD BARZAN

[See also Love, Marriage, Sex]

KNOWLEDGE:

To the small part of ignorance
that we arrange and classify we give
the name knowledge.
                        AMBROSE BIERCE

Knowledge and human power are
synonymous.
                        FRANCIS BACON

Knowledge is power—if you
know it about the right people.

Much knowledge is a curse.
                        CHUANG-TZU

Knowledge is of two kinds; we
know a subject ourselves, or we
know where we can find information
upon it.
                        SAMUEL JOHNSON

A man is accepted into a church
for what he believes and he is turned
out for what he knows.
                        MARK TWAIN

Universities are full of knowledge;
the freshmen bring a little in and the
seniors take none away, and knowledge accumulates.
                        LAWRENCE LOWELL

Mistakes are their own instruc-
tors.
                        HORACE

The trouble with most folks ain't so much their ignorance as knowing so many things that ain't so.

JOSH BILLINGS

The chief knowledge that a man gets from reading books is the knowledge that very few of them are worth reading.

H. L. MENCKEN

A man who carries a cat by the tail learns something he can learn in no other way.

MARK TWAIN

[See also College, Education, Scholar, Scholarship, Teacher, Youth]

LADY:

A lady, if undrest at Church, looks silly,
One cannot be devout in dishabilly.

GEORGE FARQUHAR

An actress is not a lady; at least when she is, she is not an actress.

GEORGE BERNARD SHAW

[See also Woman]

LANDLORD:

Give a landlord an inch and he'll build an apartment house.

AMERICAN PROVERB

He who has the property in the soil has the same up in the sky.

LATIN PROVERB

[See also Property]

LANGUAGE:

If the Romans had been obliged to learn Latin they would never have found time to conquer the world.

HEINRICH HEINE

The learned fool writes his nonsense in better language than the unlearned, but it is still nonsense.

BENJAMIN FRANKLIN

One tongue is sufficient for a woman.

JOHN MILTON

It was Greek to me.

WILLIAM SHAKESPEARE

Foreign sounds, like foreign servants, ought not to be introduced to the disadvantage of the natives.

C. C. COLTON

LAW:

Under the laws of this country a man is innocent until he is proved guilty—then he is usually insane.

The more numerous the laws, the more corrupt the state.

TACITUS

When you have no basis for an argument, abuse the plaintiff.

CICERO

The law itself follows gold.

PROPERTIUS

If nature had as many laws as the State, God Himself could not reign over it.

LUDWIG BOERNE

I have forgotten more law than you ever knew but allow me to say, I have not forgotten much.
SIR JOHN MAYNARD, to a British magistrate

Legality is killing us.

J. G. VIENNET

'Tis easier to make some things legal than to make them legitimate.

SÉBASTIEN CHAMFORT

The trouble with law is lawyers.

CLARENCE DARROW

The English laws punish vice; the Chinese laws do more, they reward virtue.

OLIVER GOLDSMITH

If you laid all our laws end to end, there would be no end.

ARTHUR "BUGS" BAER

"Legally" is a robust adverb—it justifies many ill-gotten gains.

HONORÉ DE BALZAC

Law is a ass, a idiot.

CHARLES DICKENS

The law can take a purse in open court,
While it condemns a less delinquent for't.

SAMUEL BUTLER

Let him whose coat a court has taken,
Sing his song and go his way.

THE TALMUD

Where law ends, tyranny begins.

WILLIAM PITT

Where lawyers enter, tyranny begins.

GREGORY NUNN

Self-defense is the clearest of all laws, and for this reason: lawyers didn't make it.

DOUGLAS JERROLD

He who goes to law for a sheep loses his cow.

SPANISH PROVERB

The law is a system that protects everybody who can afford to hire a good lawyer.

There is no end to the laws, and no beginning to the execution of them.

MARK TWAIN

Law and equity are two things which God hath joined, but which man has put asunder.

C. C. COLTON

If the laws could speak for themselves, they would complain of the lawyers.

SIR GEORGE SAVILE

Our very freedom is secure because we're a nation governed by laws, not by men. We cannot as citizens pick and choose the laws we will or will not obey.

RONALD REAGAN

The United States is the greatest law factory the world has ever known.

CHARLES EVANS HUGHES

America, where, thanks to Congress, there are forty million laws to enforce ten commandments.

The law is fair to all. In its fairness for equality it forbids the rich as well as the poor to beg in the streets and to steal bread.

ANATOLE FRANCE

Some laws of state aimed at curbing crime are even more criminal.

FRIEDRICH ENGELS

Law is a strange thing. It makes a man swear to tell the truth, and every time he shows signs of doing so, some lawyer objects.

Laws are like cobwebs. If a trifling or powerless thing falls into them they hold it fast; while, if it is something weightier, it breaks through them and is off.

SOLON

[See also Court, Crime, Judge, Jury, Justice, Lawsuit, Lawyer, Punishment]

LAWSUIT:

I was never ruined but twice, once when I lost a lawsuit and once when I won one.

VOLTAIRE

I can't do no literary work for the rest of this year because I'm meditating another lawsuit and looking around for a defendant.

MARK TWAIN

Fond of lawsuits, little wealth; fond of doctors, little health.

HEBREW PROVERB

[See also Law]

LAWYER:

It is unfair to believe everything we hear about lawyers—some of it might not be true.

GERALD F. LIEBERMAN

Woe unto ye . . . lawyers! for ye lade men with burdens grievous to bear.

THE BIBLE

Let's kill all the lawyers.

WILLIAM SHAKESPEARE

Ignorance of the law excuses no man.

JOHN SELDEN

Ignorance of the law excuses no man from practicing it.

ADDISON MIZNER

He is no lawyer who cannot take two sides.

CHARLES LAMB

Every once in a while you meet a fellow in some honorable walk of life that was once admitted to the bar.

KIN HUBBARD

A contingency fee is an arrangement in which if you lose your lawyer gets nothing—and if you win you get nothing.

It has been said that the course to be pursued by a lawyer was first to get on, second to get honor, and third to get honest.

GEORGE M. PALMER

A good lawyer is a bad neighbor.

FRENCH PROVERB

The sharp employ the sharp; ver-

ily, a man may be known by his lawyer.

DOUGLAS JERROLD

Whene'er a bitter foe attack thee
Sheathe thy sword, thy wrath re-
    strain;
Or else will magistrates and law-
    yers
Divide thy wealth, thy purse re-
    tain.

ARCHEVOLTI, 16TH CENTURY

He is wondering whether he made God, or God made him.

RUFUS CHOATE, on what a lawyer thinks.

To succeed in other trades, capacity must be shown; in the law, concealment of it will do.

MARK TWAIN

God works wonders now and
    then;
Behold a lawyer, an honest man.

BENJAMIN FRANKLIN

Where there's a rift in the lute, the business of the lawyer is to widen the rift and gather the loot.

ARTHUR GARFIELD HAYS

Lawyers earn a living by the sweat of their browbeating.

JAMES G. HUNEKER

Young lawyers attend the courts, not because they have business there but because they have no business anywhere else.

WASHINGTON IRVING

[*See also* Law]

LEADERSHIP:

Anyone can steer the ship when the sea is calm.

PUBLILIUS SYRUS

The shepherd always tries to persuade the sheep that their interests and his own are the same.

STENDHAL

The emperor sent his troops to the field with immense enthusiasm; and he will lead them in person, when they return.

MARK TWAIN

In enterprise of martial kind,
    When there was any fighting,
He led his regiment from behind—
    He found it less exciting.
But when away his regiment ran,
    His place was at the fore, O—
That celebrated,
    Cultivated,
Underrated Nobleman,
The Duke of Plaza-Toro.

W. S. GILBERT

[*See also* Courage, Coward]

LIAR:

Liar: The very basis of civilized society.

OSCAR WILDE

Some persons make promises for the pleasure of breaking them.

WILLIAM HAZLITT

[*See also* Lie, Lying, Politician]

LIBEL:

The greater the truth, the greater the libel.

LORD MANSFIELD

[*See also* Truth, Slander]

LIBERAL:

I can remember way back when a liberal was one who was generous with his own money.

WILL ROGERS

A liberal is a man who will give away everything he doesn't own.

FRANK DANE

Liberalism is trust of the people tempered by prudence; conservatism, distrust of people tempered by fear.

WILLIAM GLADSTONE

A man who has both feet planted firmly in the air can be safely called a liberal.

AMERICAN PROVERB

A man who has both feet planted firmly in the air can be safely called a liberal; as opposed to the conservative, who has both feet firmly planted in his mouth.

GERALD BARZAN

A liberal is a man who is right most of the time, but he's right too soon.

GREGORY NUNN

He that defers his charity until he is dead is, if a man weighs it rightly, rather liberal of another man's goods than his own.

FRANCIS BACON

[See also Conservative, Democrat, Politician, Politics]

LIBERTY:

Liberty: One of Imagination's most precious possessions.

AMBROSE BIERCE

Dictatorship naturally arises out of democracy, and the most aggravated form of tyranny and slavery out of the most extreme liberty.

PLATO

The people never give up their liberties but under some delusion.

EDMUND BURKE

The true character of liberty is independence, maintained by force.

VOLTAIRE

Proclaim liberty throughout all the land unto all the inhabitants.

THE BIBLE

They that can give up essential liberty to obtain a little temporary safety deserve neither liberty nor safety.

BENJAMIN FRANKLIN

In America we believe in Life, Liberty—and the pursuit.

[See also Democracy, Government]

LIBRARY:

Your library is your Paradise.

ERASMUS

There are seventy million books in American libraries, but the one you want is always out.

TOM MASSON

[See also Book]

LIE:

I do not mind lying, but I hate inaccuracy.

SAMUEL BUTLER

There are a terrible lot of lies going about the world, and the worst of it is that half of them are true.

WINSTON CHURCHILL

A lie with a purpose is one of the worst kind, and the most profitable.

FINLEY PETER DUNNE

There are three kinds of lies: lies, damned lies, and statistics.

BENJAMIN DISRAELI

He who comes from afar may lie without fear of contradiction as he is sure to be listened to with the utmost attention.

FRENCH PROVERB

'Tis hard a new-formed fable to express,
And make it seem your own well-managed mess.

LATIN PROVERB

[See also History, Lying, Politician, Politics]

LIFE:

The trouble with life is that there are so many beautiful women, and so little time.

JOHN BARRYMORE

Life is a tragedy for those who feel, and a comedy for those who think.

JEAN DE LA BRUYÈRE

It's a good thing that life is not as serious as it seems to a waiter.

DON HEROLD

On with the dance, let joy be unconfined, is my motto; whether there's any dance to dance or any joy to unconfine.

MARK TWAIN

A precipice in front of you, and wolves behind you, in your rear; that is life.

LATIN PROVERB

Where there is life there is wishful thinking.

GERALD F. LIEBERMAN

Life is like an onion. Why is life like an onion? Because you peel away layer after layer and when you come to the end you have nothing.

YIDDISH PROVERB

Life's but a walking shadow, a poor player
That struts and frets his hour upon the stage,
And then is heard no more; it is a tale
Told by an idiot, full of sound and fury,
Signifying nothing.

WILLIAM SHAKESPEARE

Life is short, but it's long enough to ruin any man who wants to be ruined.

JOSH BILLINGS

I've read the last page of the Bible. It's going to turn out all right.

BILLY GRAHAM

Life may not be beautiful but it is interesting.

SIR JOHN ROBERT SEELEY

The enjoyments of this life are not equal to its evils.

PLINY THE ELDER

Life is one long process of getting tired.

SAMUEL BUTLER

No matter how bad things get you got to go on living, even if it kills you.

SHOLEM ALEICHEM

The first hundred years are the hardest.

WILSON MIZNER

Life is a waste of wearisome
    hours,
Which seldom the rose of enjoy-
    ment adorns;
And the heart that is soonest
    awake to the flowers
Is always the first to be touch'd by
    the thorns.

THOMAS MOORE

There is a period of life when we go backwards as we advance.

JEAN-JACQUES ROUSSEAU

Why are we so fond of that life which begins with a cry and ends with a groan?

MARY, COUNTESS OF WARWICK

The world itself is but a large prison, out of which some are daily led to execution.

SIR WALTER RALEIGH

The great business of life is, to be, to do, to do without, and to depart.

JOHN MORLEY

In our sad condition our only con-solation is the expectancy of another life. Here below all is incomprehen-sible.

MARTIN LUTHER

Life can only be understood back-wards, but it must be lived forwards.

SØREN KIERKEGAARD

The Book of Life begins with a man and a woman in a garden, and ends with Revelations.

OSCAR WILDE

The hour of departure has ar-rived and we go our ways; I to die, and you to live. Which is better? Only God knows.

SOCRATES

Not to be born is best.

SOPHOCLES

All some people expect in life is a fair advantage.

[See also Death, Noise]

LIPS:

Lips, however rosy, must be fed.

SCOTTISH PROVERB

Graze on my lips, and when those
    mounts are dry
Stray lower, where the pleasant
    fountains lie.

GERVASE MARKHAM

139

LONELINESS

[*See also* Kiss]

LITERATURE:

Only the more rugged mortals should attempt to keep up with current literature.

GEORGE ADE

I have the conviction that excessive literary production is a social offense.

GEORGE ELIOT

People do not deserve to have good writings; they are so pleased with bad.

RALPH WALDO EMERSON

[*See also* Book, Writer, Writing]

LIVING TOGETHER:

Today couples live together until they learn to detest one another. Then they get married.

Companionate marriage is so-called because the people involved are not married and will rapidly cease to be companions.

G. K. CHESTERTON

[*See also* Marriage, Sex, Women's Lib]

LOAN:

It is better to give than to lend, and it costs about the same.

PHILIP GIBBS

[*See also* Banker, Friendship]

LOGIC:

Logic is the technique by which we add conviction to truth.

JEAN DE LA BRUYÈRE

The heated mind resents the chill touch and relentless scrutiny of logic.

WILLIAM GLADSTONE

There is a danger that if the Court does not temper its doctrinaire logic with a little practical wisdom, it will convert the constitutional Bill of Rights into a suicide pact.

ROBERT JACKSON

[*See also* Reason]

LONELINESS:

Be good and you will be lonely.

MARK TWAIN

It is very lonely sometimes, trying to play God.

OLIVER WENDELL HOLMES

I'm lonesome, they are all dying; I have hardly a warm personal enemy left.

JAMES McNEILL WHISTLER

In Genesis it says that it is not good for a man to be alone, but sometimes it is a great relief.

JOHN BARRYMORE

LOOKS:

Looks are deceiving. A man with a vacant look may have a full house.

LOSER:

It's better to have loved and lost, much better.

There are two tragedies in life. One is to lose your heart's desire, the other is to gain it.

GEORGE BERNARD SHAW

It's the good loser who finally loses out.

KIN HUBBARD

LOVE:

First love is a little foolishness and a lot of curiosity.

GEORGE BERNARD SHAW

There are people who would never have fallen in love if they had never heard of love.

FRANÇOIS DE LA ROCHEFOUCAULD

To be in love is merely to be in a perpetual state of anesthesia.

H. L. MENCKEN

Love: A grave mental illness.

PLATO

Love is the delightful interval between meeting a beautiful girl and discovering that she looks like a haddock.

JOHN BARRYMORE

Love is said to be blind but I know some fellows in love who can see twice as much in their sweethearts as I do.

JOSH BILLINGS

Unless you can muse in a crowd all day
  On the absent face that fixed you;
Unless you can love as the angels may
  With the breadth of heaven betwixt you;
Unless you can dream that his faith is fast
  Through behoving and unbehoving;
Unless you can die when the dream is past—
  Oh, never call it loving.

ELIZABETH BARRETT BROWNING

Love is the triumph of imagination over intelligence.

H. L. MENCKEN

How do I love thee? Let me count
the ways.
I love thee to the depth and
breadth and height
My soul can reach. . . .

ELIZABETH BARRETT BROWNING

Love is not altogether a delirium,
yet it has many points in common
therewith.

THOMAS CARLYLE

A false enchantment can all too
easily last a lifetime.

W. H. AUDEN

There is no living with thee, nor
without thee.

MARTIAL

It is better to have loved your
wife than never to have loved at all.

EDGAR SALTUS

Love and war are the same thing.

MIGUEL DE CERVANTES

Ah Love! Could you and I with
him conspire
To grasp this sorry Scheme of
Things entire
Would we not shatter it to bits—
and then
Re-mould it nearer to the Heart's
Desire?

OMAR KHAYYÁM

One is never too old to yearn.

ITALIAN PROVERB

Women are made to be loved, not
understood.

OSCAR WILDE

When a scholar goes to seek out a
bride he should take along an ignoramus as an expert.

THE TALMUD

Let the first impulse pass, wait for
the second.

BALTASAR GRACIÁN

They love too much that die for
love.

JOHN RAY

Love is based on a view of women
that is impossible to those who have
had any experience with them.

H. L. MENCKEN

Love is a state in which a man
sees things most decidedly as they
are not.

FRIEDRICH NIETZSCHE

It is difficult to lay aside a
confirmed passion.

CATULLUS

The heart has its reasons which
reason does not understand.

BLAISE PASCAL

Love: An ocean of emotions surrounded entirely by expenses.

THOMAS R. DEWAR

One should always be in love. That is the reason one should never marry.

OSCAR WILDE

No more we meet in yonder
  bowers;
Absence has made me prone to
  roving;
But older, firmer hearts than ours
Have found monotony in loving.

LORD BYRON

One must have loved a woman of genius to appreciate what happiness there is in loving a fool.

CHARLES MAURICE DE TALLEYRAND

A truce to your volumes, your
  studies give o'er;
For books cannot teach you
  love's marvelous lore.

HAFIZ OF PERSIA

Like the measles, love is most dangerous when it comes late in life.

LORD BYRON

The loves of some people are but the result of good suppers.

SÉBASTIEN CHAMFORT

The way to a man's heart is through his stomach.

TRADITIONAL PROVERB

The way to a woman's heart is through your wallet.

FRANK DANE

All the world loves a lover, but not while the love-making is going on.

ELBERT HUBBARD

Subdue your passion or it will subdue you.

HORACE

[See also Affection, Man, Marriage, Sex, Woman, Women's Lib]

LOVE LETTER:

Wrong no man and write no woman.

ELBERT HUBBARD

LOVER:

A lover teaches a wife all her husband kept hidden from her.

HONORÉ DE BALZAC

A lover is a man who tries to be more amiable than is his nature.

SÉBASTIEN CHAMFORT

The quarrels of lovers are the resuscitation of love.

TERENCE

[See also Adultery, Infidelity, Love]

LOYALTY:

He who by his prince too blindly
  does obey,

Keeps his faith, his virtue throws away.

JOHN DRYDEN

Loyalty to petrified opinion never yet broke a chain or freed a human soul.

MARK TWAIN

[See also Patriotism]

LUCK:

He dances well to whom fortune pipes.

ITALIAN PROVERB

Substance is not enough, accident is also required.

GREEK PROVERB

The man who has always been fortunate cannot easily have great reverence for virtue.

CICERO

Just my luck! If I had been bred a hatter, little boys would have come into the world without heads.

E. R. BULWER-LYTTON

The Devil's children have the Devil's luck.

ENGLISH PROVERB

I'm a great believer in luck and I find the harder I work the more I have of it.

STEPHEN LEACOCK

Yes, there's luck in most things, and in none more than being born at the right time.

EDMUND CLARENCE STEDMAN

Luck can be assisted. It is not all chance with the wise.

BALTASAR GRACIÁN

Better a lucky physician than a learned one.

ENGLISH PROVERB

Wait till a man's life is ended; till then call him not happy but lucky.

SOLON

He is so unlucky that he runs into accidents which started out to happen to somebody else.

DON MARQUIS

The only sure thing about luck is that it will change.

WILSON MIZNER

[See also Fate, Fortune]

LYING:

The best liar is he who makes the smallest amount of lying go the longest way.

SAMUEL BUTLER

A wise man does not waste so good a commodity as lying for naught.

MARK TWAIN

[See also Lie, Politician, Politics, Propaganda, United Nations]

MADNESS:

Better mad with the rest of the world than wise alone.

BALTASAR GRACIÁN

All are lunatics, but he who can analyze his delusion is called a philosopher.

AMBROSE BIERCE

[See also Insanity]

MAGIC:

The magic of the tongue is the most dangerous of all spells.

E. R. BULWER-LYTTON

MAIL:

The ideal love affair is one conducted by post.

GEORGE BERNARD SHAW

I have received no more than one or two letters in my life that were worth the postage.

HENRY DAVID THOREAU

Neither snow nor rain nor heat nor gloom of night stays these couriers from the swift completion of their appointed rounds.

HERODOTUS
(The motto of the U.S. Postal Service)

[See also Christmas]

MAJORITY:

The majority is always wrong; the minority is rarely right.

HENRIK IBSEN

If fifty million people say a foolish thing it is still a foolish thing.

ANATOLE FRANCE

We go by the major vote, and if the majority are insane, the sane must go to the hospital.

HORACE MANN

The oppression of a majority is detestable and odious: the oppression of a minority is only one degree less detestable and odious.

WILLIAM GLADSTONE

[See also Minority]

MAN:

Somebody must take a chance. The monkeys who did became men, and the monkeys who didn't are still jumping around in trees making faces at the monkeys who did.

LINCOLN STEFFENS

Man is a two-legged animal without feathers.

PLATO

I hate mankind, for I think of myself as one of the best of them, and I know how bad I am.

SAMUEL JOHNSON

Are you a man or a mouse? Squeak up!

Man is the only animal that blushes. Or needs to.

MARK TWAIN

Methinks we might elevate ourselves a little more. We might climb a tree, at least.

HENRY DAVID THOREAU

Man is stark mad. He cannot make a worm, yet he makes gods by the dozens.

MICHEL DE MONTAIGNE

Man cannot live by incompetence alone.

LAURENCE PETER

How great in number are the little-minded men.

PLAUTUS

I wonder men dare trust themselves with men.

WILLIAM SHAKESPEARE

Have you ever watched a crab on the shore crawling backward in search of the Atlantic Ocean, and missing it? That's the way the mind of man operates.

H. L. MENCKEN

Man is an incomprehensible monster.

BLAISE PASCAL

Man's inhumanity to man
Makes countless thousands mourn!

ROBERT BURNS

The mass of men lead lives of quiet desperation.

HENRY DAVID THOREAU

Breathes there a man with hide so tough
Who says two sexes aren't enough?

SAMUEL HOFFENSTEIN

Man that is born of a woman is of few days, and full of trouble.

THE BIBLE

Though I've belted you and flayed you,
By the livin' Gawd that made you,
You're a better man than I am, Gunga Din!

RUDYARD KIPLING

It was a pity he couldna be hatched o'er again, an' hatched different.

GEORGE ELIOT

Of all the ways of defining man, the worst is the one which makes him out to be a rational animal.

ANATOLE FRANCE

Man's life is a warfare against the malice of men.

BALTASAR GRACIÁN

Every man has a sane spot somewhere.

ROBERT LOUIS STEVENSON

All that I care to know is that a man is a human being, that is enough for me; he can't be any worse.

MARK TWAIN

The more I see of men, the more I like dogs.

MME. DE STAËL

It is strange that men should see sublime inspiration in the ruins of an old church, and see none in the ruins of a man.

G. K. CHESTERTON

Darwinian Man, though well-
behaved,
At best is only a monkey shaved!

W. S. GILBERT

Man, in his anxiety to refute evidence that he is a monkey, manages to further the belief that he is an ass.

GERALD F. LIEBERMAN

[See also Woman, Women's Lib]

MANAGEMENT:

So much of what we call management consists in making it difficult for people to work.

PETER DRUCKER

[See also Unions (Labor)]

MANNERS:

What once were vices are manners now.

SENECA

If a man has good manners and is not afraid of other people he will get by, even if he is stupid.

DAVID ECCLES

The highest perfection of politeness is only a beautiful edifice, built, from the base to the dome, of ungraceful and gilded forms of charitable and unselfish lying.

MARK TWAIN

When a Roman was returning from a trip he used to send someone ahead to inform his wife, so as not to surprise her in the act.

MICHEL DE MONTAIGNE

Never argue at the dinner table, for the one who is not hungry always gets the best of the argument.

RICHARD WHATELY

To be cordial is like roughing a man's head to jolly him up or kissing a child that doesn't want to be kissed. You are relieved when it's over.

GEORGE SANTAYANA

He is every other inch a gentleman.

REBECCA WEST

Naught must disturb a man of worth at dinner.

FRENCH PROVERB

The best-mannered people make the most absurd lovers.

DENIS DIDEROT

Be kind and considerate of others, depending somewhat upon who they are.

DON HEROLD

Be always pert and insolent, and behave yourself as if you were the injured person.

JONATHAN SWIFT

These passengers, by reason of
  their clinging to a mast,
Upon a desert island were eventually cast.
They hunted for their meals, as
  Alexander Selkirk used,
But they couldn't chat together—
  they had not been
  introduced.

W. S. GILBERT

Be polite, write diplomatically; even in a declaration of war one observes the rules of politeness.

OTTO VON BISMARCK

A patronizing disposition always has its meaner side.

GEORGE ELIOT

Talk to every woman as if you loved her, and to every man as if he bored you, and at the end of your first season you will have the reputation of possessing the most perfect social tact.

OSCAR WILDE

[See also Charm, Gentleman, Tact]

MARRIAGE:

Marriage is the process whereby love ripens into vengeance.

Make 'im take 'er, and keep 'er,
That's 'ell for 'em both.

RUDYARD KIPLING

By all means marry. If you get a good wife you will become happy—and if you get a bad one you will become a philosopher.

SOCRATES

When two people are under the influence of the most violent, most insane, most delusive and most transient of passions, they are required to swear that they will remain in that excited, abnormal and exhausting condition continuously until death do them part.

GEORGE BERNARD SHAW

Marriage is the sunset of love.

FRENCH PROVERB

Courtship is to marriage as a very witty prologue to a very dull play.
WILLIAM CONGREVE

Marriage, if one will face the truth, is an evil, but a necessary evil.
MENANDER

Second Marriage: The triumph of hope over experience.
SAMUEL JOHNSON

The deed involves sacrifice and risk.
MARTIN BUBER

Concubinage has been corrupted by marriage.
FRIEDRICH NIETZSCHE

It destroys one's nerves to be amiable every day to the same human being.
BENJAMIN DISRAELI

Any intelligent woman who reads the marriage contract, and then goes into it, deserves all the consequences.
ISADORA DUNCAN

It's a funny thing that when a man hasn't anything on earth to worry about, he goes off and gets married.
ROBERT FROST

Marriage is popular because it combines the maximum of temptation with the maximum of opportunity.
GEORGE BERNARD SHAW

What delight we married people have to see these poor fools decoyed into our condition.
SAMUEL PEPYS

My wife was too beautiful for words—but not for arguments.
JOHN BARRYMORE

None but the brave can live with the fair.
KIN HUBBARD

There's nothing wrong with marriage. It's just the living together afterward that's murder.
SAM LEVENSON

It is commonly a weak man, who marries for love.
SAMUEL JOHNSON

He who marries for money earns it.
HEBREW PROVERB

Keep thy eyes wide open before marriage, and half shut afterward.
THOMAS FULLER

Here they come, the couple plighted—
On life's journey gaily start them,
Soon to be for aye united,
Till divorce or death shall part them.
W. S. GILBERT

Marriage is an adventure, like going to war.
G. K. CHESTERTON

Men are April when they woo,
December when they wed; maids are
May when they are maids, but the
sky changes when they are wives.
WILLIAM SHAKESPEARE

Marriage is a romance in which
the hero dies in the first chapter.

A husband should tell his wife everything that he is sure she will find
out.
THOMAS R. DEWAR

My notion of a wife at forty is
that a man should be able to change
her, like a bank note, for two
twenties.
DOUGLAS JERROLD

Monotony: The system that
allows a man only one wife.

Bigamy is one way of avoiding
the painful publicity of divorce and
the expense of alimony.
OLIVER HERFORD

In marriage, as in war, it is permitted to take every advantage of the
enemy.
SAMUEL JOHNSON

How gently glides the marriage
life away
When she who rules still seems
but to obey.
PUBLILIUS SYRUS

A termagant unto her husband
said,

One time when matrimonial
squalls blew high,
"You and the devil are surely re-
lated,"
—"Only by marriage," was his
quaint reply.

Don't marry for money. You can
borrow it cheaper.

A young man married is a man
that's marred.
WILLIAM SHAKESPEARE

Marriage is a ghastly public confession of a strictly private intention.
IAN HAY

Music played at weddings always
reminds me of the music played for
soldiers before they go into battle.
HEINRICH HEINE

It is too hard a knot for me
t'untie.
WILLIAM SHAKESPEARE

A husband and wife who have
separate bedrooms have either
drifted apart or found happiness.
HONORÉ DE BALZAC

Men marry because they are tired,
women because they are curious;
both are disappointed.
OSCAR WILDE

As father Adam first was fool'd,
A case that's all too common,
Here lies a man a woman rul'd,
The Devil rul'd the woman.
ROBERT BURNS

There are some good marriages, but practically no delightful ones.

FRANÇOIS DE LA ROCHEFOUCAULD

Socrates died from an overdose of wedlock.

ANSWER TO A COLLEGE EXAM QUESTION

[See also Divorce]

MASTURBATION:

Philosophy stands in the same relation to the study of the actual world as masturbation to sexual love.

KARL MARX

MATCHMAKING:

Pleasing ware is half sold.

ITALIAN PROVERB

When I lost my wife every family in town offered me another; but when I lost my horse no one offered to make him good.

FRENCH SAYING

[See also Marriage]

MEDICATION:

After quitting radio I was able to live on the money I saved on aspirins.

FRED ALLEN

Half of the modern drugs could well be thrown out the window, except that the birds might eat them.

MARTIN H. FISCHER

[See also Drugs, Medicine]

MEDICINE:

There are three subjects on which the knowledge of the medical profession in general is woefully weak; they are manners, morals and medicine.

GERALD F. LIEBERMAN

They do certainly give very strange, and newfangled, names to diseases.

PLATO

If anybody comes to I,
I physic, bleeds and sweats 'em;
If after that they like to die,
Why what care I?—I. Lettsom.

ATTRIBUTED TO A DR. ISAAC LETTSOM, 19TH CENTURY

The best medicine I know for rheumatism is to thank the Lord it ain't the gout.

JOSH BILLINGS

The oldest man alive today is reported to have celebrated his one hundred and thirty-ninth birthday. His case is regarded as a triumph of nature over medical knowledge.

I firmly believe that if the whole materia medica could be sunk to the bottom of the sea, it would be all the better for mankind—and all the worse for the sea.

OLIVER WENDELL HOLMES

Dunces, rejoice; forgive all censures past;
The greatest dunce has killed your foe at last.

ALEXANDER POPE, on the physicians who attended him during his last illness

Medicine is a collection of uncertain prescriptions, the results of which, taken collectively, are more fatal than useful to mankind.

NAPOLEON

I am dying from the treatment of too many physicians.

ALEXANDER THE GREAT

They had me on the operating table all day. They looked into my stomach, my gall bladder, they examined everything inside of me. Know what they decided? I need glasses.

JOE E. LEWIS

Medicine can only cure curable diseases, and then not always.

CHINESE PROVERB

God help the patient.

LORD MANSFIELD

Medicine is a science which hath been, as we have said, more professed than laboured, and yet more laboured than advanced. The labour having been, in my judgment, rather in circle than in progression.

FRANCIS BACON

MEDIOCRITY:

Mediocrity obtains more with application than superiority without it.

BALTASAR GRACIÁN

In my opinion we are in danger of developing a cult of the Common Man, which means a cult of mediocrity.

HERBERT HOOVER

MEMBERSHIP:

I won't belong to any organization that would have me as a member.

GROUCHO MARX

MEMORY:

If you tell the truth you don't have to remember anything.

MARK TWAIN

God gave us memories so that we might have roses in December.

JAMES M. BARRIE

I've a grand memory for forgetting.

ROBERT LOUIS STEVENSON

I always have trouble remembering three things: faces, names, and —I can't remember what the third thing is.

FRED ALLEN

The right honorable gentleman is indebted to his memory for his jests —and to his imagination for his facts.

RICHARD BRINSLEY SHERIDAN

I'm still chasing girls. I don't remember what for, but I'm still chasing them.

JOE E. LEWIS

It is well known that the older a man grows the faster he could run as a boy.

RED SMITH

When you are right no one remembers; when you are wrong no one forgets.

IRISH PROVERB

The best memory is that which forgets nothing but injuries. Write kindness in marble and write injuries in the dust.

PERSIAN PROVERB

No man has a good enough memory to make a successful liar.

ABRAHAM LINCOLN

MERCY:

An attribute beloved of detected offenders.

AMBROSE BIERCE

There is a mercy which is weakness, and even treason against the common good.

GEORGE ELIOT

The court is most merciful when the accused is most rich.

HEBREW PROVERB

Nothing emboldens sin so much as mercy.

WILLIAM SHAKESPEARE

Mercy but murders, pardoning those that kill.

WILLIAM SHAKESPEARE

[See also Crime, Justice]

METAPHYSICS:

When the speaker and he to whom he speaks do not understand, that is metaphysics.

VOLTAIRE

[See also Knowledge, Philosophy]

MILITARY:

Set them to simmer and take off the scum,

And a Heavy Dragoon is the residuum.

W. S. GILBERT

I am not one of those who believe that a great army is the means of maintaining peace, because if you build up a great profession those who form parts of it want to exercise their profession.

WOODROW WILSON

War is too important to be left to the generals.

GEORGES CLEMENCEAU

All through history it's the nations that have given most to the generals and the least to the people that have been the first to fall.

HARRY S. TRUMAN

It's one to a million
That any civilian
My figure and form'll surpass.

W. S. GILBERT

To me the officer is a separate race.

MATA HARI

[See also Army, Stupidity, War]

MIND:

Merely having an open mind is nothing; the object of opening the mind, as of opening the mouth, is to shut it again on something solid.

G. K. CHESTERTON

[See also Brain, Ignorance, Knowledge, Stupidity]

MINORITY:

In a democracy the majority has every right to act as stupid as the minority.

FRANK DANE

A minority is always compelled to think. That is the blessing of being in the minority.

LEO BAECK

It is unnatural for a majority to rule, for a majority can seldom be organized for united and specific action, and a minority can.

JEAN-JACQUES ROUSSEAU

Suspicion is ever on the suffering side.

PUBLILIUS SYRUS

Beware the tyranny of the minority.

LATIN PROVERB

[See also Majority]

MIRACLE:

An act or event out of the order of nature and unaccountable, as beating a normal hand of four kings and an ace with four aces and a king.

AMBROSE BIERCE

An event described by those to whom it was told by men who did not see it.

ELBERT HUBBARD

Many a man who is now willing to be shot down for . . . his belief in a miracle would have doubted, if he had been present, the miracle itself.

G. C. LICHTENBERG

[See also Faith, Religion]

MISER:

Misers part with nothing until they die. Then they give up the ghost.

LATIN PROVERB

How easy it is for a man to die rich, if he will but be contented to live miserable.

HENRY FIELDING

'Tis strange the miser should his cares employ
To gain those riches he can ne'er enjoy;
It is less strange the prodigal should waste
His wealth to purchase what he can ne'er taste.

ALEXANDER POPE

Misers amass wealth for those who wish them dead.

POLISH PROVERB

He bewails the loss of the water when he washes himself.

PLAUTUS

Misers aren't fun to live with, but they make wonderful ancestors.

DAVID BRENNER

[See also Avarice, Money]

MISFORTUNE:

With man, most of his misfortunes are occasioned by man.

PLINY THE ELDER

In the misfortune of our friends we find something which is not displeasing to us.

FRANÇOIS DE LA ROCHEFOUCAULD

We all have enough strength to bear the misfortunes of others.

FRANÇOIS DE LA ROCHEFOUCAULD

[See also Fortune, Luck]

MISTAKE:

The worst mistake we make is teaching children that money isn't everything.

JOSEPH MANKIEWICZ

I have made mistakes, but I never made the mistake of claiming that I never made one.

JAMES GORDON BENNETT

Mistakes. Life would be dull without them.

OSCAR WILDE

[*See also* Experience]

MISTRESS:

Next to the pleasure of making a new mistress is that of being rid of an old one.

WILLIAM WYCHERLEY

Chaste to her husband, frank to all beside,
A teeming mistress, but a barren bride.

ALEXANDER POPE

MOB:

It is the proof of a bad cause when it is applauded by the mob.

SENECA

The nose of a mob is its imagination. By this, at any time, it can be quietly led.

EDGAR ALLAN POE

Mob law does not become due process of law by securing the assent of a terrorized jury.

OLIVER WENDELL HOLMES

You can talk a mob into anything.

JOHN RUSKIN

It is an easy and a vulgar thing to please the mob, and no very arduous task to astonish them.

C. C. COLTON

[*See also* Demagogue, People]

MODERATION:

He who drinks a glass a day
Shall live to die another way.

STANLICUS

Be moderate in everything, including moderation.

HORACE PORTER

I can abstain; but I can't be moderate.

SAMUEL JOHNSON

Moderation in temper is always a virtue; but moderation in principle is always a vice.

THOMAS PAINE

[*See also* Abstinence]

MODESTY:

Great artists are modest almost as seldom as they are faithful to their wives.

H. L. MENCKEN

At least I have the modesty to admit that lack of modesty is one of my failings.

HECTOR BERLIOZ

No modest man ever did or ever will make a fortune.

LADY MARY WORTLEY MONTAGU

The English instinctively admire any man who has no talent, and is modest about it.

JAMES AGATE

A candidate is a modest man who shrinks from the publicity of private life to seek the obscurity of public office.

AMBROSE BIERCE

The man who is ostentatious of his modesty is twin to the statue that wears a fig-leaf.

MARK TWAIN

MONARCHY:

Kings have long hands.

OVID

The type of government they have in England is called a limited mockery.

ANSWER ON A COLLEGE EXAM

Do you not know that I am above the law?

JAMES II

Democracy: A hectic interlude between monarchies.

WILL AND ARIEL DURANT

MONEY:

If you want to know what God thinks of money, look at the people he gives it to.

YIDDISH PROVERB

It is better to have a permanent income than to be fascinating.

OSCAR WILDE

If you would know the value of money try to borrow some.

BENJAMIN FRANKLIN

All heiresses are beautiful.

JOHN DRYDEN

There's only one thing money won't buy, and that's poverty.

JOE E. LEWIS

Add little to little and there will be a great heap.

OVID

The reason some people are stingy is also the reason they are rich.

AMERICAN PROVERB

The love of money grows as the money itself grows.

JUVENAL

A great fortune is a great slavery.

SENECA

There is no fortress so strong that money cannot take it.

CICERO

Wealth is not without its advantages.

JOHN KENNETH GALBRAITH

Ready money is Aladdin's lamp.

LORD BYRON

Marry for money, my little sonny, a rich man's joke is always funny.

HEBREW PROVERB

Every man now worships gold, all other reverence being done away.

PROPERTIUS

When we hang the capitalists they will sell us the rope we use.

JOSEPH STALIN

He catches the best fish who angles with a golden hook.

LATIN PROVERB

If money be not thy servant, it will be thy master. The covetous man cannot so properly be said to possess wealth, as that may be said to possess him.

FRANCIS BACON

So we get the chinks we will bear the stinks.

ENGLISH PROVERB

There is nothing so comfortable as a small bankroll; a big one is always in danger.

WILSON MIZNER

There are persons who are chained to gold and silver.

THE TALMUD

It ain't so much trouble to get rich as it is to tell when we have got rich.

JOSH BILLINGS

Money begets money.

ITALIAN PROVERB

Where gold speaks every tongue is silent.

ITALIAN PROVERB

Finance, like time, devours its own children.

HONORÉ DE BALZAC

Every crowd has a silver lining.

P. T. BARNUM

I've never been poor, but I've been broke.

MIKE TODD

Money no longer talks. It just goes without saying.

I don't think you can spend yourself rich.

GEORGE HUMPHREY

He who has plenty of pepper can afford to season his cabbage well.

LATIN PROVERB

Thanks a billion, fellas. Since I'm on the Appropriations Committee

I'd feel like a cheapskate if I said "Thanks a million."
ANONYMOUS AMERICAN CONGRESS-MAN

[See also Avarice, Religion]

MONOGAMY:

The Western custom of one wife and hardly any mistresses.
H. H. MUNRO

Monogamy: A synonym for monotony.
GREGORY NUNN

[See also Marriage]

MONOPOLY:

These capitalists generally act harmoniously and in concert, to fleece the people.
ABRAHAM LINCOLN

When I want to buy up any politicians I always find the anti-monopolists the most purchasable. They don't come so high.
WILLIAM H. VANDERBILT

A holding company is a thing where you hand an accomplice the goods while the policeman searches you.
WILL ROGERS

[See also Business, Money, Wealth]

MONUMENT:

Reminders of those who have been forgotten.
AMERICAN PROVERB

Deeds, not stones, are the true monuments of the great.
J. L. MOTLEY

MORALITY:

We know no spectacle so ridiculous as the British public in one of its periodical fits of morality.
THOMAS BABINGTON MACAULAY

Don't be too moral. You may cheat yourself out of much life so.
HENRY DAVID THOREAU

Morality is simply the attitude we adopt towards people whom we dislike.
OSCAR WILDE

How high can you stoop?
OSCAR LEVANT, when asked to comment on Eddie Fisher's affair with Elizabeth Taylor

Might was the measure of right.
LUCAN

When morals fail the stains of vice disgrace
The noble honors of the human race.
HORACE

Moral codes adjust themselves to environmental conditions.

WILL DURANT

The new morality is terrible. It's taken all the sting out of gossip.

[*See also* Justice, Vice]

MORTGAGE:

An empty purse and a new house make a man wise, but too late.

PORTUGUESE PROVERB

[*See also* Home, Landlord]

MOTHER:

The old-time mother who used to wonder where her boy was now has a grandson who wonders where his mother is.

KIN HUBBARD

For one on the ocean of crime
   long tossed,
Who loves his mother, is not quite
   lost.

THOMAS DUNN ENGLISH

Mother always said that honesty was the best policy, and money isn't everything. She was wrong about other things too.

GERALD BARZAN

God could not be everywhere, so therefore he made mothers.

THE TALMUD

Some of the dirtiest dogs, past and present, had mothers.

GREGORY NUNN

What a price we pay for the glories of motherhood.

ISADORA DUNCAN

When I was born my mother was terribly disappointed. Not that she wanted a girl—she wanted a divorce.

WOODY ALLEN

My mother could have boarded and lodged the three musketeers and D'Artagnan for twenty years without discovering their sex; and they would no more have obtruded it on her than they would have ventured to smoke in her drawing-room.

GEORGE BERNARD SHAW

The God to whom little boys say their prayers has a face very like their mother's.

JAMES M. BARRIE

[*See also* Children, Family, Father]

MOTHER-IN-LAW:

Be kind to your mother-in-law but pay for her board at some good hotel.

JOSH BILLINGS

My wife is the kind of girl who will not go anywhere without her

mother, and her mother will go anywhere.

JOHN BARRYMORE

Behind every successful man
stands a surprised mother-in-law.

HUBERT HUMPHREY

The chain of wedlock is so heavy
that it takes two to carry it—and
sometimes three.

ALEXANDER DUMAS

[See also Marriage]

MOUSE:

Mouse: An animal which strews
its path with fainting women.

AMBROSE BIERCE

In baiting a mouse-trap with
cheese, always leave room for the
mouse.

H. H. MUNRO

A mouse never entrusts his life to
only one hole.

PLAUTUS

[See also Man]

MOVIES:

Over in Hollywood they almost
made a great picture, but they
caught it just in time.

WILSON MIZNER

We are on the track of something
absolutely mediocre.

BILLY WILDER

Hollywood is a place where people from Iowa mistake each other
for movie stars.

FRED ALLEN

The movies enable an actor not
only to act but also to sit down in
the theater and clap for himself.

WILL ROGERS

A director must be a policeman, a
midwife, a psychoanalyst, a syco-
phant and a bastard.

BILLY WILDER

In Hollywood the woods are full
of people that learned to write but
evidently can't read. If they could
read their stuff, they'd stop writing.

WILL ROGERS

The teen years are fraught with
any number of hazards, but none so
perilous as that which manifests itself as a tendency to consider movies
an important art form.

FRAN LEBOWITZ

What seems to make them more
adult than ours is that we don't understand the dialogue.
BILLY WILDER, on European films.

Nobody in TV makes as much
money as Robert Redford, who likes
to make movies for several million
dollars only on the condition that

they contain some sort of social message. I can't take very seriously a social message delivered by an actor who's paid nine million dollars to deliver it, and who charges you five dollars to see it.

DAVID BRINKLEY

[See also Hollywood]

MURDER:

Never murder a man who is about to commit suicide.

GERMAN PROVERB

There are glances of hatred that stab, and raise no cry of murder.

GEORGE ELIOT

For murder, though it have no tongue,
Will speak with most miraculous organ.

WILLIAM SHAKESPEARE

[See also Crime, Justice]

MUSIC:

Nothing soothes me more after a long and maddening course of pianoforte recitals than to sit and have my teeth drilled.

GEORGE BERNARD SHAW

Music hath charms to soothe the savage beast.

JAMES BRAMSTON

Music hath charm to soothe a savage beast—but I'd try a revolver first.

JOSH BILLINGS

Modern music is as dangerous as narcotics.

PIETRO MASCAGNI

Wagner's music is better than it sounds.

MARK TWAIN

Nothing is capable of being well set to music that is not nonsense.

JOSEPH ADDISON

Military justice is to justice what military music is to music.

GEORGES CLEMENCEAU

Preposterous ass, that never read so far
To know the cause why music was ordain'd!
Was it not to refresh the mind of man,
After his studies or his usual pain?

WILLIAM SHAKESPEARE

I know only two tunes. One of them is "Yankee Doodle"—and the other isn't.

ULYSSES S. GRANT

After silence that which comes nearest to expressing the inexpressible is music.

ALDOUS HUXLEY

The history of a people is found in its songs.

GEORGE JELLINEK

. . . music, moody food
Of us that trade in love.

WILLIAM SHAKESPEARE

O Music! Miraculous art! A blast of thy trumpet and millions rush forward to die; a peal of thy organ and uncounted nations sink down to pray.

BENJAMIN DISRAELI

Some cry up Haydn, some Mozart,
Just as the whim bites. For my part,
I do not care a farthing candle
For either of them, nor for Handel.

CHARLES LAMB

[See also Dance, Marriage]

MYSTERY:

The unknown is ever imagined.

GREEK PROVERB

[See also Faith, Religion]

MYTHOLOGY:

The body of a primitive people's beliefs concerning its origin, early history, heroes, deities and so forth, as distinguished from the true accounts which it invents later.

AMBROSE BIERCE

[See also Religion]

NAME:

I have been known to the peanut munchers as "The Great Profile."

JOHN BARRYMORE

Fools' names, like fools' faces,
Are often seen in public places.

THOMAS FULLER

I would rather make my name than inherit it.

WILLIAM MAKEPEACE THACKERAY

A good name is better than a girdle of gold.

FRENCH PROVERB

Who steals my purse steals trash;
'tis something, nothing;
'Twas mine, 'tis his, and has been slave to thousands;
But he that filches from me my good name
Robs me of that which not enriches him,
And makes me poor indeed.

WILLIAM SHAKESPEARE

Good name in man and woman, dear my lord,
Is the immediate jewel of their souls.

WILLIAM SHAKESPEARE

What's in a name? That which we
call a rose
By any other name would smell as
sweet.

WILLIAM SHAKESPEARE

NATURE:

Nature never makes any blunders;
when she makes a fool she means it.

JOSH BILLINGS

Nature has given women so much
power that the law has very wisely
given them little.

SAMUEL JOHNSON

Nature can do more than physicians.

OLIVER CROMWELL

It is too late to go back to the
order of nature or the truth in history.

J. R. PAXTON

Of all the wonders of nature, a
tree in summer is perhaps the most
remarkable; with the possible excep-
tion of a moose singing "Embracea-
ble You" in spats.

WOODY ALLEN

A nature lover is a person who,
when treed by a bear, enjoys the
view.

NECESSITY:

Necessity is the mother of invention.

LATIN PROVERB

To need nothing is divine, and the
less a man needs the nearer does he
approach to divinity.

SOCRATES

Necessity makes the best soldiers.

JOSEPHUS

Give us the luxuries of life and
we will dispense with its necessities.

J. L. MOTLEY

NEIGHBOR:

One whom we are commanded to
love as ourselves, and who does all
he knows how to make us disobe-
dient.

AMBROSE BIERCE

Love your neighbor as yourself;
but don't take down the fence.

CARL SANDBURG

Your own safety is at stake when
your neighbor's house is in flames.

HORACE

A good neighbor is a fellow who
smiles at you over the back fence
but doesn't climb over it.

ARTHUR "BUGS" BAER

NEUTRALITY:

When in doubt who will win, be neutral.

SWISS PROVERB

They are neutral against us.

WORLD WAR II SERVICEMEN'S DESCRIPTION OF THE SPANISH AND PORTUGUESE

NEWS:

No news is good news.

LUDOVIC HALÉVY

None loves the messenger who brings bad news.

SOPHOCLES

The news of any politician's death should be listed under "Public Improvements."

FRANK DANE

[See also Editor, Journalism, Newspaper]

NEWSPAPER:

Nothing can . . . be believed which is seen in a newspaper.

THOMAS JEFFERSON

Newspapers have degenerated. They may now be absolutely relied upon.

OSCAR WILDE

If a newspaper prints a sex crime it's smut, but when the New York Times prints it, it's a sociological study.

ADOLPH S. OCHS

Well, I found by talking to every person who had any involvement with the Pentagon Papers that the situation within the Nixon Administration was not unlike that on the New York Times. That is to say, a lot of time they didn't know what they were doing either.

HARRISON E. SALISBURY

The old saw says, "Let a sleeping dog lie." Right! Still, when there is much at stake it is better to get a newspaper to do it.

MARK TWAIN

They misrepresent, they distort, they color, they blackguard, they lie.

HAROLD L. ICKES

Half the council aren't crooks.

NEWSPAPER RETRACTION, TO CORRECT AN EDITORIAL SAYING HALF THE COUNCIL WERE CROOKS

I'll give anything for a good copy now, be it true or false, so it be news.

BEN JONSON

Advertisements contain the only truth to be relied on in a newspaper.

THOMAS JEFFERSON

The feeling has existed for years that newspapers must be courageously outspoken, and that to prove they are so, they must proclaim editorial opinion every day. Obviously, this attitude does not take into account the embarrassing possibility that there may be days when even the most informed editor will lack a sensible idea worth expressing.

ROBERT MCHUGH

Give them a corrupt House of Lords, give them a venal House of Commons, give them a tyrannical prince, give them a truckling court, and let me have an unfettered press —[and] I will defy them to encroach a hair's-breadth upon the liberties of England.

RICHARD BRINSLEY SHERIDAN

In America the President reigns for four years, and journalism governs for ever and ever.

OSCAR WILDE

The press is like the air, a chartered libertine.

WILLIAM PITT THE ELDER

A newspaper is a circulating library with high blood pressure.

ARTHUR "BUGS" BAER

The man who reads nothing at all is better educated than the man who reads nothing but newspapers.

THOMAS JEFFERSON

Not all the news that's fit to print is fit to read.

[*See also* Editor, Journalism, Press]

NEW YEAR:

God send you happy, God send you happy,
We pray God send you a happy New Year.

SONG OF THE OLD ENGLISH CAROLERS

I can no longer bring myself to wish anyone a happy New Year. Not when I think of what would make them happy.

GERALD F. LIEBERMAN

Ring out the old, ring in the new,
Ring, happy bells, across the snow;
The year is going, let him go;
Ring out the false, ring in the true.

ALFRED, LORD TENNYSON

NEW YORK:

The posthumous revenge of the Merchant of Venice.

ELBERT HUBBARD

The city of Brotherly Shove.

What else can you expect from a town that's shut off from the world

by the ocean on one side and New
Jersey on the other?

O. HENRY

New York, the nation's thyroid
gland.

CHRISTOPHER MORLEY

There is more sophistication and
less sense in New York than anywhere else on the globe.

DON HEROLD

Coming to New York and not
going to the theater is like going to
bed with a beautiful woman and not
making love.

GREGORY NUNN

The world is grand, beautiful,
thrilling. But I love New York.

DOROTHY KILGALLEN

NOISE:

A mountain was in labor, sending
forth dreadful groans, and there was
in the region highest expectations.
After all that, it brought forth a
mouse.

PHAEDRUS

As with narrow-necked bottles:
the less in them, the more noise they
make in pouring it out.

JONATHAN SWIFT

Noise: A stench in the ear.

AMBROSE BIERCE

[See also Speech]

NOMINATION:

The call of the vile.

ELBERT HUBBARD

[See also Politician, Politics]

NON-CONFORMIST:

You'll non-conform when I tell
you to non-conform.

TELEVISION PRODUCER'S MEMO TO
HIS WRITERS

A man who stands up for his
rights, when it pays.

GERALD BARZAN

[See also Courage, Coward]

NONSENSE:

No one is exempt from talking
nonsense; the mistake is to do it solemnly.

MICHEL DE MONTAIGNE

A little nonsense now and then
Is relished by the wisest men.

[See also Stupidity]

NOTHING:

Out of nothing nothing can come,
and nothing can become nothing.

PERSIUS

NUDITY:

I have seen three emperors in their nakedness, and the sight was not inspiring.

OTTO VON BISMARCK

I never expected to see the day when girls would get sunburned in the places they do today.

WILL ROGERS

Having spent my entire vacation in a nudist colony, I was somewhat taken back when a lady shook my hand and said: "Good-by, Mr. Nunn, I hope to see more of you."

GREGORY NUNN

NUMBERS:

Say what you will about the Ten Commandments, you must always come back to the pleasant fact that there are only ten of them.

H. L. MENCKEN

NUN:

Women give themselves to God when the Devil wants nothing more to do with them.

SOPHIE ARNOULD

When a woman gets too old to be attractive to men she turns to God.

HONORÉ DE BALZAC

Get thee to a nunnery: why wouldst thou be a breeder of sinners?

WILLIAM SHAKESPEARE

OATH:

A liar freely gives his oath.

PIERRE CORNEILLE

In lapidary inscriptions a man is not upon oath.

SAMUEL JOHNSON

If I ever utter an oath again may my soul be blasted to eternal damnation.

GEORGE BERNARD SHAW

I'll take thy word for faith, not as
thine oath;
Who shuns not to break one will
sure crack both.

WILLIAM SHAKESPEARE

[See also Lie, Lying]

OBITUARY:

I never wanted to see anybody die, but there are a few obituary notices I have read with pleasure.

CLARENCE DARROW

[See also Death]

OBSCENITY:

It is the grossness of the spectator that discovers nothing but grossness in the subject.

WILLIAM HAZLITT

Obscenity is such a tiny kingdom that a single tour covers it completely.

HEYWOOD BROUN

OCCUPATION:

The ugliest of trades have their moments. Were I a grave digger, or perhaps a hangman, there are some people I could work for with a great deal of pleasure.

DOUGLAS JERROLD

Hamlet's experience simply could not have happened to a plumber.

GEORGE BERNARD SHAW

[See also Union, Work]

OCEAN:

Seas but join the regions they divide.

ALEXANDER POPE

Ocean: A body of water occupying about two-thirds of a world made for man—who has no gills.

AMBROSE BIERCE

ODOR:

Fish and guests smell in three days.

BENJAMIN FRANKLIN

Where all stink, one is not smelt.

ST. BERNARD

He shines and stinks, like rotten mackerel by moonlight.

JOHN RANDOLPH

[See also Politician, Politics]

OMEN:

When a man's dog turns against him it is time for a wife to pack her trunk and go home to mama.

MARK TWAIN

Omen: A sign that something will happen if nothing happens.

AMBROSE BIERCE

Without a sign, his sword the
  brave man draws,
And asks no omen, but his country's cause.

HOMER

The leaves fall before the tree dies.

FRENCH PROVERB

OPERA:

A supreme social challenge.

CLEVELAND AMORY

Opera in English is, in the main, just about as sensible as baseball in Italian.

H. L. MENCKEN

Anything that is too stupid to be spoken is sung.

VOLTAIRE

The banging and slamming and booming and crashing were something beyond belief.

MARK TWAIN, on *Lohengrin*

[*See also* Music]

OPINION:

Maternity is a matter of fact, paternity is a matter of opinion.

AMERICAN PROVERB

No one can have a higher opinion of him than I have; and I think he's a dirty little beast.

W. S. GILBERT

He never chooses an opinion, he just wears whatever happens to be in style.

LEO TOLSTOY

The public buys its opinions as it buys its meat, or takes in its milk, on the principle that it is cheaper to do this than to keep a cow. So it is, but the milk is more likely to be watered.

SAMUEL BUTLER

If one man says to thee, "Thou art a donkey," pay no heed. If two speak thus, purchase a saddle.

THE TALMUD

It is difference of opinion that makes horse races.

MARK TWAIN

The foolish and the dead never change their opinions.

JAMES RUSSELL LOWELL

A mass of men equals a mass of opinions.

LATIN PROVERB

Inconsistencies of opinion, arising from changes of circumstances, are often justifiable.

DANIEL WEBSTER

In negligence cases the injured party is always torn between two professional opinions: his doctor's, who says he no longer needs crutches, and his lawyer's, who says he does.

[*See also* Majority, Minority]

OPPORTUNITY:

Do when ye may, or suffer ye the nay, in love 'tis the way.

ENGLISH PROVERB

The first half of life consists of the capacity to enjoy without the chance; the last half consists of the chance without the capacity.

MARK TWAIN

There is a tide in the affairs of men,
Which, taken at the flood, leads on to fortune;
Omitted, all the voyage of their life
Is bound in shallows and in miseries.

WILLIAM SHAKESPEARE

There is a tide in the affairs of women,
Which, taken at the flood, leads—God knows where.

LORD BYRON

He missed an invaluable opportunity to hold his tongue.

ANDREW LANG

We consume our tomorrows fretting about our yesterdays.

PERSIUS

The just man may sin with an open chest of gold before him.

ITALIAN PROVERB

Men never moan over the opportunities lost to do good, only the opportunities to be bad.

GREEK PROVERB

[See also Fate, Fortune, Success]

OPPOSITION:

Given a sufficient number of people and an adequate amount of time you can create insurmountable opposition to the most inconsequential idea.

[See also Enemy, Politics]

OPTIMIST:

A proponent of the doctrine that black is white.

AMBROSE BIERCE

An optimist is a fellow who believes a housefly is looking for a way to get out.

GEORGE JEAN NATHAN

Where there is life there is hope.
PATRICK BRONTË, father of the Bronte sisters; his last words

An optimist is a girl who mistakes a bulge for a curve.

RING LARDNER

An optimist proclaims that we live in the best of all possible worlds—the pessimist fears this is true.

JAMES BRANCH CABELL

Optimism: The doctrine or belief that everything is beautiful, including what is ugly, everything good, especially the bad, and everything right that is wrong. . . . An intellectual disorder, yielding to no treatment but death . . . Hereditary, but fortunately not contagious.

AMBROSE BIERCE

Optimist: A man who calls bull-shit fertilizer.

FRANK DANE

[See also Hope, Pessimist]

ORATOR:

What orators want in depth they give you in length.

BARON DE LA BRÈDE ET DE MONTESQUIEU

Our public men are speaking every day on something—but they ain't saying anything.

WILL ROGERS

Orators are most vehement when their cause is weak.

CICERO

A good speaker makes a good liar.

GERMAN PROVERB

[See also Demagogue, Speech]

ORIGINALITY:

If they haven't heard it before, it's original.

GENE FOWLER

Originality is nothing but judicious imitation.

VOLTAIRE

I see nothing in it new and valuable. What is valuable is not new, and what is new is not valuable.

DANIEL WEBSTER

There is nothing new but that which is forgotten.

MLLE. BERTIN, modiste to Marie Antoinette, when asked if a dress was new

There is nothing new under the sun.

THE BIBLE

[See also Invention]

ORPHAN:

A living person whom death has deprived of the power of filial in-gratitude.

AMBROSE BIERCE

[See also Children]

ORTHODOXY:

A man must be orthodox upon most things or he will never have time to preach his own heresy.

G. K. CHESTERTON

[See also Faith, Religion]

PAIN:

Pain is life.

CHARLES LAMB

Pain: An uncomfortable frame of mind that may have a physical basis in something that is being done to the body, or may be purely mental, caused by the good fortune of others.

AMBROSE BIERCE

One pain is lessen'd by another's anguish.

WILLIAM SHAKESPEARE

The least pain in our little finger gives us more concern than the destruction of millions of our fellow beings.

WILLIAM HAZLITT

Time heals old pain, while it creates new ones.

HEBREW PROVERB

PARENT:

My parents were neither very poor nor conspicuously honest.

MARK TWAIN

The first half of our lives is ruined by our parents and the second half by our children.

CLARENCE DARROW

You are the bows from which your children, as living arrows, are sent forth.

KAHLIL GIBRAN

Parents were invented to make children happy by giving them something to ignore.

OGDEN NASH

Diogenes struck the father when the son swore.

ROBERT BURTON

[See also Father, Mother]

PARIS:

The American arrives in Paris with a few French phrases he has culled from a conversational guide or picked up from a friend who owns a beret.

FRED ALLEN

The first thing that strikes a visitor to Paris is a taxi.

Paris, a city of gaieties and pleasures, where four fifths of the inhabitants die of grief.

SÉBASTIEN CHAMFORT

[See also American, Heaven]

PARTNERSHIP:

In business partnerships and marriage partnerships, oh, the cheating that goes on.

AMERICAN PROVERB

Forty for you, sixty for me
And equal partners we will be.

GERALD BARZAN

[See also Business]

PASSION:

The ruling passion, be it what it
will,
The ruling passion conquers reason still.

ALEXANDER POPE

[See also Love]

PAST:

The good of other times let people
state;
I think it lucky I was born so late.

OVID

I cannot sing the old songs,
Or dream those dreams again.

CHARLOTTE BARNARD

The past, at least, is secure.

DANIEL WEBSTER

What's past is prologue.

WILLIAM SHAKESPEARE

It used to be a good hotel, but
that proves nothing—I used to be a
good boy.

MARK TWAIN

Anyone who doesn't miss the past
never had a mother.

GREGORY NUNN

The past always looks better than
it was because it isn't here.

FINLEY PETER DUNNE

[See also Future]

PATIENCE:

O' the mass of arms, the brilliant
leadership, the courage and magnitude of the ancient armies of
Greece, combined to conquer the
city of Troy; all that, and ten years
of perseverance.

HIPPONAX, THE SATIRIST

Patience is the key to paradise.

TURKISH PROVERB

Heaven grant us patience with a
man in love.

RUDYARD KIPLING

Everything comes to him who
hustles while he waits.

THOMAS A. EDISON

Patience is a necessary ingredient
of genius.

BENJAMIN DISRAELI

[See also Perseverence]

PATRIOTISM:

It is the patriotic duty of every man to lie for his country.

ALFRED ADLER

Patriotism is your conviction that this country is superior to all other countries because you were born in it.

GEORGE BERNARD SHAW

Every man loves his native land, whether he was born there or not.

IRISH SAYING, attributed to THOMAS FITCH

Patriotism is the last refuge of a scoundrel.

SAMUEL JOHNSON

Many a bum show has been saved by the flag.

GEORGE M. COHAN

Though I love my country, I do not love my countrymen.

LORD BYRON

But in spite of all temptations
To belong to other nations,
He remains an Englishman.

W. S. GILBERT

No man, I fear, can effect great benefits for his country without some sacrifice of the minor virtues.

SYDNEY SMITH

You'll never have a quiet world till you knock the patriotism out of the human race.

GEORGE BERNARD SHAW

Patriotism varies, from a noble devotion to a moral lunacy.

WILLIAM R. INGE

Our country, right or wrong.

STEPHEN DECATUR

My country, always wrong.

STUDENT SLOGAN

PEACE:

Peace is preferable to a place in history.

JUSTO PASTOR BENITEZ

To be prepared for war is one of the most effectual means of preserving peace.

GEORGE WASHINGTON

There is a peace more destructive of the manhood of living man than war is destructive of his material body.

DOUGLAS JERROLD

Peace: In international affairs, a period of cheating between two periods of fighting.

AMBROSE BIERCE

Strange to see how a good dinner and feasting reconciles everybody.

SAMUEL PEPYS

When monarchs through their bloodthirsty commanders lay waste a country, they dignify their atrocity by calling it "making peace."

TACITUS

If a man would live in peace he should be blind, deaf, and dumb.

TURKISH PROVERB

If they want peace, nations should avoid the pin-pricks that precede cannon-shots.

NAPOLEON

There may come a time when the lion and the lamb will lie down together, but I am still betting on the lion.

JOSH BILLINGS

[See also War]

PEDIGREE:

Do well and you will have no need of ancestors.

VOLTAIRE

[See also Ancestry]

PEOPLE:

You may fool all the people some of the time, you can even fool some of the people all of the time; but you can't fool all of the people all the time.

ABRAHAM LINCOLN

You can fool some of the people all of the time and all of the people some of the time—but most of the time they will make fools of themselves.

As long as people believe in absurdities they will continue to commit atrocities.

VOLTAIRE

The people people work with best
Are sometimes very queer;
The people people own by birth
Quite shock your first idea.
The people people have for friends
Your common sense appall,
But the people people marry
Are the queerest folks of all.

CHARLOTTE P. GILMAN

The people are to be taken in small doses.

RALPH WALDO EMERSON

I have found little that is good about human beings. In my experience most of them, on the whole, are trash.

SIGMUND FREUD

It is the nature of all people to believe every calamity happening to them a trial, and every one happening to others a judgment.

We are inclined to believe those whom we do not know because they have never deceived us.

SAMUEL JOHNSON

People can be divided into three groups: those who make things happen, those who watch things happen —and those who wonder, What Happened?

People in groups tend to agree on courses of action which as individuals they know are stupid.

Some people are electrifying— they light up a room when they leave.

We are all schlemiels.
YIDDISH PROVERB

[See also Man, Woman]

PERFORMANCE:

No matter how well you perform there's always somebody of intelligent opinion who thinks it's lousy.
SIR LAURENCE OLIVIER

All lovers swear more performance than they are able.
WILLIAM SHAKESPEARE

[See also Theater]

PERSEVERANCE:

No man drowns if he perseveres in praying to God—and can swim.
RUSSIAN PROVERB

Everyone has a mass of bad work

in him which he will have to work off and get rid of before he can do better; and, indeed, the more lasting a man's ultimate work, the more sure he is to pass through a time, and perhaps a very long one, in which there seems to be very little hope for him.
SAMUEL BUTLER

[See also Patience]

PESSIMIST:

Always borrow from a pessimist —he never expects to get it back.

A pessimist is a man who thinks all women are bad. An optimist is a man who hopes they are.
CHAUNCEY DEPEW

The man who is a pessimist before forty-eight knows too much; the man who is an optimist after forty-eight knows too little.
MARK TWAIN

A pessimist is a man who, faced with the choice of two evils, chooses both.

A pessimist is a man who thinks everybody is as nasty as himself.
GEORGE BERNARD SHAW

[See also Optimist]

PHILADELPHIA:

I once spent a year in Philadelphia. I think it was on a Sunday.

W. C. FIELDS

In Boston they ask, How much does he know? In New York, How much is he worth? In Philadelphia, Who were his parents?

MARK TWAIN

PHILANTHROPIST:

A philanthropist is a man who gives away what he should be giving back.

Take egotism out and you would castrate the benefactors.

RALPH WALDO EMERSON

With one hand he put a penny in the urn of poverty, and with the other took a shilling out.

ROBERT POLLOK

He is one of those wise philanthropists who, in a time of famine, would vote for nothing but a supply of toothpicks.

DOUGLAS JERROLD

PHILANTHROPY:

Those who give hoping to be rewarded with honor are not giving, they are bargaining.

PHILO

To enjoy a good reputation give publicly, and steal privately.

JOSH BILLINGS

The worst of charity is that the lives you are asked to preserve are not worth preserving.

RALPH WALDO EMERSON

Steal the hog, and give the feet for alms.

GEORGE HERBERT

The shining example of philanthropy is often tarnished when thought is given to how the philanthropist got it in the first place.

[See also Charity]

PHILOSOPHER:

There is nothing so absurd that some philosopher has not already said.

CICERO

If I wished to punish a province, I would have it governed by philosophers.

FREDERICK THE GREAT

The origins of disputes between philosophers is, that one class of them have undertaken to raise man by displaying his greatness, and the other to debase him by showing his miseries.

BLAISE PASCAL

A philosopher will not believe what he sees because he is too busy speculating on what he does not see.
BERNARD DE FONTENELLE

There is no record in history of a happy philosopher.
H. L. MENCKEN

If he really thinks there is no distinction between vice and virtue, when he leaves our houses let us count our spoons.
SAMUEL JOHNSON

All are lunatics, but he who can analyze his delusion is called a philosopher.
AMBROSE BIERCE

[See also Marriage]

PHILOSOPHY:

When he who hears does not know what he who speaks means, and when he who speaks does not know what he himself means—that is philosophy.
VOLTAIRE

Philosophy: A route of many roads leading from nowhere to nothing.
AMBROSE BIERCE

Philosophy may teach us to bear with equanimity the misfortunes of our neighbors.
OSCAR WILDE

Philosophy is utterly useless and fruitless, and for this reason is the sublimest of all pursuits.
GEORG WILHELM FREDERICK HEGEL

[See also Knowledge, Wisdom]

PHYSICIAN:

Every physician . . . hath his favorite disease.
HENRY FIELDING

Though physician to others, yet himself full of sores.
LATIN PROVERB

No matter what conditions
Dyspeptic come to feaze,
The best of all physicians
Is apple-pie and cheese!
EUGENE FIELD

The kind physician grants the husband's pray'rs,
Or gives relief to long-expecting heirs.
JONATHAN SWIFT

[See also Doctor, Medicine]

PIETY:

I'm religiously opposed to religion.
VICTOR HUGO

Those who had loved God most have loved man least.
ROBERT GREEN INGERSOLL

Thou villain, thou art full of piety.

WILLIAM SHAKESPEARE

[See also Faith, Religion]

PILGRIM:

If they hadn't landed there would be some reason for celebrating the fact.

MARK TWAIN

The Pilgrim Fathers landed on the shores of America and fell on their knees; then they fell upon the aborigines.

AMERICAN SAYING

A Pilgrim Father was one who, leaving Europe in 1620 because not permitted to sing psalms through his nose, followed it to Massachusetts, where he could personate God according to the dictates of his conscience.

AMBROSE BIERCE

PIONEER:

Pioneers are always kicked in the teeth when the thing they pioneered starts to pay off. Look at Jesus.

FRANK DANE

PITY:

If a madman were to come into this room with a stick in his hand no doubt we should pity his state of mind, but our primary consideration would be to take care of ourselves. We should knock him down first, and pity him afterward.

SAMUEL JOHNSON

If you pity rogues you are no great friend to honest men.

THOMAS FULLER

Pardon: To remit a penalty and restore to a life of crime. To add to the lure of crime the temptation of ingratitude.

AMBROSE BIERCE

[See also Charity, Mercy]

PLAGIARISM:

When a thing has been said and said well, have no scruple. Take it and copy it.

ANATOLE FRANCE

The immature artist imitates. The mature artist steals.

LIONEL TRILLING

When 'Omer smote 'is bloomin' lyre,
He'd 'eard men sing by land an' sea;
An' what he thought 'e might require,
'E went an' took—the same as me!

RUDYARD KIPLING

Instead of forming new words I recommend to you any kind of artful management by which you are able to give cost to old ones.

HORACE

Taking something from one man and making it worse is plagiarism.

GEORGE MOORE

There is much difference between imitating a man and counterfeiting him.

BENJAMIN FRANKLIN

They castrate the books of other men in order that with the fat of their works they may lard their own lean volumes.

JOVIUS

Genius borrows nobly.

RALPH WALDO EMERSON

In comparing various authors with one another, I have found that some of the gravest and latest writers have transcribed, word for word, from former works, without making acknowledgement.

PLINY THE ELDER

Originality is undetected plagiarism.

WILLIAM R. INGE

Great literature must spring from an upheaval in the author's soul. If that upheaval is not present then it must come from the works of any other author which happens to be handy and easily adapted.

ROBERT BENCHLEY

Nothing is said which has not been said before.

TERENCE

What a good thing Adam had. When he said a good thing, he knew nobody had said it before.

MARK TWAIN

The only good copies are those which make us see the absurdities of bad originals.

FRANÇOIS DE LA ROCHEFOUCAULD

No productive author can remain a productive author without other productive authors.

Plagiarists are always suspicious of being stolen from.

SAMUEL TAYLOR COLERIDGE

Perish those who said our good things before we did.

DONATUS

If you steal from one author it's plagiarism. If you steal from many, it's research.

WILSON MIZNER

PLAN:

Plan: To bother about the best method of accomplishing an accidental result.

AMBROSE BIERCE

It is a bad plan that admits of no modification.

PUBLILIUS SYRUS

The best laid schemes o' mice and men
Gang aft a-gley.

ROBERT BURNS

PLEASURE:

The rule of my life is to make business a pleasure, and pleasure my business.

AARON BURR

When pleasure interferes with business, give up business.

AMERICAN PROVERB

Pleasures are like poppies spread:
You seize the flower, its bloom is shed;
Or like the snow falls in the river:
A moment white—then melts forever.

ROBERT BURNS

In everything satiety closely follows the greatest pleasures.

CICERO

Rich the treasure;
Sweet the pleasure.

JOHN DRYDEN

There is no pleasure in having nothing to do; the fun is in having lots to do and not doing it.

MARY LITTLE

[*See also* Love, Sin]

POET:

A mighty good sausage stuffer was spoiled when the man became a poet.

EUGENE FIELD

A person born with an instinct for poverty.

ELBERT HUBBARD

The man is either mad, or he is making verses.

HORACE

Homer has taught all other poets the art of telling lies skillfully.

ARISTOTLE

War talk by men who have been in a war is always interesting; whereas moon talk by a poet who has not been in the moon is likely to be dull.

MARK TWAIN

A poet can survive anything but a misprint.

OSCAR WILDE

Poets are born, not paid.

ADDISON MIZNER

A poet in history is divine, but a poet in the next room is a joke.

MAX EASTMAN

[*See also* Writer]

POETRY:

I've read some of your modern free verse and wonder who set it free.

JOHN BARRYMORE

This poem will never reach its destination.

VOLTAIRE, on Rousseau's *Ode to Posterity*

A work where nothing's just or fit; One glaring chaos and wild heap of wit.

ALEXANDER POPE

I would as soon write free verse as play tennis with the net down.

ROBERT FROST

Free verse is like free love; it is a contradiction in terms.

G. K. CHESTERTON

Publishing a volume of verse is like dropping a rose petal down the Grand Canyon and waiting for the echo.

DON MARQUIS

Poetry should only occupy the idle.

LORD BYRON

[*See also* Writing]

POLICY:

When policy fails try thinking.

AMERICAN BUSINESS MAXIM

Deny it!

SIGN IN THE EXECUTIVE WASHROOM OF A MAJOR OIL COMPANY

Be generous, good and just— when anything is to be gained by virtue.

BILLY BOY FRANKLIN

POLITICIAN:

An honest politician is one who when he's bought stays bought.

SIMON CAMERON

The world is weary of statesmen whom democracy has degraded into politicians.

BENJAMIN DISRAELI

It is hard to say why politicians are called servants, unless it's because a good one is hard to find.

GERALD F. LIEBERMAN

If there is anything a public servant hates to do it's something for the public.

KIN HUBBARD

Politician: An eel in the fundamental mud upon which the superstructure of organized society is reared. When he wriggles he mistakes the agitation of his tail for the trembling of the edifice. As compared with the statesman, he suffers the disadvantage of being alive.

AMBROSE BIERCE

Fleas can be taught nearly anything that a Congressman can.

MARK TWAIN

Spain has her matadors. The United States has her Senators.

JOE LAURIE, JR.

Too bad ninety percent of the politicians give the other ten percent a bad reputation.

HENRY KISSINGER

Everybody except us is running for governor.

BARRY GRAY

He knows nothing and he thinks he knows everything. That points clearly to a political career.

GEORGE BERNARD SHAW

When a man assumes a public trust he should consider himself a public property.

THOMAS JEFFERSON

Politicians are the same all over. They promise to build a bridge where there is no river.

NIKITA S. KHRUSHCHEV

Everything is organized today. I called my Congressman a jack-ass, and I heard from the jack-ass lobby.

FRANK DANE

Any man with a fine shock of hair, a good set of teeth, and a bewitching smile can park his brains, if he has any, and run for public office.

FRANK DANE

[*See also* Election, Lying, Politics, President, Vice]

POLITICS:

In politics stupidity is not a handicap.

NAPOLEON

Now and then an innocent man is sent to the legislature.

KIN HUBBARD

Politics is the diversion of trivial men who, when they succeed at it, become important in the eyes of more trivial men.

GEORGE JEAN NATHAN

I always voted at my party's call,
And never thought of thinking for myself at all
I thought so little, they rewarded me
By making me the Ruler of the Queen's Navee!

W. S. GILBERT

When a leader is in the Democratic Party he's a boss, and when he's in the Republican Party he's a leader.

HARRY S. TRUMAN

In politics the choice is constantly between two evils.

JOHN MORLEY

The two maxims of any great man at court are, always to keep his countenance and never to keep his word.

JONATHAN SWIFT

Politics is not a bad profession. If you succeed there are many rewards, if you disgrace yourself you can always write a book.

RONALD REAGAN

Politics ain't worrying this country one-tenth as much as where to find a parking space.

WILL ROGERS

The cure for admiring the House of Lords is to go and look at it.

WALTER BAGEHOT

Politics is a profession where the paths of glory lead but to the gravy.

BILLY BOY FRANKLIN

You can fool too many people too much of the time.

JAMES THURBER

I think that in public affairs stupidity is more dangerous than knavery, because it is harder to fight.

WOODROW WILSON

No political party has exclusive patent rights on prosperity.

FRANKLIN D. ROOSEVELT

There are hardly two creatures of a more differing species than the same man, when pretending to a place and when in possession of it.

SIR GEORGE SAVILE

You don't have to fool all the people all of the time; you just have to fool enough to get elected.

GERALD BARZAN

The right man, in the right place, at the right time—can steal millions.

GREGORY NUNN

You mustn't enthrone ignorance just because there is so much of it.

AMERICAN PROVERB

Reagan won because he ran against Jimmy Carter. If he ran unopposed he would have lost.

MORT SAHL

Nepotism: Appointing your grandmother to office for the good of the party.

AMBROSE BIERCE

Politics: A strife of interests masquerading as a contest of principles. The conduct of public affairs for private advantage.

AMBROSE BIERCE

Politics makes strange postmasters.

KIN HUBBARD

What we need in appointive positions are men of knowledge and ex-

perience with sufficient character to
resist temptations.

CALVIN COOLIDGE

O, that estates, degrees, and
offices
Were not deriv'd corruptly, and
that clear honour
Were purchased by the merit of
the wearer.

WILLIAM SHAKESPEARE

In politics nothing is contemptible.

BENJAMIN DISRAELI

We have not fit men for the times.

JOHN ADAMS

[See also Government, Hypocrisy,
Politician, Stupidity]

POLLUTION:

People should speak now, or forever hold their breaths.

CONSERVATIONISTS' MOTTO

The air of Athens is pure, whence
the inhabitants have more piercing
apprehension and quicker reflexes
than the rest of Greece. Thebes, on
the other hand, is thick and foggy,
its inhabitants dull and slow.

CICERO

Fresh air is good if you don't take
too much of it; most of the achievements and pleasures of life are in
bad air.

OLIVER WENDELL HOLMES

POLYGAMY:

An endeavor to get more out of
life than there is in it.

ELBERT HUBBARD

The greatest testimony to man's
willingness to take chances.

JOE LAURIE, JR.

[See also Marriage, Monogamy]

POPULARITY:

If you wish to be loved, show
more of your faults than your
virtues.

E. R. BULWER-LYTTON

Many men and women enjoy popular esteem not because they are
known, but because they are not
known.

SÉBASTIEN CHAMFORT

[See also Applause]

POSTERITY:

He hungered for posterity, and he
died from hunger.

GREGORY NUNN

Posterity is that which is denied
an author until he is in the public
domain.

FRANK DANE

[See also Ancestry]

POVERTY:

Honest poverty is a gem that even a king might be proud to call his own—but I wish to sell out.

MARK TWAIN

It's no disgrace to be poor, but it might as well be.

KIN HUBBARD

Poverty is a wonderful thing. It sticks to a man after all his friends have forsaken him.

HEBREW PROVERB

I know a fellow who's as broke as the Ten Commandments.

JOHN MARQUAND

No man can worship God or love his neighbor on an empty stomach.

WOODROW WILSON

Remember the poor—it costs nothing.

JOSH BILLINGS

One of the strangest things about life is that the poor, who need the money the most, are the ones that never have it.

FINLEY PETER DUNNE

Show me a man with very little money and I'll show you a bum.

JOE E. LEWIS

It is a difficult matter to argue with the belly since it has no ears.

CATO

Always the gods give small things to the small.

CALLIMACHUS

Poverty sits by the cradle of all our great men and rocks all of them to manhood.

HEINRICH HEINE

Poverty is no disgrace to a man, but it is confoundedly inconvenient.

SYDNEY SMITH

The poor would never be able to live at all if it weren't for the poor.

GEORGE MOORE

All the arguments which are brought to represent poverty as no evil show it to be evidently a great evil.

SAMUEL JOHNSON

Poverty is no disgrace—and that's the only good thing you can say about poverty.

[See also Money]

POWER:

Power tends to corrupt; absolute power corrupts absolutely.

LORD ACTON

In the United States though power corrupts, the expectation of power paralyzes.

JOHN KENNETH GALBRAITH

Power is what men seek and any group that gets it will abuse it.

LINCOLN STEFFENS

Woman's influence is powerful, especially when she wants something.

JOSH BILLINGS

A woman seen by all is a woman wished for; hence the terrible power of actresses.

HONORÉ DE BALZAC

Every man who possesses power is impelled to abuse it.

BARON DE LA BRÈDE ET DE MONTESQUIEU

Power does not corrupt men; fools, however, if they get into a position of power, corrupt power.

GEORGE BERNARD SHAW

The secret of power is the knowledge that others are more cowardly than you are.

LUDWIG BOERNE

Power, after love, is the first source of happiness.

STENDHAL

A cock has influence on his own dunghill.

PUBLILIUS SYRUS

[See also Government, Politics]

PRAISE:

We wish to attract praise to ourselves even as we seem to be praising others.

FRANÇOIS DE LA ROCHEFOUCAULD

The highest praise that can ever be given a General Assembly of Maryland is it might have been worse. It is also the highest praise that can ever be given to a dead cat.

H. L. MENCKEN

[See also Applause, Flattery]

PRAYER:

Father of Light, great God Heaven!
Hear'st thou the accents of despair?
Can guilt like man's be e'er forgiven?
Can vice atone for crimes by prayer?

LORD BYRON

Heaven grant that the burden you carry may have as easy an exit as it had an entrance.

ERASMUS: *Prayer for a Pregnant Woman*

When the gods wish to punish us they answer our prayers.

OSCAR WILDE

More than once I had seen a noble who had gotten his enemy at a disadvantage stop to pray before cutting his throat.

MARK TWAIN

Of Course—I prayed—
And did God Care?

EMILY DICKINSON

Do not ask for what you will wish you had not got.

SENECA

There are more tears shed over answered prayers than over unanswered prayers.

ST. THERESA

[*See also* Faith, God, Religion]

PREACHING:

Hear how he clears the points o'
  Faith
Wi' rattlin' an thumpin'—!
Now meekly calm, now wild in
  wrath.
He's stampin', and he's jumpin'—!

ROBERT BURNS

The worst scoundrels make the best preachers.

GERMAN PROVERB

[*See also* Sin]

PREFACE:

Read all the prefaces of Dryden,
For these our critics much
  confide-in.

(Tho' merely writ at first for
  filling
To raise the volume's price a shilling.)

JONATHAN SWIFT

Preface: That part of a book which is never read.

PREJUDICE:

If my theory of relativity is proven successful, Germany will claim me as a German and France will declare that I am a citizen of the world. Should my theory prove untrue, France will say I am a German and Germany will declare that I am a Jew.

ALBERT EINSTEIN

He had only one eye, and the popular prejudice runs in favor of two.

CHARLES DICKENS

Opinions founded on prejudice are always sustained with the greatest violence.

HEBREW PROVERB

Inequality is as dear to the American heart as liberty itself.

WILLIAM DEAN HOWELLS

[*See also* Jew]

PRESIDENT:

There's some folks standing behind the President that ought to get
around where he can watch 'em.

KIN HUBBARD

When I was a boy I was told that
anyone could be President. I'm beginning to believe it.

CLARENCE DARROW

I would rather be right than be
President.

HENRY CLAY

All a man needs to be elected
President is the kind of profile that
looks good on a postage stamp.

BILLY BOY FRANKLIN

President: The leading figure in a
small group of men of whom—and
of whom only—it is positively
known that immense numbers of
their countrymen did not want any
of them for President.

AMBROSE BIERCE

[*See also* Politician, Politics, Vice-
President]

PRESS:

Freedom of the press is limited to
those who own one.

A. J. LIEBLING

It is very difficult to have a free,
fair, and honest press anywhere in
the world. In the first place, as a
rule, papers are largely supported by
advertising, and that immediately
gives the advertisers a certain hold
over the medium which they use.

ELEANOR ROOSEVELT

Freedom of the press is useless
when people do not understand what
they read.

GERALD F. LIEBERMAN

[*See also* Newspaper]

PRIDE:

You can't hold your head high
with your hand out.

YIDDISH PROVERB

Pride goeth before destruction,
and an haughty spirit before a fall.

THE BIBLE

Why was man created on the sixth
day? To teach that if he is ever swol-
len with pride, it can be said: A flea
came ahead of thee in Creation.

THE TALMUD

I might have gone to West Point
but I was too proud to speak to a
congressman.

WILL ROGERS

[*See also* Vanity]

PRINCIPLE:

When a fellow says it ain't the money but the principle of the thing, it's the money.

KIN HUBBARD

It is easier to fight for one's principles than to live up to them.

ALFRED ADLER

Prosperity is the best protector of principle.

MARK TWAIN

A precedent embalms a principle.

BENJAMIN DISRAELI

Success is the ability to rise above principle.

GERALD BARZAN

PRISON:

The most anxious man in a prison is the warden.

GEORGE BERNARD SHAW

Prison: A place of punishments, and rewards.

AMBROSE BIERCE

To a warden Utopia is an escape-proof jail.

It is easier to stay out than get out.

MARK TWAIN

PRIZE:

What we have we prize not to the worth
Whiles we enjoy it, but being lacked and lost,
Why, then we rack the value; then we find
The virtue that possession would not show us.

WILLIAM SHAKESPEARE

PROBLEM:

Science is always wrong—it never solves a problem without creating ten more.

GEORGE BERNARD SHAW

What do you do with the problem solvers after the problem is solved?

If you keep your head when all about you are losing theirs—you don't understand the problem.

PROCRASTINATION:

Don't put off till tomorrow what can be enjoyed today.

JOSH BILLINGS

Procrastination is the art of keeping up with yesterday.

DON MARQUIS

PRODUCER:

An associate producer is the only guy in Hollywood who will associate with a producer.

FRED ALLEN

I hate a man who always says "yes" to me. When I say "no" I like a man who also says "no."

SAM GOLDWYN

[*See also* Hollywood]

PROFESSION:

Somebody must get the incompetent lawyers and doctors.

GEORGE BERNARD SHAW

All professions are conspiracies against the laity.

GEORGE BERNARD SHAW

Every person who has mastered a profession is a sceptic concerning it.

GEORGE BERNARD SHAW

[*See also* Occupation]

PROFESSOR:

Those who go to college and never get out are called professors.

GEORGE GIVOT

College professors are people who get what's left over after the football coach is paid off.

[*See also* Teacher]

PROFIT:

A man profits more by the sight of an idiot than by the orations of the learned.

ARABIAN PROVERB

It is a socialist idea that making profits is a vice; I consider the real vice is making losses.

WINSTON CHURCHILL

Nobody ever lost money taking a profit.

BERNARD BARUCH

[*See also* Business, Partnership]

PROGRESS:

Unquestionably, there is progress. The average American now pays twice as much in taxes as he formerly got in wages.

H. L. MENCKEN

A hundred years ago Hester Prynne of *The Scarlet Letter* was given an A for adultery. Today she would rate no better than a C-plus.

PETER DE VRIES

All progress is based upon a universal innate desire on the part of every organism to live beyond its income.

SAMUEL BUTLER

There is more required today to make a single man wise than formerly to make Seven Sages.

BALTASAR GRACIÁN

What we call progress is the exchange of one nuisance for another.

HAVELOCK ELLIS

Every step of progress the world has made has been from scaffold to scaffold, and from stake to stake.

WENDELL PHILLIPS

[See also Change, Science]

PROHIBITION:

There is a crying for wine in the streets, all joy is darkened, the mirth of the land is gone.

THE BIBLE

In 1927 a speakeasy proprietor whose premises were raided sued the local precinct captain for breach of promise.

Prohibition may be a disputed theory, but none can say that it doesn't hold water.

TOM MASSON

A prohibitionist is the sort of man one wouldn't care to drink with, even if he drank.

H. L. MENCKEN

Prohibition helped to beautify American home life. It got rid of the rings around the bathtubs.

GERALD F. LIEBERMAN

[See also Temperance]

PROMISE:

Promises and piecrust are made to be broken.

JONATHAN SWIFT

Books of poetry by young writers are usually promissory notes that are never met.

OSCAR WILDE

It's useless to hold a person to anything he says while he's in love, drunk, or running for office.

SHIRLEY MACLAINE

Some persons make promises for the pleasure of breaking them.

WILLIAM HAZLITT

If you wish to be a success in the world, promise everything, deliver nothing.

NAPOLEON

[See also Lie, Lying, Politician, Politics]

PROMPTNESS:

I owe all my success in life to having been always a quarter of an hour before my time.

LORD NELSON

Laugh and the world laughs with
you, be prompt and you dine alone.
GERALD BARZAN

I am a believer in punctuality
though it makes me very lonely.
E. V. VERRALL

PROPAGANDA:

The great masses of the people
will more easily fall victims to a big
lie than to a small one.
ADOLF HITLER

If a lie is repeated often enough
all the dumb jackasses in the world
not only get to believe it, they even
swear by it.
BILLY BOY FRANKLIN

[See also Lie, Lying]

PROPERTY:

Thieves respect property. They
merely wish the property to become
their property that they may more
perfectly respect it.
G. K. CHESTERTON

Property is robbery.
LATIN PROVERB

By right or wrong
Lands and goods go to the strong.
RALPH WALDO EMERSON

[See also Landlord, Real Estate]

PROPHET:

The wisest prophets make sure of
the event first.
HORACE WALPOLE

Prophecy: The art and practice of
selling one's credibility for future
delivery.
AMBROSE BIERCE

[See also Dream]

PROSPERITY:

The very bond of love.
WILLIAM SHAKESPEARE

I'll say this for adversity: people
seem to be able to stand it, and
that's more than I can say for prosperity.
KIN HUBBARD

Few of us can stand prosperity—
another man's, I mean.
MARK TWAIN

Americans have mastered the art
of being prosperous though broke.
BILLY BOY FRANKLIN

You know not how to live in
clover.
MENANDER

Prosperity discovers vice, adversity discovers virtue.
FRANCIS BACON

Ten ancient commandments lousing up the fun.
Along came prosperity—and then there were none.

GERALD BARZAN

Everything in the world may be endured except continual prosperity.

JOHANN WOLFGANG VON GOETHE

Prosperity: That condition which attracts the lively interest of lawyers, and warrants your being sued for damages, or indicted; or both.

ELBERT HUBBARD

Americans have always been able to handle austerity and even adversity. Prosperity is what's doing us in.

JAMES RESTON

Prosperity is the surest breeder of insolence I know.

MARK TWAIN

[See also Adversity, Inflation, Money, Success]

PROSTITUTION:

It has been said that politics is the second oldest profession. I have learned that it bears a striking resemblance to the first.

RONALD REAGAN

These [prostitutes] are the highest-paid professional women in America.

GAIL SHEEHY

Females are not the only species who prostitute themselves for money; they are the only ones that are honest about it.

FRANK DANE

[See also Hypocrisy, Lawyer, Politician, Politics]

PROTEST:

The lady doth protest too much, methinks.

WILLIAM SHAKESPEARE

War hath no fury like a noncombatant.

CHARLES E. MONTAGUE

PROVERB:

A proverb is a short sentence based on long experience.

MIGUEL DE CERVANTES

A country can be judged by the quality of its proverbs.

GERMAN PROVERB

The nation that is richest in proverbs [Spain] is the one that has proved itself the least wise in action.

JOSEPH JACOBS

Two thousand years of experience have indeed shown that the Fear or Love of the Lord forms a very good foundation for practical wisdom. But it has to be supplemented by some such corollary as "Keep your powder dry" before it becomes of direct service in the conduct of life.

JOSEPH JACOBS

In the multitude of proverbs consists the greatest proof of their uselessness as guides to action, for by this means we get proverbs at cross purposes.

JOSEPH JACOBS

[See also Epigram]

PSYCHIATRY:

Psychiatry has emerged as a new science, the aim of which is to chart our symptoms at the expense of our amusements. It is a form of horizontal confession subscribed to by those who would like to know why they do things that have always been done. It is a diversion for the rich, a palliative for the poor, and a boon to the furniture industry. To the sex connotation of the common couch it has added the luster of a college diploma.

GERALD F. LIEBERMAN

Psychoanalysts seem to be long on information and short on application.

GENE FOWLER

A psychiatrist is a fellow who asks you a lot of expensive questions your wife asks for nothing.

JOEY ADAMS

The alienist is not a joke.
He finds you cracked and leaves you broke.

KEITH PRESTON

Just because you're paranoid doesn't mean you're not being followed.

PSYCHOANALYSIS:

Daughters go into analysis hating their fathers, and come out hating their mothers. They never come out hating themselves.

LAURIE JO WOJCIK

Psychoanalysis is the disease it claims to cure.

KARL KRAUS

Psychoanalysis is confession without absolution.

G. K. CHESTERTON

PUBLICITY:

What kills a skunk is the publicity it gives itself.

ABRAHAM LINCOLN

PUBLISHING:

A multitude of books distracts the mind.

SENECA

Manuscript: Something submitted in haste and returned at leisure.

OLIVER HERFORD

The great American novel has not only already been written, it has already been rejected.

FRANK DANE

[See also Author, Book, Writer, Writing]

PUNISHMENT:

Young man, you will soon have to appear before another, and perhaps a better, judge than I.
WESTERN JUDGE, on pronouncing the death sentence

A man in jail has more room, better food, and commonly better company.

SAMUEL JOHNSON

The sin ye do by two and two ye must pay for one by one.

RUDYARD KIPLING

Every unpunished delinquency has a family of delinquencies.

HERBERT SPENCER

He hurts the good who spares the bad.

PUBLILIUS SYRUS

It is for the general good of all that the wicked should be punished.

EURIPIDES

[See also Crime, Justice, Mercy, Pity]

PURITAN:

A puritan is a person who pours righteous indignation into the wrong things.

G. K. CHESTERTON

The objection to Puritans is not that they try to make us think as they do, but that they try to make us do as they think.

H. L. MENCKEN

The Puritan hated bear-baiting, not because it gave pain to the bear, but because it gave pleasure to the spectators.

THOMAS BABINGTON MACAULAY

Puritanism: The haunting fear that someone, somewhere, may be happy.

H. L. MENCKEN

PUSH:

One of the two things mainly conducive to success, especially in politics. The other is pull.

AMBROSE BIERCE

QUARREL:

What stronger breastplate than a heart untainted!

Thrice is he armed that hath his
quarrel just,
And he but naked, though locked
up in steel,
Whose conscience with justice is
corrupted.

WILLIAM SHAKESPEARE

Thrice is he armed that hath his
quarrel just,
And four times he who gets his
fist in fust.

ARTEMUS WARD

Those who in quarrels interpose
Must often wipe a bloody nose.

JOHN GAY

When you see a married couple
coming down the street, the one who
is two or three steps ahead is the one
that's mad.

HELEN ROWLAND

The fiercest quarrels do not always argue the greatest offenses.

TERENCE

In all private quarrels the duller
nature is triumphant by reason of
dullness.

GEORGE ELIOT

The full potentialities of human
fury cannot be reached until a friend
of both parties tactfully intervenes.

G. K. CHESTERTON

[See also Love, War]

QUOTATION:

The act of repeating erroneously
the words of another.

AMBROSE BIERCE

Classical quotation is the parole
of literary men all over the world.

SAMUEL JOHNSON

By necessity, by proclivity, and by
delight, we all quote.

RALPH WALDO EMERSON

I often quote myself. It adds spice
to my conversation.

GEORGE BERNARD SHAW

The wisdom of the wise and the
experience of the ages are perpetu-
ated by quotations.

BENJAMIN DISRAELI

A quotation at the right moment
is like bread to the famished.

THE TALMUD

I have made it a rule, whenever I
say something stupid, to immediately
attribute it to Samuel Johnson, the
President of these United States—or
the Bible.

BILLY BOY FRANKLIN

[See also Epigram, Wisdom]

RACE:

The human race was always interesting and we know by its past

that it will always continue so, monotonously.

MARK TWAIN

The end of the human race is that it will die of civilization.

RALPH WALDO EMERSON

Don't overestimate the decency of the human race.

H. L. MENCKEN

After all there is but one race—humanity.

GEORGE MOORE

Rattlesnake: Our   prostrate brother.

AMBROSE BIERCE

Civil Rights Movement: The struggle of the black race to show that, if given the chance, it can screw up as good as the white race.

FRANK DANE

There are times when one would like to hang the whole human race, and finish the farce.

MARK TWAIN

[See also Life, Man, Woman]

RADICAL:

More than once I should have lost my soul to radicalism if it had been the originality it was mistaken for by its young converts.

ROBERT FROST

The radical of one century is the conservative of the next. The radical invents the views. When he has worn them out the conservative adopts them.

MARK TWAIN

[See also Conservative]

RAILROAD:

A road on rails, faster'n the eye can flicker
So east and west kin swap their lies quicker.

19TH CENTURY SONG

Since I moved to suburbia I found out the purpose of those railroad timetables. Without them there would be no way of knowing how late your train is.

GREGORY NUNN

[See also Transportation, Travel]

RASCAL:

Make yourself a good man, then you can be sure there is at least one less skunk in the world.

19TH CENTURY WESTERN AMERICAN PRAYER

The world belongs to the rascals, Heaven belongs to the good.

PERSIAN PROVERB

Rascals are always sociable.

ARTHUR SCHOPENHAUER

Lash the rascals naked through the world.

WILLIAM SHAKESPEARE

[See also Bastard]

REAL ESTATE:

Never build after you are five and forty; have five years income in hand before you lay a brick; and always calculate the expense at double the estimate.

HENRY KETT

The meek shall inherit the earth; and . . . delight . . . in the peaceful abundance.

THE BIBLE

If the real estate gang could, they'd raise the rents in the graveyards.

FRANK DANE

[See also Landlord]

REASON:

Many are destined to reason wrongly; others, not to reason at all, and others to persecute those who reason.

VOLTAIRE

He is next to the gods whom reason impels.

CLAUDIAN

Reason is the enemy of faith.

MARTIN LUTHER

Among civilized nations reason has always been an occupational hazard.

Nothing is ever accomplished by a reasonable man.

AMERICAN PROVERB

[See also Brain, Judgment]

REBELLION:

Insurrection of thought always precedes insurrection of arms.

WENDELL PHILLIPS

Rebellions of the belly are the worst.

FRANCIS BACON

Men seldom, or rather never for a length of time, and deliberately, rebel against anything that does not deserve rebelling against.

THOMAS CARLYLE

Rebellion: A system devised to replace one form of tyranny with another.

[See also Conformity, Non-Conformist]

RECOLLECTION:

Take notes on the spot, a note is worth a cart-load of recollections.

RALPH WALDO EMERSON

Recollection: To remember in great detail something that never happened.

FRANK DANE

[See also Autobiography, Memory]

REFORM:

I think I am better than the people who are trying to reform me.

ED HOWE

A sinner can reform, but stupidity is forever.

[See also Change, Progress]

REINCARNATION:

We do not know what to do with this short life, yet we yearn for another that will be eternal.

ANATOLE FRANCE

The biggest hoax perpetrated by the human mind is its "life after death" valentine.

H. L. MENCKEN

How many ages hence
Shall this our lofty scene be acted o'er,

In states unborn and accents yet unknown!

WILLIAM SHAKESPEARE

[See also Death, Life]

REJECTION:

In the fields of art the art of rejection is, for the most part, artless . . . Oriental propriety, however, demands a warmer approach. And so, early in the century, the following standard rejection form was used [by a Chinese publisher]: "Illustrious brother of the sun and moon look upon the slave who rolls at thy feet, who kisses the earth before thee, and demands of thy charity permission to speak and live. We have read the manuscript with delight. By the bones of our ancestors we swear that never before have we encountered such a masterpiece. Should we print it His Majesty, the Emperor, would order us to take it as a criterion and never again print anything which was not equal to it. As that would not be possible before ten thousand years, all trembling we return this manuscript and beg thee ten thousand pardons. See my head at thy feet, and I am the slave of thy servant.–The Editor."

Quoted by GERALD F. LIEBERMAN

[See also Books, Publishing, Writer, Writing]

RELIGION:

When it is a matter of money, all men are of the same religion.

VOLTAIRE

Democracy is also a form of religion; it is the worship of jackals by jackasses.

H. L. MENCKEN

In a temple everything should be serious except the thing that is being worshipped.

OSCAR WILDE

I don't believe in God because I don't believe in Mother Goose.

CLARENCE DARROW

Most people have some sort of religion, at least they know which church they're staying away from.

JOHN ERSKINE

In religion we believe only what we do not understand, except in the instance of an intelligible doctrine that contradicts an incomprehensible one. In that case we believe the former as a part of the latter.

AMBROSE BIERCE

An idea isn't responsible for the people who believe in it.

DON MARQUIS

You can always borrow a corkscrew from a member of the Protestant Episcopal Church.

CHAUNCEY DEPEW

Men are swayed more by fear than by reverence.

ARISTOTLE

Not one of them who took up in his youth with this opinion that there are no gods ever continued until old age faithful to his conviction.

PLATO

A great perhaps.

FRANÇOIS RABELAIS

We have just enough religion to make us hate but not enough to make us love one another.

JONATHAN SWIFT

If men are so wicked with religion what would they be without it?

BENJAMIN FRANKLIN

Irreligious men are often better suited for godly missions.

HASIDIC SAYING

Religions revolve madly around sexual questions.

REMY DE GOURMONT

Religion is what keeps the poor from murdering the rich.

NAPOLEON

I am afraid the clergyman's God is often the head of the clerical profession.

WILLIAM R. INGE

The church has always been willing to swap off treasures in heaven for cash down.

ROBERT GREEN INGERSOLL

A clergyman is a man who undertakes the management of our spiritual affairs as a method of bettering his temporal ones.

AMBROSE BIERCE

Every dogma has its day.

ISRAEL ZANGWILL

The man who is always worrying whether or not his soul would be damned generally has a soul that isn't worth a damn.

OLIVER WENDELL HOLMES

There is only one religion, though there are a hundred versions of it.

GEORGE BERNARD SHAW

We think the ancients were foolish who worshipped the sun. I would worship it forever if I had grace to do so.

HENRY DAVID THOREAU

No gold, no Holy Ghost.

SAMUEL BUTLER

I won't take my religion from any man who never works except with his mouth.

CARL SANDBURG

Religion is the opiate of the masses.

KARL MARX

All religions issue Bibles against Satan, and say the most injurious things against him, but we never hear his side.

MARK TWAIN

Intelligence, I admit, is no safeguard if one is determined to leap into disbelief.

BARBARA HARRISON

There are few among us who have not suffered from too early familiarity with the Bible and the conceptions of religion.

HAVELOCK ELLIS

The only objection against the Bible is a bad life.

EARL OF ROCHESTER

Scratch the Christian and you find the pagan, spoiled.

ISRAEL ZANGWILL

Redemption is the fundamental mystery of our holy religion, and who believeth in it shall not perish, but have everlasting life in which to try to understand it.

AMBROSE BIERCE

[See also Christian, Faith, God, Jew]

REMEDY:

There is a remedy for everything; it is called death.

PORTUGUESE PROVERB

'Tis a sharp remedy, but a sure one for all ills.

SIR WALTER RALEIGH, on feeling the cutting edge of the ax with which he was to be beheaded

To do nothing is also a good remedy.

HIPPOCRATES

For a desperate disease, a desperate cure.

LATIN PROVERB

[See also Medicine]

REPENTANCE:

If I repent anything it is very likely to be my good behavior.

HENRY DAVID THOREAU

Repentance: The faithful attendant and follower of Punishment. It is usually manifest in a degree of reformation that is not inconsistent with continuity of sin.

AMBROSE BIERCE

Then turns repentant, and his
    God adores
With the same spirit that he
    drinks and whores.

ALEXANDER POPE

[See also Confession, Sin]

REPORT:

When some men discharge an obligation you can hear the report for miles around.

MARK TWAIN

[See also News, Rumor]

REPORTER:

A would-be satirist, a hired
    buffoon,
A monthly scribbler of some low
    lampoon,
Condemn'd to drudge, the meanest of the mean,
And furbish falsehoods for a magazine.

LORD BYRON

[See also Journalism]

REPUBLICAN:

Anybody can be a Republican when the stock market is up. But when stocks is selling for no more than they're worth, let me tell you, being a Republican is a sacrifice.

WILL ROGERS

If you shoot a Republican out of season, the fine will be ten dollars and costs.

19TH CENTURY MISSISSIPPI SAYING

Republicans will do anything for the poor except get off their backs.

AMERICAN PROVERB

Republicans are men who made their money under the Democrats, and wish to see that nobody else is faced with the same dastardly sin on their consciences.

BILLY BOY FRANKLIN

Trickle, trickle,
Trickle, trickle.
Give me a buck
And I'll give you a nickel.

GERALD BARZAN

Republicans are for both the man and the dollar, but in case of conflict, the man before the dollar.

ABRAHAM LINCOLN

As to the Democrats or the Republicans, let a man choose which he will, he is sure to repent.

GREGORY NUNN

[See also Conservative, Liberal, Money, Politics]

REPUTATION:

I am better than my reputation.

JOHANN [CHRISTOPH] FRIEDRICH VON SCHILLER

How many people live on the reputation of the reputation they might have made!

OLIVER WENDELL HOLMES

How many worthy men can survive their own reputations?

MICHEL DE MONTAIGNE

A man may write himself out of reputation when nobody else can do it.

TOM PAINE

Nothing deflates so fast as a punctured reputation.

THOMAS R. DEWAR

Judge a man by the reputation of his enemies.

ARABIAN PROVERB

[See also Fame]

RESEARCH:

I have not been able to devise a satisfactory method of research myself. I constantly read about historians who spend years on their particular subject and make millions of notations on little three-by-five cards. Everything is there when they get done . . . I have never been able to use those little cards. Maybe you have to be a professor to do it, one with a lot of Ph.D. students. Maybe *they* do the (little) cards.

HARRISON E. SALISBURY

The more research I do the more I find everything is at random. Somebody goes off in this direction, somebody in that, and who knows what the end result is going to be?

HARRISON E. SALISBURY

I find that a great part of the information I have was acquired by

looking up something and finding something else on the way.
FRANKLIN P. ADAMS

It is not worth while to go round the world to count the cats in Zanzibar.
HENRY DAVID THOREAU

[See also Knowledge, Science]

RESIGNATION:

Resign: To renounce an advantage for a greater advantage.
AMBROSE BIERCE

RESPECT:

I get no respect. The way my luck is running, if I was a politician I'd be honest.
RODNEY DANGERFIELD

If you steal something small you are a petty thief, but if you steal millions you are a gentleman of society.
GREEK PROVERB

Since when was genius found respectable?
ELIZABETH BARRETT BROWNING

Virtue has never been as respectable as money.
MARK TWAIN

Treating your adversary with respect is giving him an advantage to which he is not entitled.
SAMUEL JOHNSON

Men have to do some awfully mean things to keep up their respectability.
GEORGE BERNARD SHAW

Respectability: The offspring of a liaison between a bald head and a bank account.
AMBROSE BIERCE

In his private heart no man much respects himself.
MARK TWAIN

[See also Manners, Money]

RESPONSIBILITY:

Diogenes struck the father when the son swore.
ROBERT BURTON

REST:

Death after life.
EDMUND SPENSER

It is no disgrace to rest a bit.
GENE FOWLER

[See also Death, Retirement]

RESTITUTION:

The founding or endowing of universities and public libraries by gift or bequest.
AMBROSE BIERCE

[*See also* Crime, Philanthropist, Philanthropy]

RETIREMENT:

When some fellers decide to retire nobody knows the difference.

KIN HUBBARD

Walk sober off before the sprightlier age
Comes titt'ring on, and shoves you from the stage.

ALEXANDER POPE

[*See also* Age]

RETREAT:

In the first and foremost flight, ha, ha!
You always find that knight, ha, ha!
    That celebrated,
    Cultivated,
    Underrated Nobleman,
The Duke of Plaza-Toro!

W. S. GILBERT

In all the trade of war no feat
Is nobler than a brave retreat.

SAMUEL BUTLER

[*See also* Courage, War]

RETRIBUTION:

Curious how Napoleon's greatest detractors have all come to horrible ends. Londonderry cut his throat. Ludwig XVIII rotted on his throne, and Professor Saalfeld of Goettingen is still professor of Goettingen.

HEINRICH HEINE

[*See also* Revenge]

RETROSPECT:

A year hence, or five years, we shall in retrospect think of our present bomb-ridden era of murder and international mayhem as a day spent in the Garden of the Gods.

GENE FOWLER

As lousy as things are now, tomorrow they will be somebody's good old days.

GERALD BARZAN

[*See also* History, Lie, Lying, Past]

REVENGE:

No one returns with good will to the place which has done him a mischief.

PHAEDRUS

One should always get even in some way, else the sore place will go on hurting.

MARK TWAIN

Jimmy Carter is the South's revenge for Sherman's march through Georgia.

RONALD REAGAN

Revenge is sweet, sweeter than life itself. So say fools.

JUVENAL

One good act of vengeance deserves another.

JOHN JEFFERSON

Success is the best revenge.

FRENCH PROVERB

Vengeance to God alone belongs;
But when I think of all my wrongs,
My blood is liquid flame!

SIR WALTER SCOTT

REVOLUTION:

Let the ruling classes tremble at a Communist revolution. The proletarians have nothing to lose but their chains. . . . Workers of the world, unite!

KARL MARX

So they united, and the Communist revolution took the chain from their legs and wound it around their necks.

SAMUEL BONOM

Never wear your best trousers when you go out to fight for freedom and truth.

HENRIK IBSEN

The excessive increase of anything causes a reaction in the opposite direction.

PLATO

The bitterest reactionaries are always found among those raised high by a popular upheaval.

HONORÉ DE BALZAC

Revolution: In politics, an abrupt change in the form of misgovernment.

AMBROSE BIERCE

He who devours the substance of the poor will find it at length a bone to choke him.

FRENCH PROVERB

When the people contend for their liberty they seldom get anything for their victory, but new masters.

SIR GEORGE SAVILE

A man may build himself a throne of bayonets, but he cannot sit on it.

WILLIAM R. INGE

Two forces which are the worst enemies of civil freedom are the absolute monarchy and the revolution.

LORD ACTON

Inferiors revolt in order that they may be equal, and equals that they may be superior. Such is the state of mind which creates revolutions.

ARISTOTLE

Poverty is the parent of revolution and crime.

ARISTOTLE

Declarations of Independence make nobody really independent.

GEORGE SANTAYANA

[See also Conformity, Non-Conformist, Rebellion]

RICH:

Ah, if the rich were rich as the poor fancy riches.

RALPH WALDO EMERSON

A rich man is either a scoundrel or the heir of a scoundrel.

SPANISH PROVERB

Get what you can and keep what you have. That's the way to get rich.

SCOTTISH PROVERB

He who enjoys good health is rich, though he knows it not.

ITALIAN PROVERB

It is an easy matter for a stingy man to get rich—but what's the use?

AMERICAN PROVERB

It is the wretchedness of being rich that you have to live with rich people.

LOGAN PEARSALL SMITH

[See also Miser, Money, Wealth]

RIGHTS:

If some people got their rights

they would complain of being deprived of their wrongs.

OLIVER HERFORD

[See also Democracy, Equality, Law]

ROMANCE:

Nothing spoils a romance so much as a sense of humor in the woman.

OSCAR WILDE

There once was a man not unique
Who imagined himself quite a shique;
But the girls didn't fall
For the fellow at all.
He made only twenty a wique.

Nudity has taken all the romance out of semi-nudity.

GREGORY NUNN

[See also Love, Man, Sex, Woman]

ROME:

The true key to the declension of the Roman Empire . . . may be stated in two words: the imperial character overlaying, and finally destroying, the national character.

SAMUEL TAYLOR COLERIDGE

I found Rome brick and I leave it marble.

AUGUSTUS

Rome had Senators too, that's why it declined.

> FRANK DANE

Who goes to Rome a beast returns a beast.

> ITALIAN PROVERB

Would that the people of Rome had but one neck.

> CALIGULA

RUMOR:

What some invent the rest enlarge.

> JONATHAN SWIFT

I cannot tell how the truth may be;
I say the tale as 'twas said to me.

> SIR WALTER SCOTT

Rumor is a pipe
Blown by surmises, jealousies, conjectures . . .

> WILLIAM SHAKESPEARE

[See also Gossip]

RUSSIA:

The mass trials have been a great success, comrades. In the future there will be fewer but better Russians.

> NINOTCHKA

Russia has abolished God but so far God has been more tolerant.

> JOHN CAMERON SWAYZE

The policy of Russia is changeless. Its methods, its tactics, its maneuvers may change, but the polar star of its policy, world domination, is a fixed star.

> KARL MARX

Russia is a riddle wrapped in a mystery inside an enigma.

> WINSTON CHURCHILL

Any time a politician tells you "The Russians are coming" hang onto your wallet. It's just another raid on the treasury.

> GORE VIDAL

The trees in Siberia are miles apart—that's why the dogs are so fast.

> BOB HOPE

SABBATH:

The Sabbath was made for man, and not man for the Sabbath.

> THE BIBLE

Sabbath: A weekly festival having its origin in the fact that God made the world in six days and was arrested on the seventh.

> AMBROSE BIERCE

Some keep the Sabbath going to Church—

I keep it, staying at Home—
With a Bobolink for a Chorister—
And an Orchard, for a Dome—
EMILY DICKINSON

Only one day's rest of seven?
    That's a difficult ration.
I hold that at least one off-day
    Was lost in translation.
GERALD BARZAN

SAFETY:

When you're safe at home you
wish you were having an adventure;
when you're having an adventure
you wish you were safe at home.
THORNTON WILDER

Here lies Reverend Zekiel Bone;
Met his death in a safety zone.
EPITAPH IN AN ENGLISH CEMETERY

As if there were safety in stupidity
alone.
HENRY DAVID THOREAU

The best safety lies in fear.
WILLIAM SHAKESPEARE

[See also Caution, Fear]

SAINT:

The only difference between the
saint and the sinner is that every
saint has a past, and every sinner
has a future.
OSCAR WILDE

Some reputed saints that have
been canonized ought to have been
cannonaded.
C. C. COLTON

SALARY:

Let us all be happy and live
within our means—even if we have
to borrow money to do it.
ARTEMUS WARD

Draw your salary before spending
it.
ARTEMUS WARD

It's best to save a little while your
earnings are small. It's impossible to
save after you begin making money.

College man: At twenty he thinks
he can save the world, at thirty he
begins to wish he could save part of
his salary.

[See also Wages]

SANITY:

An asylum for the sane would be
empty in America.
GEORGE BERNARD SHAW

Who, then, is sane?
HORACE

[See also Insanity, Madness]

SATIRE:

In times like these it is difficult not to write satire.

JUVENAL

Bitter the jest when satire comes too near the truth and leaves a sting behind it.

TACITUS

Fools are my theme, let satire be my song.

LORD BYRON

[See also Wit]

SAVAGE:

I expect that Woman will be the last thing civilized by man.

GEORGE MEREDITH

Savages: Tribes of people who don't know that anything is wrong, until missionaries tell them.

[See also Mob]

SCHOLAR:

A mere scholar, who knows nothing but books, must be ignorant even of them.

WILLIAM HAZLITT

A mere scholar, a mere ass.

ROBERT BURTON

[See also College, Education]

SCHOLARSHIP:

All wish to know but none to pay the fee.

JUVENAL

When a woman turns to scholarship there is usually something wrong with her sexual apparatus.

FRIEDRICH NIETZSCHE

[See also Research, Scholar]

SCHOOL:

Sex education may be a good idea in the schools but I don't believe the kids should be given homework.

BILL COSBY

After a fellow gets famous it doesn't take long for someone to bob up that used to sit next to him in school.

KIN HUBBARD

I have never let my schooling interfere with my education.

MARK TWAIN

[See also Education]

SCIENCE:

There is no way to find out why a snorer can't hear himself snore.

MARK TWAIN

Do what we can, summer will have its flies.
RALPH WALDO EMERSON

This is the machine age. The only thing people do by hand is scratch themselves.
JOE LAURIE, JR.

There are physicists who say we have the capabilities to destroy the world twelve times over. I say once is enough.
DAVE ALLEN

I shall make electricity so cheap that only the rich can afford to burn candles.
THOMAS EDISON

Science in the modern world has many uses; its chief use, however, is to provide long words to cover the errors of the rich.
G. K. CHESTERTON

Science does not deny God, she goes one better. She makes Him unnecessary.
FREETHINKERS OF LIÈGE

It is inexcusable for scientists to torture animals; let them make their experiments on journalists and politicians.
HENRIK IBSEN

Law of Hydrodynamics: When the body is immersed in water, the telephone rings.

There are men who would be afraid to commit themselves on the doctrine that castor oil is a laxative.
CAMILLE FLAMMARION

Science has discovered it is the lower part of the face that gives away one's thoughts, not the eyes. This is especially true when one opens the lower part of the face.

One machine can do the work of fifty ordinary men. No machine can do the work of one extraordinary man.
ELBERT HUBBARD

We're about to enter the age of flight before we've developed a chair that a man can sit in comfortably.
PHILIP WYLIE

It is told that such are the aerodynamics and wing-loading of the bumblebee that in principle it cannot fly. It does, and the knowledge that it defies the august authority of Isaac Newton and Orville Wright must keep the bee in constant fear of crack-up . . . life among the bumblebees must bear a remarkable resemblance to life in the United States in recent years.
JOHN KENNETH GALBRAITH

[See also Progress, Research]

SCOTCH:

It requires a surgical operation to get a joke well into a Scotch understanding.

SYDNEY SMITH

Much may be made of a Scotchman, if he be caught young.

SAMUEL JOHNSON

The unflagging quality of Scotch and Irish whiskey is sober proof that the knowledge of water was accepted with neither hysteria nor tumult in the provinces, and will forever stand to the undiluted glory of these intelligent people.

GERALD F. LIEBERMAN

The noblest prospect which a Scotchman ever sees is the high road that leads him to England!

SAMUEL JOHNSON

SECRET:

The secret of being a bore is to tell everything.

VOLTAIRE

No man should have a secret from his own wife. She invariably finds out. Women have a wonderful instinct about things. They can discover everything except the obvious.

OSCAR WILDE

Keep to yourself the final touches of your art.

BALTASAR GRACIÁN

Where secrecy or mystery begins, vice or roguery is not far off.

SAMUEL JOHNSON

Keep no secrets of thyself from thyself.

GREEK PROVERB

Women keep no secrets, and I know many men who are women in this regard.

JEAN DE LA FONTAINE

If you would keep your secret from an enemy, tell it not to a friend.

BENJAMIN FRANKLIN

Tell your friend a lie. If he keeps it secret, then tell him the truth.

PORTUGUESE PROVERB

SECRETARY:

A secretary must think like a man, act like a lady, look like a girl —and work like a dog.

In America I had two secretaries —one for autographs and the other for locks of hair. Within six months one had died of writer's cramp, and the other was completely bald.

OSCAR WILDE

SEDUCTION:

Speech is the vestibule to the palace of love.

JAMI OF PERSIA

A little still she strove, and much
repented,
And whispering, "I will ne'er consent"—consented.

LORD BYRON

Maidens, like moths, are ever
caught by glare,
And Mammon wins his way
where seraphs might despair.

LORD BYRON

He who hesitates—is a damned
fool.

MAE WEST

A few creditable attempts at the
beginning are sufficient to arouse curiosity, without pledging one to the
final object.

BALTASAR GRACIÁN

Foul words and frowns must not
repel a lover.

WILLIAM SHAKESPEARE

She who is silent consents.

FRENCH PROVERB

Men who do not make advances
to women are apt to become victims
of women who make advances to
them.

WALTER BAGEHOT

[See also Love, Man, Sex, Woman,
Women's Lib]

SELF-CONTROL:

She who ne'er answers till a husband cools,
Or, if she rules him, never shows
she rules;
Charms by accepting, by submit-
ting, sways,
Yet has her humor most, when
she obeys.

ALEXANDER POPE

If you can keep your head when
all about you are losing theirs—
perhaps you don't understand the
situation.

[See also Patience]

SENSITIVE:

Some people are so sensitive they
feel snubbed if an epidemic over-
looks them.

KIN HUBBARD

Exaggerated sensitiveness is an ex-
pression of the feeling of inferiority.

ALFRED ADLER

The wearer knows best where the
shoe pinches.

SPANISH PROVERB

SERMON:

Let us have wine and women,
mirth and laughter,

Sermons and soda-water the day after.

LORD BYRON

One may prefer fresh eggs, though laid by a fowl of the meanest understanding, but why fresh sermons?

GEORGE ELIOT

[See also Preaching]

SERVANT:

A good servant is a real godsend; but truly 'tis a rare bird in the land.

MARTIN LUTHER

American women expect to find in their husbands a perfection that English women only hope to find in their butlers.

SOMERSET MAUGHAM

The cook was a good cook, as cooks go; and as cooks go, she went.

H. H. MUNRO

Here are all kinds of employers wanting all sorts of servants, and all sorts of servants wanting all kinds of employers, and they never seem to come together.

CHARLES DICKENS

Buttress: A butler's wife.

The difference between a man and his valet; they both smoke the same cigars, but only one pays for them.

ROBERT FROST

The tongue is the worst part of a bad servant.

JUVENAL

The more servants, the more enemies.

FRENCH PROVERB

SEX:

There is no one, no matter their size, shape or accent, who doesn't turn someone else on, somewhere, somehow.

LARRY LEVENSON

Sex is not taxed—but it can be taxing.

JOHN BARRYMORE

Too much of a good thing can be wonderful.

MAE WEST

It's not the men in my life that counts, it's the life in my men.

MAE WEST

If one were to eliminate from the presidency anyone whose flesh is weak, the White House would have been deserted since the death of Thoreau.

WILLIAM F. BUCKLEY, JR.

Who, in this era of literature about females whose legs fly open like trick compasses, cares to hear of love with its clothes on?

BEN HECHT

The sex life of a fish is nothing to brag about.

ROBERT BENCHLEY

Sex is only dirty if it's done right.

AMERICAN PROVERB

Two is company; three is terrific.

FRANK DANE

As the French say, there are three sexes—men, women, and clergymen.

SYDNEY SMITH

Much of our highly valued cultural heritage has been acquired at the cost of sexuality.

SIGMUND FREUD

There may be some things better than sex, and some things may be worse. But there is nothing exactly like it.

W. C. FIELDS

Were kisses all the joys in bed,
One woman would another wed.

WILLIAM SHAKESPEARE

I valued sexual experience because of its power of producing a celestial flood of emotion and exaltation which, however momentary, gave me a sample of the ecstasy that may one day be the normal condition of conscious intellectual activity.

GEORGE BERNARD SHAW

Children should never discuss sex in the presence of their elders.

GREGORY NUNN

Those do it best who cannot tell how it's done.

JAMES M. BARRIE

The union of the epiderms.

FRENCH SAYING

I was never duped by sex as a basis for permanent relations, nor dreamt of marriage in connection with it.

GEORGE BERNARD SHAW

If sex is such a natural phenomenon, how come there are so many books on how to?

BETTE MIDLER

'Tis the Devil inspires this evanescent ardor, in order to divert the parties from prayer.

MARTIN LUTHER

[See also Adultery, Celibacy, Chastity, Desire, Familiarity, Infidelity, Kiss, Life, Living Together, Love, Lover, Man, Marriage, Mistress, Monogamy, Morality, Nudity, Opportunity, Performance, Pleasure, Prostitution, Rest, Romance, Seduction, Self-Control, Sin, Temptation, Virgin, Virtue, Woman, Women's Lib]

SHAKESPEARE:

I don't know whether Lord Bacon wrote Shakespeare's works or not, but if he didn't he missed the greatest opportunity of his life.

HORACE RUSSELL

If we wish to know the force of human genius we should read Shakespeare. If we wish to see the insignificance of human learning we may study his commentators.

WILLIAM HAZLITT

SHAME:

If a man fools me once, shame on him. If the same man fools me twice, shame on me.

ASIAN PROVERB

Where there is shame, there is hope for virtue.

GERMAN PROVERB

SIGHT:

One sees things for the first time only once.

THEODORE H. WHITE

Television proves that sight has a definite odor.

GERALD F. LIEBERMAN

SILENCE:

If silence be good for the wise, how much the better for fools.

THE TALMUD

If you don't say anything you won't be called on to repeat it.

CALVIN COOLIDGE

Blessed are they who have nothing to say, and who cannot be persuaded to say it.

JAMES RUSSELL LOWELL

Speech is silvern; silence is golden.

THOMAS CARLYLE

The canon is definitely made up and the whole golden gospel of silence effectively compressed in thirty-five volumes.

JOHN MERLEY, on the collected works of Thomas Carlyle

[See also Speech]

SILLY:

He was born silly and had a relapse.

ARTHUR "BUGS" BAER

SIN:

Some rise by sin, and some by virtue fall.

WILLIAM SHAKESPEARE

For the sin they do by two and two they must pay for one by one.

RUDYARD KIPLING

To abstain from sin when one can no longer· sin is to be forsaken by sin, not to forsake it.

ST. AUGUSTINE

There is no sin except stupidity.
OSCAR WILDE

The worst sin towards our fellow creatures has not been to hate them but to be indifferent to them: that's the essence of inhumanity.
GEORGE BERNARD SHAW

Most sinners are cursed at not because we despise their sins but because we envy their success at sinning.
THOMAS BABINGTON MACAULAY

O Thou, who didst with pitfall
and with gin
Beset the Road I was to wander
in,

Thou wilt not with Predestined
Evil round
Enmesh, and then impute my Fall
to Sin!
OMAR KHAYYÁM

Preachers denounce sin as if it was available to everyone.
FRANK DANE

A woman who writes commits two sins: she increases the number of books, and decreases the number of women.
ALPHONSE KARR

Men who make no pretensions to being good on one day out of seven are called sinners.
MARY LITTLE

It is a sin to believe evil of others —but it is seldom a mistake.
H. L. MENCKEN

Every sin is the result of a collaboration.
STEPHEN CRANE

The reason the way of the transgressor is hard is because it's so crowded.
KIN HUBBARD

Religion has done love a great service by making it a sin.
ANATOLE FRANCE

[See also Hell, Religion]

SINCERITY:

A wit should be no more sincere than a woman constant.
WILLIAM CONGREVE

It is dangerous to be sincere unless you are also stupid.
GEORGE BERNARD SHAW

Nobody would be a charlatan who could afford to be sincere.
RALPH WALDO EMERSON

[See also Honesty, Virtue]

SLANDER:

Throw plenty of mud and some of it is bound to stick.
HIPPONAX THE SATIRIST

The greater the truth, the greater the libel.

LORD MANSFIELD

You've got to be careful quoting Ronald Reagan, because when you quote him accurately it's called mudslinging.

FRITZ MONDALE

[See also Gossip]

SLEEP:

O sleep, O gentle sleep,
Nature's soft nurse.

WILLIAM SHAKESPEARE

Most people spend their lives going to bed when they're not sleepy and getting up when they are.

CINDY ADAMS

[See also Death]

SMILE:

One may smile, and smile, and be a villain.

WILLIAM SHAKESPEARE

People worry, and God smiles.

HEBREW PROVERB

The smiles of a pretty woman are the tears of the purse.

ITALIAN PROVERB

SMOKING

Wrinkles should merely indicate where smiles have been.

MARK TWAIN

They gave each other a smile with a future in it.

RING LARDNER

SMOKING:

To cease smoking is the easiest thing I ever did. I ought to know because I've done it a thousand times.

MARK TWAIN

There are people who strictly deprive themselves of each and every eatable, drinkable and smokable which has in any way acquired a shady reputation. They pay this price for health. And health is all they get for it.

MARK TWAIN

When you smoke cigarettes you're likely to burn yourself to death; with chewing tobacco the worst thing you can do is drown a midget.

FRED ALLEN

I have seen many a man turn his gold into smoke, but you are the first who has turned smoke into gold.

ELIZABETH I, to Sir Walter Raleigh

It is now proven, beyond a doubt, that smoking is a leading cause of statistics.

FLETCHER KNEBEL

220 SNOB

May never lady press his lips,
   His proffered love returning,
Who makes a furnace of his
   mouth,
And keeps its chimney burning.
May each true woman shun his
   sight,
   For fear the fumes might choke
   her;
And none but those who smoke
   themselves
Have kisses from a smoker.

19TH CENTURY ANTI-SMOKING CAMPAIGN

It has always been my rule never
to smoke when asleep, and never to
refrain when awake.

MARK TWAIN

I kissed my first woman and
smoked my first cigarette on the
same day. I have never had time for
tobacco since.

ARTURO TOSCANINI

A woman is only a woman, but a
good cigar is a smoke.

RUDYARD KIPLING

A cigarette is the perfect type of
a perfect pleasure. It is exquisite,
and it leaves one unsatisfied.

OSCAR WILDE

I always sleep with one shoe in
my hand to put out any fires I may
accidentally ignite.

GENE FOWLER

A good cigar is as great a comfort
to a man as a good cry to a woman.

E. R. BULWER-LYTTON

SNOB:

I knew a woman once whose
name was Mrs. Mabel Jallup. She
had taste. One day she saw a vase at
an auction. She bought it. She
brought it home and put it on her
table. It was Ming, and it made the
Grand Rapids furniture look cheap.
She was very sad, so she sold the
Grand Rapids furniture and bought
period. But the period furniture
made her mail-order house look
cheap. So she sold the house and
took an exclusive apartment in town.
But this apartment was so exclusive
it made Mr. Jallup look cheap. Naturally she got a divorce, and married
a Mr. Preston Potter. But she was
stymied. Mr. Preston Potter made
her look cheap.

DOROTHY RICE SIMS

In Heaven an angel is nobody in
particular.

GEORGE BERNARD SHAW

Asses speak only of horses.

HEINRICH HEINE

It's the high-class people you have
to give passes to.

FLORENZ ZIEGFELD

Snobs talk as if they had forgotten
their ancestors.

HERBERT AGAR

Rectitude, platitude, high-hatitude.

MARGOT ASQUITH

That which we call a snob, by any other name would still be snobbish.

WILLIAM MAKEPEACE THACKERAY

The man who worships mere wealth is a snob.

ANTHONY TROLLOPE

There is no being so poor and contemptible, who does not think there is somebody still poorer and still more contemptible.

SAMUEL JOHNSON

God is satisfied with one *d* but the Todds need two.

ABRAHAM LINCOLN, when asked the spelling of his wife's maiden name

The whole strength of England lies in the fact that the enormous majority of English people are snobs.

GEORGE BERNARD SHAW

Whosoever changes the pronunciation of their name, after getting rich, is a snob.

GERALD BARZAN

I can enjoy flowers quite happily without translating them into Latin.

CORNELIA OTIS SKINNER

A highbrow is a person educated beyond his intelligence.

BRANDER MATTHEWS

One of the very best temporary cures for pride and affectation is seasickness. A man who wants to vomit never puts on airs.

JOSH BILLINGS

He was not brought by the stork, he was delivered by a man from the Audubon Society, personally.

FRED ALLEN

There are no people quite so vulgar as the over-refined ones.

MARK TWAIN

Whoever is rich is my brother.

RUSSIAN PROVERB

A highbrow is the kind of person who looks at a sausage and thinks of Picasso.

ALAN PATRICK HERBERT

[*See also* Status]

SOBRIETY:

The worst thing about some men is that when they are not drunk they are sober.

WILLIAM BUTLER YEATS

Water, taken in moderation, cannot hurt anybody.

MARK TWAIN

[*See also* Drink, Intoxication]

SOCIALISM:

Many people consider the things government does for them to be social progress—but they consider the things government does for others as socialism.

EARL WARREN

American Politics: A form of socialism for the rich, including the politicians.

GREGORY NUNN

I don't look for much to come out of government ownership as long as we have Democrats and Republicans.

KIN HUBBARD

[See also Government]

SOCIAL SECURITY:

The Republican Party is a friend of Social Security the way Colonel Sanders was a friend of chickens.

CHARLES T. MANATT

SOCIETY:

A system in which the two great commandments are to hate your neighbor and to love your neighbor's wife.

THOMAS BABINGTON MACAULAY

Society is composed of two great classes—those who have more din-

ners than appetite, and those who have more appetite than dinners.

SÉBASTIEN CHAMFORT

Society is a hospital of incurables.

RALPH WALDO EMERSON

Society everywhere is in conspiracy against the manhood of every one of its members.

RALPH WALDO EMERSON

Society is now one polish'd horde,
Form'd of two mighty tribes, the bores and bored.

LORD BYRON

Nature makes only dumb animals; we owe the fools to society.

HONORÉ DE BALZAC

If you wish to be popular in society you must consent to be taught many things you already know.

CHARLES MAURICE DE TALLEYRAND

In polite society one laughs at all the jokes, including the ones one's heard before.

FRANK DANE

I suppose society is wonderfully delightful. To be in it is merely a bore. But to be out of it is simply a tragedy.

OSCAR WILDE

SOLDIER:

When the military man approaches, the world locks up its spoons and packs off its womankind.

GEORGE BERNARD SHAW

The worse the man the better the soldier. If soldiers be not corrupt they ought to be made so.

NAPOLEON

[See also Military, War]

SONG:

Our sweetest songs are those that tell of saddest thought.

PERCY BYSSHE SHELLEY

I am saddest when I sing. So are those who hear me; they are sadder even than I.

ARTEMUS WARD

Song: The licensed medium for bawling in public things too silly or sacred to be uttered in ordinary speech.

OLIVER HERFORD

You have Van Gogh's ear for music.

BILLY WILDER, to a singing actor

There are German songs which can make a stranger to the language cry.

MARK TWAIN

[See also Music, Opera]

SOUL:

Four thousand volumes of metaphysics will not teach us what the soul is.

VOLTAIRE

Alas, my soul, pleasing companion of this body, fleeting thing, art thou now deserting it? Whither do you fly?

HADRIAN

[See also Faith, Religion, Heaven]

SOUP:

The soup is never hot enough if the waiter can keep his thumb in it.

WILLIAM COLLIER

Only the pure in heart can make a good soup.

LUDWIG VON BEETHOVEN

There is only one thing harder than looking for a dewdrop in the dew, and that is fishing for a clam in the clam chowder.

NEW ENGLAND PROVERB

[See also Cooking, Food]

SPACE:

Space has no top, no bottom; in fact, it is bottomless both at the bottom and the top.

BILL NYE

Somewhere, behind space and time,
Is wetter water, slimier slime.

RUPERT BROOKE

SPAIN:

The Spaniards have it that a buxom widow must be either married, buried, or shut up in a convent.

SAM SLICK

To the Spaniards has been well applied the witticism about Charles II: They never said a foolish thing and never did a wise one.

JOSEPH JACOBS

A whale stranded upon the coast of Europe.

EDMUND BURKE

SPEAKER:

He multiplied words without knowledge.

THE BIBLE

In biblical days it was considered a miracle for an ass to speak. Now it would be a miracle if one kept quiet.

No one is exempt from talking nonsense; the misfortune is to do it solemnly.

MICHEL DE MONTAIGNE

[See also Politician, Speech]

SPECIALIST:

One who limits himself to his chosen mode of ignorance.

ELBERT HUBBARD

There is nothing so stupid as an educated man, if you get off the thing he was educated in.

WILL ROGERS

No man can be a pure specialist without being in the strict sense an idiot.

GEORGE BERNARD SHAW

An expert is one who knows more and more about less and less.

NICHOLAS MURRAY BUTLER

[See also Doctor, Medicine]

SPECULATION:

If the world were good for nothing else, it is a fine subject for speculation.

WILLIAM HAZLITT

October. This is one of the peculiarly dangerous months to speculate in stock. The others are July, January, September, April, November, May, March, June, December, August and February.

MARK TWAIN

[See also Stock Market]

SPEECH:

Did I say something that stupid? PHOCION, Greek statesman-general to an aide, when the people of Athens interrupted his speech with thunderous applause.

When at a loss how to go on, cough.

GREEK PROVERB

I have never seen an ass who talked like a human being, but I have met many human beings who talked like asses.

HEINRICH HEINE

We make more enemies by what we say than friends by what we do.

JOHN C. COLLINS

Speech was given man to disguise his thoughts.

CHARLES MAURICE DE TALLEYRAND

There was a maiden speech, so inaudible that it was doubted whether, after, the young orator really did lose his virginity.

BENJAMIN DISRAELI

Better never begin than never make an end.

GEORGE HERBERT

It is not by speeches and resolutions of majorities that the great questions of the time are decided . . . but by iron and blood.

OTTO VON BISMARCK

Small wits have the gift of speaking much and saying nothing.

FRANÇOIS DE LA ROCHEFOUCAULD

A closed mouth gathers no feet.

AMERICAN PROVERB

He who has little silver in his pouch must have the more silk on his tongue.

E. R. BULWER-LYTTON

No member needs so great a number of muscles as the tongue.

LEONARDO DA VINCI

It ain't a bad plan to keep still occasionally, even when you know what you're talking about.

KIN HUBBARD

Blessed is the man who, having nothing to say, abstains from giving in words evidence of the fact.

GEORGE ELIOT

When I can't talk sense I talk metaphor.

J. P. CURRAN

For more than forty years I have been speaking prose without knowing it.

MOLIÈRE

What orators lack in depth they make up for in length.

BARON DE LA BRÈDE ET DE MONTESQUIEU

You taught me language; and my profit on't
Is, I know how to curse.

WILLIAM SHAKESPEARE

Adlai Stevenson has a genius for saying the right thing, at the right time, to the wrong people.

JOE E. LEWIS

A word too much always defeats its purpose.

ARTHUR SCHOPENHAUER

Lisp: To call a spade a thpade.

OLIVER HERFORD

Oratory is the art of making a loud noise seem like a deep thought.

Woman's word is never done.

AMERICAN PROVERB

A closed mouth catches no flies.

FRENCH PROVERB

[See also Lying, Politician, Silence]

SPELLING:

I hold that a man has as much right to spell a word as it is pronounced as he has to pronounce it the way it ain't spelled.

JOSH BILLINGS

I don't give a damn for a man that can spell a word only one way.

MARK TWAIN

SPINSTER:

When there is an old maid in the house a watchdog is unnecessary.

HONORÉ DE BALZAC

When spinsterhood is bliss, 'tis folly to be wived.

[See also Marriage, Women's Lib]

SPORT:

No man is fit to be called a sportsman what doesn't kick his wife out of bed an average of once every three weeks.

ROBERT SMITH SURTREES

All is fair in love and golf.

AMERICAN PROVERB

The difference between an amateur and a professional athlete is, the latter is paid by check.

I took up golf for the exercise—
and all I keep getting is holes-in-one.
                          GREGORY NUNN

I throw a ball and get paid for it.
Others do it by throwing the bull.
                          JEROME DEAN

Magellan went around the world
in 1521—which isn't too many
strokes when you consider the distance.
                          JOE LAURIE, JR.

Caution is a most valuable asset in
fishing, especially if you are the fish.

There are two kinds of colleges in
this country: those that fired the
football coach before the season
started, and those that wish they
had.

I listened to a football coach who
spoke straight from the shoulder—at
least I could detect no higher origin
in anything he said.
                          DIXON RYAN FOX

The battle of Waterloo was won
on the playing fields of Eton.
                          DUKE OF WELLINGTON

[See also Games]

SPRING:

A little Madness in the Spring
Is wholesome even for the King.
                          EMILY DICKINSON

Spring makes everything young
again—but man.
                          JEAN PAUL RICHTER

In the spring a young man's fancy
lightly turns—and turns—and turns.
                          HELEN ROWLAND

SPY:

Every government has spies in
every other country, and every other
country knows about them. It is
merely a form of international cour-
tesy, like exchange professors.
                          ROBERT BENCHLEY

Spies are of no use nowadays.
Their profession is over. The newspapers do their work instead.
                          OSCAR WILDE

[See also United Nations]

STAGE:

The stage is the refuge of the too
fascinating.
                          OSCAR WILDE

There is that smaller world which
is the stage, and that larger stage
which is the world.
                          ISAAC GOLDBERG

[See also Actor, Theater]

STATESMAN:

In statesmanship get the formalities right, never mind about the moralities.

MARK TWAIN

A statesman is a politician who's been dead ten or fifteen years.

HARRY S. TRUMAN

You can always get the truth from an American statesman after he has turned seventy, or given up all hope of the Presidency.

WENDELL PHILLIPS

Honest statesmanship is the wise employment of individual meanness for the public good.

ABRAHAM LINCOLN

Metternich approaches close to being a great statesman. He lies very well.

NAPOLEON

The fastest way for a politician to become an elder statesman is to lose an election.

EARL WILSON

A statesman is one who lies in state.

[See also Lie, Lying, Politician, Politics]

STATISTICS:

He uses statistics as a drunken man uses lampposts—for support rather than for illumination.

ANDREW LANG

A single death is a tragedy, a million deaths is a statistic.

JOSEPH STALIN

Statistics: A group of numbers looking for an argument.

STATUS:

No matter her past, when a chambermaid marries a lord she becomes a lady.

LATIN PROVERB

Training is everything. The peach was once a bitter almond; cauliflower is nothing but cabbage with a college education.

MARK TWAIN

I would rather be the first man here than the second man in Rome.

JULIUS CAESAR, on his way to Spain.

Beautiful sins, like beautiful things, are the privilege of the rich.

OSCAR WILDE

I would rather sit on a pumpkin, and have it all to myself, than be crowded on a velvet cushion.

HENRY DAVID THOREAU

Abstention from labor is the conventional evidence of wealth and is therefore the conventional mark of social standing.

THORSTEIN VEBLEN

Rank is a great beautifier.

E. R. BULWER-LYTTON

Archbishop: A Christian ecclesiastic of a rank superior to that attained by Christ.

H. L. MENCKEN

He flourishes with hereditary honors.

LATIN PROVERB

He who liveth in the palace hall
Waneth fast and spendeth all.

RALPH WALDO EMERSON

That which is called firmness in a king is called obstinacy in a jackass.

LORD ERSKINE

Some men never feel small, but these are the few men who are.

G. K. CHESTERTON

O let us love our occupations,
Bless the squire and his relations,
Live upon our daily rations,
And always know our proper stations.

CHARLES DICKENS

Arguments are extremely vulgar, for everybody in good society holds exactly the same opinions.

OSCAR WILDE

Some movie stars wear their sunglasses even in church. They're afraid God might recognize them and ask for autographs.

FRED ALLEN

Never have a companion who casts you in the shade.

BALTASAR GRACIÁN

Nothing is more harsh than a low man when raised to a certain height.

CLAUDIAN

A mighty pomp, though made of little things.

VIRGIL

At a round table there is no dispute about place.

ITALIAN PROVERB

Hasty climbers have sudden falls.

ITALIAN PROVERB

You cannot separate the monarchy from its trappings.

JOHN MILTON

I am his Highness' dog at Kew;
Pray tell me, sir, whose dog are you?

ALEXANDER POPE

When science discovers the center of the universe a lot of people will be disappointed to find they are not it.

BERNARD BAILY

You should study the Peerage.
. . . It is the best thing in fiction the
English have ever done.

OSCAR WILDE

The Pedigree of Honey
  Does not concern the Bee—
A Clover, any time, to him,
  Is Aristocracy.

EMILY DICKINSON

Exclusiveness is a characteristic of
recent riches, high society, and the
skunk.

AUSTIN O'MALLEY

My folks didn't come over on the
Mayflower but they were here to
meet the boat.

WILL ROGERS

The Astors are a country,
bounded on the north, south, east
and west—by the Astors.

1920s SAYING

When a fox has his hour of importance, bow to him.

THE TALMUD

Fit yourself for the best society,
and then, never enter it.

JOHN RUSKIN

Away with these trappings to the
vulgar; I know them in and out.

PERSIUS

[See also Money, Snob]

STOCK MARKET:

My family wasn't affected by the
crash of '29. They went broke in
'28.

GERALD BARZAN

The market is a place set apart
where men may deceive each other.

ANARCHASIS

What a falling off was there!

WILLIAM SHAKESPEARE

I made a fortune getting out too
soon.

J. P. MORGAN

There are two times in a man's
life when he should not speculate—
when he cannot afford it, and when
he can.

MARK TWAIN

Want to make money?
Here's a plan to try:
Buy stocks when they are low,
Sell them when they're high.

[See also Broker, Gambling]

STUDENT:

You are young, my son, and, as
the years go by, time will change
and even reverse many of your
present opinions. Refrain, therefore,
awhile from setting yourself up as a
judge of the highest matters.

PLATO

As pliable as wax in being bent towards vice but rough and rude to their counselors.

HORACE

The idiot who praises, with enthusiastic tone,
All centuries but this, and every country but his own.

W. S. GILBERT

The progress of the times . . . is such, that little children who can neither walk nor talk, may be seen cursing their Maker!

BOYLE ROCHE

In America, the young are always ready to give to those who are older the benefits of their inexperience.

OSCAR WILDE

[See also Age, Education, Youth]

STUDY:

There is no royal road to geometry.

EUCLID

A learned man is an idler who kills time by study.

GEORGE BERNARD SHAW

Study: Concentration of the mind on whatever will ultimately put something in the pocket.

ELBERT HUBBARD

[See also College, Education, Knowledge, Student]

STUPIDITY:

When a stupid man is doing something he is ashamed of, he always declares that it is his duty.

GEORGE BERNARD SHAW

He was born stupid and greatly improved his birthright.

SAMUEL BUTLER

Rascality has limits; stupidity has not.

NAPOLEON

Stupidity often saves a man from going mad.

OLIVER WENDELL HOLMES

Some men, though patrician, are also stupid.

CICERO

Stupidity is a force unto itself.

LATIN PROVERB

He was not only stupid, he was also ignorant; an unbeatable parlay.

BILLY BOY FRANKLIN

Genius may have its limitations, but stupidity is ,not thus handicapped.

ELBERT HUBBARD

Never underestimate the power of stupid people in large groups.

Ordinarily he is insane. But he has lucid moments when he is only stupid.

HEINRICH HEINE

Against stupidity the gods are helpless.

JOHANN [CHRISTOPH] FRIEDRICH VON SCHILLER

[See also Ignorance, United Nations]

STYLE:

Style is the dress of thoughts.

LORD CHESTERFIELD

Ignorance is never out of style. It was in fashion yesterday, it is the rage today and it will set the pace tomorrow.

FRANK DANE

[See also Fashion]

SUBSIDY:

There is a great discovery still to be made in literature, that of paying literary men by the quantity they do not write.

THOMAS CARLYLE

It is not the policy of the government in America to give aid to works of any kind. They let things take their natural course without help or impediment, which is generally the best policy.

THOMAS JEFFERSON

[See also Charity]

SUBSTITUTE:

A substitute shines brightly as a king
Until a king be by.

WILLIAM SHAKESPEARE

SUBWAY:

There were thirty million fewer riders on the New York subways last year—and nobody noticed the difference.

The average straphanger's complaint is one of long standing.

The traveler with empty pockets pursues his journey in perfect safety.

OVID

SUCCESS:

'Tis more by fortune, lady, than by merit.

WILLIAM SHAKESPEARE

Successful and fortunate crime is called virtue.

SENECA

Dare to do things worthy of imprisonment if you mean to be of consequence.

JUVENAL

His demerits keep pace with his acquirements.

PUBLILIUS SYRUS

All you need in this life is ignorance and confidence, and then success is assured.

MARK TWAIN

If at first you don't succeed, you're running about average.

When smiling Fortune spreads her
     golden ray,
All crowd around to flatter and
     obey.
But when she wanders from an
     angry sky,
Our friends, our flatterers—our
     lovers—fly!

OVID

It is to their crimes that great men are indebted for their palaces.

LATIN PROVERB

Horatio Alger started by shining shoes and within one year made a million dollars. He must have used very little polish.

SAM LEVENSON

It's them as take advantage that get advantage in this world.

GEORGE ELIOT

Success is counted sweetest
     By those who ne'er succeed.

EMILY DICKINSON

Nothing is so good as it seems beforehand.

GEORGE ELIOT

A successful lawsuit is one worn by a policeman.

ROBERT FROST

Success, the mark no mortal wit,
Or surest hand, can always hit:
For whatsoe'er we perpetrate,
We do but row, we're steer'd by
     fate.

SAMUEL BUTLER

A man must have a certain amount of intelligent ignorance to get anywhere.

CHARLES F. KETTERING

It takes twenty years to become an overnight success.

EDDIE CANTOR

As long as we are lucky we attribute it to our smartness; our bad luck we give the gods credit for.

JOSH BILLINGS

The penalty of success is to be bored by the attentions of people who formerly snubbed you.

MARY LITTLE

Watch out when you're getting all you want. Fattening hogs ain't in luck.

JOEL CHANDLER HARRIS

Behind every successful man is a woman with nothing to wear.

'Tis an old lesson; time approves
it true,
And those who know it best, de-
plore it most;
When all is won that all desire to
woo,
The paltry prize is hardly worth
the cost.

LORD BYRON

Success is having ten honeydew melons and eating only the top half of each one.

BARBRA STREISAND

It's harder for a poor man to be successful than it is for a rich man.

GREGORY NUNN

To establish oneself in the world, one must do all one can to seem established there.

FRANÇOIS DE LA ROCHEFOUCAULD

A man is truly a success when he can afford to double-cross his friends.

BILLY BOY FRANKLIN

The best way to get on in the world is to make people believe it's to their advantage to help you.

JEAN DE LA BRUYÈRE

The business of an orthodox preacher is about as successful as that of a celluloid dog chasing an asbestos cat through hell.

ELBERT HUBBARD

He who makes the most of him-self doesn't make much.

OLIVER WENDELL HOLMES

Success covers a multitude of blunders.

GEORGE BERNARD SHAW

Everything bows to success, even grammar.

VICTOR HUGO

If it's worth fighting for, it's worth fighting dirty for.

AMERICAN BUSINESS PROVERB

Success: The one unpardonable sin against one's fellows.

AMBROSE BIERCE

Success is the necessary misfor-tune of life, but it is only to the very unfortunate that it comes early.

ANTHONY TROLLOPE

She's the kind of woman who climbed the ladder of success—wrong by wrong.

MAE WEST

About all some men accomplish in life is to send a son to Harvard.

ED HOWE

Want makes people lucky; luck makes them worse.

THE TALMUD

We can't all be lions in this world. There must be some lambs, and

235 SUPERIORS

harmless, kindly, gregarious creatures for eating and shearing.

WILLIAM MAKEPEACE THACKERAY

Let us be thankful for fools. But
for them the rest of us could not succeed.

MARK TWAIN

The success of any man with any
woman is apt to displease even his
best friends.

MME. DE STAËL

If I die prematurely, at any rate I
shall be saved from being bored by
my own success.

SAMUEL BUTLER

There is no more fatal blunder
than he who consumes the greater
part of his life getting his living.

HENRY DAVID THOREAU

There is always room at the top.

DANIEL WEBSTER

Success is full of promise till a
man gets it; and then it is a last
year's nest from which the birds
have flown.

HENRY WARD BEECHER

[See also Bastard, Business]

SUICIDE:

Before shooting one's self one
should deliver a soliloquy.

HEINRICH HEINE

The fellow that tries to commit
suicide with a razor, and fails, would
fail at anything.

KIN HUBBARD

I hate all the bleeders, the bleed-
ing, the bled,
The sucking, the kissing of getting
ahead;
No wonder so many have killed
themselves dead.

GERALD BARZAN

Suicide is confession.

DANIEL WEBSTER

When you go to drown yourself
always take off your clothes, they
may fit your wife's next husband.

GREGORY NUNN

SUPERMARKET:

With the supermarket as our temple and the singing commercial as
our litany, are we likely to fire the
world with an irresistible vision of
America's exalted purposes and inspiring way of life?

ADLAI E. STEVENSON

Law of the Supermarket: The
other line moves faster.

SUPERIORS:

Avoid victories over superiors.
They will allow a man to help them
but not to surpass them, and will

have any advice tendered them appear like a recollection of something they have forgotten, rather than as a guide to something they cannot find.

BALTASAR GRACIÁN

SUPERSTITION:

Superstition is the religion of feeble minds.

EDMUND BURKE

Superstition is to religion what astrology is to astronomy: the mad daughter of a wise mother.

VOLTAIRE

It is bad luck to fall out of a thirteenth-story window on Friday.

AMERICAN PROVERB

Let me make the superstitions of a nation, and I care not who makes its laws or its songs.

MARK TWAIN

[See also Religion]

SURPRISE:

The husband who desires to surprise is often very much surprised himself.

VOLTAIRE

Be not surprised if thou findest thyself in possession of unexpected wealth. Allah will provide an unexpected use for it.

JAMES J. ROCHE

SURRENDER:

By yielding you may obtain victory.

OVID

Love conquers all; let us surrender to Love.

VIRGIL

SURVIVAL:

One can survive everything nowadays, except death.

OSCAR WILDE

Man has developed an obvious capacity for surviving the pompous reiteration of the commonplace.

JOHN KENNETH GALBRAITH

Nature has made up her mind that what cannot defend itself shall not be defended.

RALPH WALDO EMERSON

[See also Life]

SUSPICION:

Look for the woman.

ALEXANDER DUMAS THE ELDER

We are always paid for our suspicion by finding what we suspect.

HENRY DAVID THOREAU

I wished my wife to be not so much as suspected.

JULIUS CAESAR

But, O! what damned minutes tell
he o'er
Who dotes, yet doubts; suspects,
yet soundly loves.

WILLIAM SHAKESPEARE

[*See also* Doubt]

SWEARING:

The existing phrasebooks are inadequate. They are well enough as far as they go, but when you fall down and skin your leg they don't tell you what to say.

MARK TWAIN

When angry, count four; when very angry, swear.

MARK TWAIN

[*See also* Oath]

SYMPATHY:

Kind words will never die—neither will they buy groceries.

BILL NYE

Sympathy is what you usually give to a relative when you don't want to lend him money.

My friends, and family, know there are two things they can always come to me for, and I will supply in abundance: sympathy and advice.

BILLY BOY FRANKLIN

If there was less sympathy in the world, there would be less trouble in the world.

OSCAR WILDE

[*See also* Advice]

TACT:

To have the reputation of possessing the most perfect social tact, talk to every woman as if you loved her, and to every man as if he bored you.

OSCAR WILDE

There are people who can do all fine and heroic things but one: keep from telling their happiness to the unhappy.

MARK TWAIN

A spoonful of honey will catch more flies than a gallon of vinegar.

BENJAMIN FRANKLIN

Women and foxes, being weak, are distinguished by superior tact.

AMBROSE BIERCE

Tact is the art of making a point without making an enemy.

The most difficult thing in the world is to know how to know how to do a thing and to watch someone else doing it wrong, without commenting.

T. H. WHITE

I've never been in Georgia, but I had a relative in the army down there—General Sherman.

FRANK CHURCH, to Jimmy Carter

I can live for two months on a good compliment.

MARK TWAIN

It is bad judgment to speak of halters in the house of a man who was hanged.

MIGUEL DE CERVANTES

[See also Diplomacy, Manners]

TALENT:

Premature development of the powers of both mind and body leads to an early grave.

QUINTILIAN

Talent is a loan from God for the relief of man's estate.

JELAL AD-DIN OF PERSIA

The audience was reserved and quietly attentive—until Rita Hayworth danced onto the screen in a flaming red dress, cut to show a major part of her acting ability.

GERALD F. LIEBERMAN

A great deal of talent is lost to the world for want of a little courage.

SYDNEY SMITH

Many a young man resembles both his parents: his mother's talent for spending money, and his father's for not making it.

Talent is commonly developed at the expense of character.

RALPH WALDO EMERSON

[See also Genius]

TARIFF:

A protective tariff is a typical conspiracy in restraint of trade.

THORSTEIN VEBLEN

Tariff: A scale of taxes on imports, designed to protect the domestic producer against the greed of his consumer.

AMBROSE BIERCE

TASTE:

A different man, a different taste.

GREEK PROVERB

Bad taste is better than no taste at all.

ARNOLD BENNETT

Taste cannot be controlled by law.

THOMAS JEFFERSON

There is no accounting for tastes.
LATIN PROVERB

Lots of money, lots of taste;
Little money, lots of waste.
GERALD BARZAN

He that tastes woman, ruin meets.
JOHN GAY

Things sweet to taste prove in digestion sour.
WILLIAM SHAKESPEARE

[See also Fashion, Style]

TAXES:

The way to crush the bourgeoisie is to grind them between millstones of taxation and inflation.
V. I. LENIN

Taxation without representation is tyranny.
Attributed to JAMES OTIS

Taxation with representation ain't so hot either.
GERALD BARZAN

When there is an income tax, the just will pay more and the unjust less.
PLATO

It is the duty of a good shepherd to shear his flock, not flay them.
TIBERIUS

What is the difference between a taxidermist and a tax collector? The taxidermist takes only your skin.
MARK TWAIN

Make use of a costly vessel today, and enjoy it, for it may be taken from you tomorrow.
THE TALMUD

The wages of sin are unreported.
AMERICAN PROVERB

The wisest men have not stopped their enemies from gathering revenue, they have prevented them from spending it.
LATIN PROVERB

It is getting harder and harder to support the government in the style to which it has become accustomed.

No matter how bad a child is, he is still good for a tax deduction.
AMERICAN PROVERB

Even when you make a tax form out on the level, you don't know when it's through if you are a crook or a martyr.
WILL ROGERS

In this world nothing is certain but death and taxes.
BENJAMIN FRANKLIN

The way taxes are, you might as well marry for love.
JOE E. LEWIS

The art of taxation consists in so plucking the goose as to obtain the largest amount of feathers with the least possible amount of hissing.
Attributed to JEAN-BAPTISTE COLBERT

He is fast rising from affluence to poverty.
MARK TWAIN

Every dish of fish brought to the table is paid for once to the fisherman and six times to the state.
J. R. McCULLOCH

Taxes have grown up like Topsy in this country.
FRANKLIN D. ROOSEVELT

In levying taxes and in shearing sheep it is well to stop when you get down to the skin.
AUSTIN O'MALLEY

Milk the cow but do not pull off the udder.
GREEK PROVERB

I'm proud to be paying taxes in the United States. The only thing is, I could be just as proud for half the money.
ARTHUR GODFREY

The principle of spending money to be paid by posterity, under the name of funding, is but swindling futurity on a large scale.
THOMAS JEFFERSON

Nothing hurts more than having to pay an income tax, unless it's not having to pay an income tax.
THOMAS R. DEWAR

The wisdom of man never yet contrived a system of taxation that would operate with perfect equality.
ANDREW JACKSON

The marvel of all history is the patience with which men and women submit to burdens unnecessarily laid upon them by their governments.
WILLIAM E. BORAH

A hypocrite is a man who pays his taxes with a smile.

The income tax has made more liars out of American people than golf has.
WILL ROGERS

TEACHER:

The average schoolmaster is, and always must be, an ass.
H. L. MENCKEN

Teaching is the fine art of imparting knowledge without possessing it.

To be good is noble, but to teach others how to be good is nobler—and less trouble.
MARK TWAIN

The vanity of teaching doth oft tempt a man to forget that he is a blockhead.
                                    SIR GEORGE SAVILE

There is nothing so pedantic as pretending not to be pedantic.
                                    WILLIAM HAZLITT

[See also Education, Knowledge]

TEARS:

Crying is the refuge of plain women, but the ruin of pretty ones.
                                    OSCAR WILDE

She stood in tears amid the alien corn.
                                    JOHN KEATS

Every woman is wrong until she cries, and then she is right; instantly.
                                    SAM SLICK

She was always crying. In fact, she wept so much she made everybody's corns ache.
                                    ARTHUR "BUGS" BAER

The most effective water power in the world—women's tears.
                                    WILSON MIZNER

Take hand and part with laughter; touch lips and part with tears.
                                    ALGERNON CHARLES SWINBURNE

[See also Alimony, Woman]

TELEVISION:

Television is called a medium because anything good on it is rare.
                                    FRED ALLEN

To get ten per cent out of a television producer you have to be a fifty-fifty partner.
                                    BILLY BOY FRANKLIN

Whatever their faults, the Communists did not invent canned laughter.

Television made a great contribution to the elimination of harmful drug addiction. It broke millions of the sleeping pill habit.
                                    GERALD F. LIEBERMAN

In television blood is thicker than talent.
                                    GERALD F. LIEBERMAN

Television has raised writing to a new low.
                                    SAM GOLDWYN

A poor joke must invent its own laughter.
                                    LATIN PROVERB

These detective series on TV always end at precisely the right moment, after the criminal is arrested and before the court turns him loose.
                                    ROBERT ORBEN

TV commercial: The opening and closing fifteen minutes of a half-hour show.

[*See also* Entertainment, Hollywood]

TEMPER:

The worst tempered people I've ever met were people who knew they were wrong.

WILSON MIZNER

We boil at different degrees.

RALPH WALDO EMERSON

When angry, count ten before you speak. If very angry, a hundred.

THOMAS JEFFERSON

No man can think clearly when his fists are clenched.

GEORGE JEAN NATHAN

[*See also* Anger]

TEMPERANCE:

Pitted against hard drinking Christians the abstemious Mahometans go down like grass before the scythe.

AMBROSE BIERCE

Temperance is simply a disposition of the mind which binds the passions.

THOMAS AQUINAS

[*See also* Abstinence, Moderation]

TEMPTATION:

Most dangerous
Is that temptation that doth goad us on
To sin in loving virtue.

WILLIAM SHAKESPEARE

Temptation when resisted brings happiness—but when yielded to brings greater happiness.

Of two evils, choose the prettier.

CAROLYN WELLS

I can resist everything except temptation.

OSCAR WILDE

Why resist temptation? There will always be more.

DON HEROLD

Somebody ought not yield to temptation, or the thing becomes absurd.

ANTHONY HOPE

There's always free cheese in a mousetrap.

INTERNATIONAL PROVERB

Familiarity breeds attempt.

FRANK DANE

The only way to get rid of a temptation is to yield to it.

OSCAR WILDE

[*See also* Sin]

TEXAS:

If I owned Hell and Texas I'd rent out Texas and live in Hell.

GENERAL PHILIP H. SHERIDAN

Texas could exist without the United States but the United States cannot exist without Texas.

SAM HOUSTON

THEATER:

One of my chief regrets during my years in the theater is that I couldn't sit in the audience and watch me.

JOHN BARRYMORE

I should rather my play were damned by bad players, than merely saved by good acting.

OLIVER GOLDSMITH

Theaters are like brothels; one never knows what he will find inside —or whom.

What a glorious garden of wonders the lights of Broadway would be to anyone lucky enough to be unable to read.

G. K. CHESTERTON

[*See also* Actor, Actress, Critic, Entertainment]

THIEF:

The jury, passing on the prisoner's life,
May in the sworn twelve have a thief or two
Guiltier than him they try.

WILLIAM SHAKESPEARE

The robb'd that smiles steals something from the thief;
He robs himself that spends a bootless grief.

WILLIAM SHAKESPEARE

We hang the petty thieves and appoint the great ones to public office.

AESOP

There are no crooked politicians in America. They've legalized their thievery.

FRANK DANE

[*See also* Crime, Politician, Politics]

THINK:

Few people think more than two or three times a year. I have made an international reputation for myself thinking once or twice a week.

GEORGE BERNARD SHAW

Beware when the great God lets loose a thinker on this planet.

RALPH WALDO EMERSON

I was a freethinker before I knew how to think.

GEORGE BERNARD SHAW

If I look confused it's because I'm thinking.

SAM GOLDWYN

We like a man to come right out and say what he thinks—if we agree with him.

MARK TWAIN

There are lots of people who can't think seriously without injuring their minds.

JOHN JAY CHAPMAN

Think twice before you speak to a friend in need.

AMBROSE BIERCE

If everybody thought before they spoke, the silence would be deafening.

GERALD BARZAN

Think with the few and speak with the many.

BALTASAR GRACIÁN

[See also Thought]

THOUGHT:

A hundred wagonloads of thoughts will not pay a single ounce of debt.

ITALIAN PROVERB

When a woman is in a train of thought someone is bound to get run down.

Though old the thought and oft exprest,
'Tis his at last who says it best.

JAMES RUSSELL LOWELL

[See also Think]

THRIFT:

Keep adding little by little and you will soon have a big hoard.

LATIN PROVERB

Take care of your pennies and your dollars will take care of themselves.

SCOTTISH PROVERB

Take care of your pennies and your pounds will take care of your heirs and barristers.

ENGLISH PROVERB

Take care of your pennies and your dollars will take care of your widow's next husband.

AMERICAN PROVERB

A penny saved is a penny wasted.

AL DIAMOND

When one has had to work so hard to get money why should he impose on himself the hardship of trying to save it?

DON HEROLD

Economy is going without something you do want in case, perhaps, you should someday want something you probably won't want.

ANTHONY HOPE

[See also Miser]

TIME:

The Bird of Time has but a little way
To flutter—and the Bird is on the Wing.

OMAR KHAYYÁM

Time and tide wait for no man.

GEOFFREY CHAUCER

Time and tide wait for no man, but time always stands still for a woman of thirty.

ROBERT FROST

It is later than you think.

CHINESE PROVERB

Time is precious, but truth is more precious than time.

BENJAMIN DISRAELI

If you're there before it's over, you're on time.

JAMES J. WALKER

Why, when I am talking, does time seem to fly?

BOB GRANT

This time, like all times, is a very good one, if we but know what to do with it.

RALPH WALDO EMERSON

The thing that takes up the least amount of time and causes the most amount of trouble is Sex.

JOHN BARRYMORE

Time is money, especially when you're talking to a lawyer or buying a commercial.

FRANK DANE

The less one has to do, the less time one finds to do it in.

LORD CHESTERFIELD

It takes less time to do something wrong than it takes to explain why you did it wrong.

Lose an hour in the morning and you will be all day hunting for it.

RICHARD WHATELY

All my possessions for one moment of time.

QUEEN ELIZABETH I

Time is a great legalizer, even in the field of morals.

H. L. MENCKEN

Backward, turn backward, O Time, in your flight,
Make me a child again just for tonight!

ELIZABETH AKERS ALLEN

Lost, yesterday, somewhere between sunrise and sunset, two golden hours, each set with sixty diamond minutes. No reward is offered, for they are gone forever.

HORACE MANN

Leave the dead moments to bury the dead.

E. R. BULWER-LYTTON

The present will not long endure.

PINDAR

Know we how many tomorrows the gods intend for our todays?

EURIPIDES

[*See also* Life, Yesterday]

TIMING:

Some men have been worthy of a better century.

BALTASAR GRACIÁN

My time has not yet come either; some are born posthumously.

FRIEDRICH NIETZSCHE

[*See also* Fate]

TITLE:

Little men are fond of long titles.

GERMAN PROVERB

The Ancient Mariner would not have taken so well if it had been called *The Old Sailor*.

SAMUEL BUTLER

I have henceforth the privilege of adding to my name the honorable title of A double S.

GEORGE COLMAN

[*See also* Name]

TOAST:

When you constantly drink to other people's health you invariably ruin your own.

DAVE ALLEN

There is an old-time toast which is golden for its beauty. "When you ascend the hill of prosperity may you not meet a friend."

MARK TWAIN

TOGETHERNESS:

Birds of a feather will gather together.

ROBERT BURTON

We must all hang together or we will hang separately.

BENJAMIN FRANKLIN

[*See also* Friendship]

TOMORROW:

Never put off till tomorrow what you can do today.

LORD CHESTERFIELD

Do it tomorrow. You've made enough mistakes for one day.

BUMPER STICKER

All the flowers of all the tomorrows are in the seeds of today and
yesterday.

CHINESE PROVERB

Tomorrow is nothing, today is too
late; the good lived yesterday.

MARTIAL

Today's achievement is only tomorrow's confusion.

WILLIAM DEAN HOWELLS

Tomorrow, and tomorrow, and
tomorrow,
Creeps in this petty pace from day
to day
To the last syllable of recorded
time,
And all our yesterdays have
lighted fools
The way to dusty death.

WILLIAM SHAKESPEARE

Tomorrow do thy worst, I have
lived today.

JOHN DRYDEN

Never put off till tomorrow what
you can do next week.

[See also Future, Time]

TONGUE:

Many have fallen by the edge of
the sword, but more have fallen by
the tongue.

THE BIBLE

[See also Gossip, Speech]

TOWN:

A hick town is one where there is
no place to go where you shouldn't.

GEORGE D. PRENTICE

A village is a hive of glass,
Where nothing unobserved can
pass.

CHARLES H. SPURGEON

TOY:

Woman, the most dangerous of
playthings.

FRIEDRICH NIETZSCHE

A new toy is something a child
uses to break his old toys.

TRADE:

Commerce: A kind of transaction
in which A plunders from B the
goods of C, and for compensation B
picks the pocket of D of money
belonging to E.

AMBROSE BIERCE

Free trade is not a principle; it is
an expedient.

BENJAMIN DISRAELI

My trade and my art is living.

MICHEL DE MONTAIGNE

In every age and clime we see
Two of a trade can never agree.

JOHN GAY

[*See also* Business, Occupation]

TRADITION:

The less there is to justify a traditional custom, the harder it is to get rid of it.

MARK TWAIN

The tradition of preserving traditions became a tradition.

GATHORNE CRANBROOK

Tradition: A clock which tells what time it was.

ELBERT HUBBARD

Out of every hundred new ideas ninety-nine or more will probably be inferior to the traditional responses which they propose to replace.

WILL AND ARIEL DURANT

Stupidity is also a tradition.

FRANK DANE

[*See also* Change]

TRAGEDY:

In the theater there is comedy and tragedy. If the house is packed it's a comedy, otherwise it's a tragedy.

SOL HUROK

In this world there are only two tragedies. One is not getting what one wants, and the other is getting it. . . . The last is a real tragedy!

OSCAR WILDE

[*See also* Life, Theater]

TRANSPORTATION:

Methods of locomotion have improved greatly in recent years, but places to go remain the same.

DON HEROLD

The only way of catching a train I ever discovered is to miss the train before.

G. K. CHESTERTON

Of course we cannot be expected to do as much for the travelling public as the railway companies. They at times put their passengers to death; we only put them to sleep.

HORACE PORTER, speaking for the Pullman Company

[*See also* Railroad, Travel]

TRAVEL:

See one promontory, see them all.

SOCRATES

I never travel without my diary. One should always have something sensational to read in the train.

OSCAR WILDE

Whoe'er has travelled life's dull round,
Where'er his stages may have been,
May sigh to think he still has found
The warmest welcome at an inn.

WILLIAM SHENSTONE

Air travel will be much safer when they eliminate the automobile ride between the city and the airport.

If a man has anything in him travel will bring it out, especially ocean travel.

The well travelled may lie with impunity.

FRENCH PROVERB

A man travels the world over in search of what he needs and returns home to find it.

GEORGE MOORE

In all my travels the thing that has impressed me the most is the universal brotherhood of man—what there is of it.

MARK TWAIN

How much a dunce that has been sent to roam
Excels a dunce that has been kept at home.

WILLIAM COWPER

[See also Hotel, Vacation]

TREASON:

Treason doth never prosper: what's the reason?
Why, if it prosper, none dare call it treason.

SIR JOHN HARRINGTON

Caesar had his Brutus, Charles the First his Cromwell, and George the Third ["Treason!" cried the Speaker]—may profit by their example. If this be treason, make the most of it.

PATRICK HENRY

Marriage is the treasonous betrayal of love.

THE TROUBADOURS

TRIAL:

When you have no basis for an argument, abuse the plaintiff.

CICERO

A fox should not be of the jury at a goose's trial.

THOMAS FULLER

Trial: A formal inquiry designed to prove and put upon record the blameless characters of judges, advocates and jurors.

AMBROSE BIERCE

[See also Justice, Law, Lawyer]

TRIUMPH:

If a husband talks in his sleep and gives no secrets away, it's a triumph of mind over mutter.

Second marriage: The triumph of hope over experience.
                                    SAMUEL JOHNSON

[*See also* Victory]

TROUBLE:

Man that is born of woman is of few days, and full of trouble.
                                    THE BIBLE

All the trouble in the world is due to the fact that man cannot sit still in a room.
                                    BLAISE PASCAL

There is nothing so consoling as to find one's neighbor's troubles are at least as great as one's own.
                                    GEORGE MOORE

I am an old man and have known a great many troubles, but most of them never happened.
                                    MARK TWAIN

I believe in getting into hot water; it keeps you clean.
                                    G. K. CHESTERTON

Double, double toil and trouble; Fire burn, and cauldron bubble.
                                    WILLIAM SHAKESPEARE

[*See also* Misfortune, Worry]

TRUST:

Trust everybody, but cut the cards.
                                    FINLEY PETER DUNNE

One should never trust a woman who tells her real age. If she tells that, she'll tell anything.
                                    OSCAR WILDE

Grant I may never prove so fond, To trust man on his oath or bond.
                                    WILLIAM SHAKESPEARE

I would rather trust my money to a man who has no hands, and so a physical impossibility to steal, than to a man of the most honest principles.
                                    SAMUEL JOHNSON

Put your trust in God; but be sure to keep your powder dry.
                                    OLIVER CROMWELL

Trust: In American politics, a large corporation composed in greater part of thrifty working men, widows of small means, orphans in the care of guardians and the courts, with many similar malefactors and public enemies.
                                    AMBROSE BIERCE

When I consider life, 'tis all a cheat;

Yet, fooled with hope, men favor
the deceit;
Trust on, and think tomorrow will
repay.
Tomorrow's falser than the former day.

JOHN DRYDEN

[See also Honor, Oath]

TRUTH:

The truth, but not the whole
truth.

BALTASAR GRACIÁN

Truth is stranger than fiction.

INTERNATIONAL PROVERB

Truth is said to be stranger than
fiction. It is to most folks.

JOSH BILLINGS

It is easy to tell the truth, but O
the consequences.

ADAM WHEELER

Often the surest way to convey
misinformation is to tell the strict
truth.

MARK TWAIN

Ever speak the truth; for, if you
will do so, you shall never be
believed and 'twill put your adver-
saries to a loss in all their disposi-
tions and undertakings.
SIR HENRY WOTTON, advice to a
diplomat

For things said false and never
meant,
Do oft prove true by accident.

SAMUEL BUTLER

Truth is its own reward.

PLATO

Never tell the truth to a pimp, a
whore, or a corporate vice-president.

FRANK DANE

As scarce as truth is, the supply
has always been in excess of the demand.

JOSH BILLINGS

A truth spoken before its time is
dangerous.

GREEK PROVERB

There is no such thing as a harmless truth.

GREGORY NUNN

Most of the change we think we
see in life is due to truths being in
and out of favor.

ROBERT FROST

Am I therefore become your
enemy because I tell you the truth?

THE BIBLE

Men occasionally stumble over
the truth, but most of them pick
themselves up and hurry off as if
nothing had happened.

WINSTON CHURCHILL

A man should be careful never to tell tales of himself to his own disadvantage.

SAMUEL JOHNSON

I want everyone to tell me the truth, even if it costs him his job.

SAM GOLDWYN

Discovery of truth is the sole purpose of philosophy . . . and has a fair prospect of existing to the end of time.

AMBROSE BIERCE

Truth is always strange.

LORD BYRON

There is nothing so powerful as truth—and often nothing so strange.

DANIEL WEBSTER

Believe everything you hear about the world, nothing is too impossibly bad.

HONORÉ DE BALZAC

A thing is not necessarily true because a man dies for it.

OSCAR WILDE

Every man has a right to utter what he thinks truth, and every other man has a right to knock him down for it.

SAMUEL JOHNSON

I never could tell a lie that anybody would doubt, nor a truth that anybody would believe.

MARK TWAIN

I have known a vast quantity of nonsense talked about bad men not looking you in the face. Don't trust that conventional idea. Dishonesty will stare honesty out of countenance, any day in the week, if there is anything to be got by it.

CHARLES DICKENS

Truth: That which is negated by the small print.

GERALD BARZAN

[See also Doubt, Honesty, Honor, Lie, Lying, Politician, Politics]

TYRANNY:

Dictatorship naturally arises out of democracy, and the most aggravated form of tyranny and slavery out of the most extreme form of liberty.

PLATO

Smart tyrants retire rich.

VOLTAIRE

Slaves would be tyrants were the chance theirs.

VICTOR HUGO

Resistance to tyrants is obedience to God.

THOMAS JEFFERSON

It is excellent to have a giant's strength;
But it is tyrannous to use it as a giant.

WILLIAM SHAKESPEARE

[*See also* Humanity, Mob, People, Race]

UGLINESS:

God's gift to virtue.

AMBROSE BIERCE

There are no ugly women; there are only women who do not know how to look pretty.

JEAN DE LA BRUYÈRE

No object is so beautiful that, under certain conditions, it will not look ugly.

OSCAR WILDE

Her face was her chaperone.

RUPERT HUGHES

[*See also* Beauty, Cosmetics]

UNDERSTANDING:

It is not necessary to understand things in order to argue about them.

PIERRE DE BEAUMARCHAIS

I have suffered from being misunderstood, but I would have suffered a hell of a lot more if I had been understood.

CLARENCE DARROW

It is difficult to get a man to understand something when his salary depends upon his not understanding it.

UPTON SINCLAIR

Some people will never learn anything, for this reason, because they understand everything too soon.

ALEXANDER POPE

Poverty is an anomaly to rich people: It is very difficult to make out why people who want dinner do not ring the bell.

WALTER BAGEHOT

One way of getting an idea of our fellow countrymen's miseries is to go and look at their pleasures.

GEORGE ELIOT

There are those who understand everything till one puts it into words.

FRANCIS BRADLEY

Understanding: A cerebral secretion that enables one having it to know a house from a horse by the roof on the house. Its nature and laws have been exhaustively expounded by Locke, who rode a house, and Kant, who lived in a horse.

AMBROSE BIERCE

UNDERTAKER:

Doctors and undertakers
Fear epidemics of good health.

GERALD BARZAN

Honor the undertaker. He always carries out what he undertakes.

Some time ago a convention of morticians discussed the danger threatening their industry from the increasing tardiness of men in keeping their rendezvous with death.

WILL AND ARIEL DURANT

Diaulus, lately a doctor, is now an undertaker; what he does as an undertaker he used also to do as a doctor.

MARTIAL

The houses that he makes last till doomsday.

WILLIAM SHAKESPEARE

[See also Doctor, Funeral, Medicine]

UNEMPLOYMENT:

When more and more people are thrown out of work, unemployment results.

CALVIN COOLIDGE

To toil for a hard master is bitter, but to have no master to toil for is more bitter still.

OSCAR WILDE

[See also Union, Work]

UNHAPPINESS:

He's simply got the instinct for being unhappy highly developed.

H. H. MUNRO

Never speak of any time of youth as being unhappy. Stupid perhaps, but not unhappy.

ADAM WHEELER

[See also Happiness]

UNION (LABOR):

A system devised to protect the inept from the unconscionable.

FRANK DANE

Union gives firmness and solidity to the humblest men.

LABERIUS

The corporation has come to stay, just as the trade union has come to stay. Each can do and has done great good. Each should be favored as long as it does good, but each should be sharply checked where it acts against law and justice.

THEODORE ROOSEVELT

Capital organizes and therefore labor must organize.

THEODORE ROOSEVELT

In union there is strength.

LABERIUS

In unions there are strikes.

If capital an' labor ever do get together it's good night fer the rest of us.

KIN HUBBARD

If the workingman gets his hours reduced much more he will be in danger of meeting himself coming home every time he goes to work.

ROBERT FROST

Organized labor still has privileges and legal immunities that even kings and governments lost years ago.

ROSCOE POUND

My uncle is in trouble with his union. They caught him working on the job.

JOEY ADAMS

Trade Unions: A system whereby bad workmen receive the same wages as good workmen.

How could God create the world in only six days? No unions.

Militant tactics have no place in the function of any organization of government employees. A strike of public employees manifests nothing less than an intent on their part to prevent or obstruct the operation of government until their demands are satisfied. Such action, looking toward the paralysis of government by those sworn to support it, is unthinkable and intolerable.

FRANKLIN D. ROOSEVELT

[See also Inflation, Wages, Work]

UNITED NATIONS:

Nobody, not even the most rabid of democrats, can imagine without actual knowledge all the emptiness and quackery that passes for diplomacy.

OTTO VON BISMARCK

When small men begin to cast big shadows, it means that the sun is about to set.

LIN YUTANG

The United Nations is an uplifting experiment, dedicated to raising the standards of living in Africa, the consciences of democracies, and the price of prostitutes in New York.

FRANK DANE

There is nothing more horrifying than stupidity in action.

ADLAI E. STEVENSON

United Nations: Where America feeds the hands that bite it.

GREGORY NUNN

Let us do nothing, AT ONCE!
MATTHEW GORDON, chief press officer for the United Nations, translating a representative's speech for the English-speaking press corps

United Nations: Too many foreign countries living beyond our means.

[In the beginning] fifty-one nations rushed to embrace the United

Nations, and, if the UN fails it will be because all had one thing in common: the foregone conclusion that fifty of the member nations were not to be trusted.

GERALD F. LIEBERMAN

The smartest people at the United Nations are the interpreters. At least we think they are. But who can tell?

[*See also* Diplomacy]

UNIVERSE:

The solar system has no anxiety about its reputation.

RALPH WALDO EMERSON

Man . . . the glory and shame of the universe.

BLAISE PASCAL

UNRELIABLE:

You can't depend on anyone to be wrong all the time.

AMERICAN PROVERB

UTILITIES:

Honor the light brigade, oh what a charge they made.

EDITORIAL ON ELECTRICAL UTILITY COMPANY'S RATE INCREASE

VACATION:

A day away from some people is like a month in the country.

HOWARD DIETZ

No one needs a vacation so much as the person who has just had one.

ELBERT HUBBARD

With me a change of trouble is as good as a vacation.

DAVID LLOYD GEORGE

The time to enjoy a European trip is about three weeks after unpacking.

GEORGE ADE

Never take vacations
To visit relations.

GERALD BARZAN

[*See also* Travel]

VALOR:

The better part of valor is discretion.

WILLIAM SHAKESPEARE

Be valiant, but not too venturous.

JOHN LYLY

If men were just there would be no need of valor.

AGESILAUS

Brave deeds are wasted when hidden.

BLAISE PASCAL

Said the commander of the delinquent brigade, "I am persuaded that any further display of valor by my troops will bring them into collision with the enemy."

HORACE PORTER

That's a valiant flea that dare eat his breakfast on the lip of a lion.

WILLIAM SHAKESPEARE

[See also Courage]

VALUE:

Nowadays we know the price of everything and the value of nothing.

OSCAR WILDE

People exaggerate the value of things they haven't got. Everybody worships truth and unselfishness because they have no experience with them.

GEORGE BERNARD SHAW

Never underestimate the value of cold cash.

GREGORY NUNN

[See also Money]

VANITY:

The tribute of the fool to the worth of the nearest ass.

AMBROSE BIERCE

They say that hens do cackle loudest when there's nothing vital in the eggs they've laid.

AMBROSE BIERCE

Lo! the drum-major in his coat of gold,
His blazing breeches and high-towering cap—
Imperiously pompous, grandly bold,
Grim, resolute, an awe-inspiring chap!
Who'd think this gorgeous creature's only virtue
Is that in battle he will never hurt you?

AMBROSE BIERCE

In outward show so splendid and vain;
'Tis but a gilded block without a brain.

PHAEDRUS

George Moore unexpectedly pinched my behind. I felt rather honored that my behind should draw the attention of the great master of English prose.

ILKA CHASE

Wherever I sit is the head of the table.

H. L. MENCKEN

Man that is of woman born is apt to be as vain as his mother.

ROBERT FROST

All is vanity.

THE BIBLE

Vanity plays lurid tricks with our memory.

JOHN CONRAD

Nothing makes one so vain as being told that one is a sinner.

OSCAR WILDE

All our geese are swans.

ROBERT BURTON

[*See also* Ego]

VARIETY:

Oh, how various is the scene
Allowed to man for his demesne.

SAMUEL HOFFENSTEIN

Variety's the very spice of life.

WILLIAM COWPER

Spice can be found in a variety of wives.

FRANK DANE

"The time has come," the Walrus said,
    "To talk of many things:
Of shoes—and ships—and sealing-
    wax—
Of cabbages—and kings—
And why the sea is boiling hot—
And whether pigs have wings."

LEWIS CARROLL

VEGETARIAN:

Vegetarian: A person who only eats side dishes.

Equal Rights for Vegetarians.

GRAFFITO ON A CHICAGO SLAUGH-
TERHOUSE

[*See also* Cannibal]

VENEREAL DISEASE:

He who sets one foot in a bawdy-
house claps t'other in an hospital.

THOMAS FULLER

VICE:

There is no vice so simple but assumes
Some mark of virtue on his outward parts.

WILLIAM SHAKESPEARE

Welcome vice, if it comest alone.

SPANISH PROVERB

Vice is a creature of such hideous mien that the more you see it the better you like it.

FINLEY PETER DUNNE

The vices of some men are magnificent.

CHARLES LAMB

I haven't a particle of confidence in a man who has no redeeming vices.

MARK TWAIN

It is good to be without vice, but it is not good to be without temptations.

WALTER BAGEHOT

It has been my experience that folks who have no vices have very few virtues.

ABRAHAM LINCOLN

Be good and you will be lonely.

MARK TWAIN

[See also Sin, Virtue]

VICE-PRESIDENT (CORPORATE):

A vice-president is a person who finds a molehill on his desk in the morning and must make a mountain out of it by five P.M.

FRED ALLEN

A vice-president is a man who takes the simple and makes it difficult; then he takes the difficult and makes it impossible; then he compliments himself for getting something done.

GERALD BARZAN

It's not whether you win or lose but how you place the blame.

You are not supposed to initial documents before I see them. Kindly erase your initials and initial the erasure.

MEMO FROM A VICE-PRESIDENT

On ships they are called barnacles; in radio they attach themselves to desks and are called vice-presidents.

FRED ALLEN

Against stupidity and vice-presidents the gods contend in vain.

GREGORY NUNN

VICE-PRESIDENT (POLITICAL):

A cow's fifth teat.

HARRY S. TRUMAN

The man with the best job in the country is the Vice-President. All he has to do is get up every morning and say, "How's the President?"

WILL ROGERS

Once there were two brothers. One ran away to sea, the other was elected Vice-President, and nothing has been heard of either of them again.

THOMAS R. MARSHALL

[See also Politician, Politics]

VICTORY:

There is no glory in outstripping jackasses.

MARTIAL

Another such victory and we are utterly undone.

PYRRHUS

Right and victory do not always concur.

JOHN SELDEN

To elude by flight is a glorious victory.

HORACE

The only victory over love is flight.

NAPOLEON

'Tis some poor fellow's skull, who fell in victory.

ROBERT SOUTHEY

[See also Peace, War]

VILLAIN:

The most natural man in a play is the villain.

ED HOWE

And thus I clothe my naked villainy
With odd old ends stol'n forth of
   holy writ,
And seem a saint when most I
   play the devil.

WILLIAM SHAKESPEARE

VINDICATION:

The vindication of the obvious is sometimes more important than the elucidation of the obscure.

OLIVER WENDELL HOLMES

VIOLENCE:

These violent delights have violent ends.

WILLIAM SHAKESPEARE

There is always something peculiarly impotent about the violence of
a literary man.

OSCAR WILDE

[See also Justice]

VIRGIN:

The modest fan was lifted up no
   more,
And virgins smiled at what they
   blushed before.

ALEXANDER POPE

For me it will be enough that a
marble stone should declare that a
queen, having reigned such a time,
lived and died a virgin.

QUEEN ELIZABETH I

I knew her before she was a
virgin.

OSCAR LEVANT, of DORIS DAY

[Virginity is] that unwholesome
and unnatural monstrosity so con-
trary to nature and so repugnant to
true sentiment, which is love.

PAUL GAUGUIN

Virginity, for some women, is the
only virtue.

FRENCH PROVERB

'Tis chastity, my brother, chastity:
She, that has that, is clad in com-
plete steel.

JOHN MILTON

Virginity can be cured!

BUMPER STICKER

[*See also* Celibacy, Chastity, Virtue]

VIRTUE:

I prefer an interesting vice to a
virtue that bores.

MOLIÈRE

A crime preserved in a thousand
centuries ceases to be a crime and
becomes a virtue.

MARK TWAIN

It is not a fashion for the maids in
France to kiss before they are
married.

WILLIAM SHAKESPEARE

It is not only for virtue's sake that
women are virtuous.

FRANÇOIS DE LA ROCHEFOUCAULD

Virtue has never been as respectable as money.

MARK TWAIN

I am as pure as the driven slush.

TALLULAH BANKHEAD

Woman's virtue is man's greatest
invention.

CORNELIA OTIS SKINNER

She is chaste who was never
asked.

WILLIAM CONGREVE

Men lose more conquests by their
own clumsiness than by any virtue in
the woman.

NINON DE LENCLOS

I do not know if she was virtuous,
but she was ugly, and with a woman
that is half the battle.

HEINRICH HEINE

No people ever yet benefited by
riches if their prosperity corrupted
their virtue.

THEODORE ROOSEVELT

If there were more like her, the
stock of halos would give out.

ARTHUR WING PINERO

As for the virtuous poor, one can
pity them, of course, but one cannot
admire them.

OSCAR WILDE

There are nine hundred and
ninety-nine patrons of virtue to one
virtuous man.

HENRY DAVID THOREAU

Most men admire
Virtue, who follow not her love.

JOHN MILTON

I always admired virtue—but I
could never imitate it.

CHARLES II

Be virtuous and you will be eccentric.

MARK TWAIN

[See also Hypocrisy, Vice, Virgin]

VOTE:

The instrument and symbol of a freeman's power to make a fool of himself and a wreck of his country.

AMBROSE BIERCE

The oppressed are allowed once every few years to decide which particular representatives of the oppressing class are to represent and repress them.

KARL MARX

A straw vote only shows which way the hot air is blowing.

O. HENRY

Whenever a fellow tells me he's bipartisan I know he's going to vote against me.

HARRY S. TRUMAN

I have learned to hold popular opinion of no value.

ALEXANDER HAMILTON

The ballot box is the surest arbiter of disputes among freemen.

JAMES BUCHANAN

The ballot box is the surest arbiter of disputes among free men; but a machine gun is quicker.

BILLY BOY FRANKLIN

The ballot is stronger than the bullet.

ABRAHAM LINCOLN

We'd all like t' vote for th' best man, but he's never a candidate.

KIN HUBBARD

[See also Democracy, Election, Politician, Politics]

WAGES:

The wages of sin is death; but the gift of God is eternal life.

THE BIBLE

The wages of sin are high—but you get your money's worth.

FRANK DANE

Fear no more the heat o' the sun,
Nor the furious winter's rages;
Thou thy worldly task hast done,
Home art gone, and ta'en thy wages.
Golden lads and girls all must,
As chimney-sweepers, come to dust.

WILLIAM SHAKESPEARE

A fair day's wages for a fair day's work.

THOMAS CARLYLE

If you do your fair day's work, you are certain to get your fair day's wage—in praise or pudding, whichever happens to suit your taste.

ALEXANDER SMITH

Remember when $25,000 was a success? Now it's a garbage collector.

FRANK DANE

[See also Inflation, Salary, Union]

WAR:

I believe in the Providence of the most men, the largest purse, and the longest cannon.

ABRAHAM LINCOLN

World War II was over. Another in the series of wars to end wars— but not the series clincher.

GERALD F. LIEBERMAN

Man must be trained for war, and woman for the relaxation of the warriors; all else is folly.

FRIEDRICH NIETZSCHE

Soldiers win battles and generals get the medals.

NAPOLEON

He belonged to that great army known as invincible in peace, invisible in war.

WILLIAM TECUMSEH SHERMAN

Love is like war. Easy to begin but very hard to stop.

H. L. MENCKEN

God is always on the side of the strongest battalion.

VOLTAIRE

To build up cities an age is needed, but an hour destroys them.

SENECA

Grass never grows where my horse has trod.

ATTILA THE HUN

War is only a cowardly escape from the problems of peace.

THOMAS MANN

As long as there are sovereign nations possessing great power, war is inevitable.

ALBERT EINSTEIN

I joined the army, and succeeded in killing about as many of the enemy as they of me.

BILL ARP

War is neither to be timidly shunned nor unjustly provoked.

PLINY

We have heard of men celebrating their country's battles who, in war, were celebrated for keeping out of them.

GEORGE D. PRENTICE

What millions died—that Caesar might be great!

THOMAS CAMPBELL

Famine, Pestilence, Destruction, Death; those Four Horsemen of the Apocalypse. What they do not accomplish, war itself does. It is God's answer to the population explosion.

YIRME VERBENIKOV

In the last 3,421 years of recorded history only 268 have seen no war.

WILL AND ARIEL DURANT

[See also Conscription, Military, Peace, Victory]

WASHINGTON, D.C.:

Washington is no place for a good actor. The competition from bad actors is too great.

FRED ALLEN

Where the criminals cover their crimes by making them legal.

FRANK DANE

Washington is like a lovely woman: nice to look at but only God knows what she has on her mind.

Congress doesn't need a gun to rob the people. They have the voice vote.

GREGORY NUNN

[See also Lie, Lying, Politician, Politics]

WATER:

Wha'? The stuff ye give 'orses?

COCKNEY DEFINITION OF WATER

When I was two years of age she asked me not to drink, and then I made a resolution of total absti-
nence. That I have adhered to it and enjoyed the beneficent effect of it through all time, I owe to my grandmother. I have never drunk a drop from that day to this of any kind of water.

MARK TWAIN

Water, water, everywhere,
And all the boards did shrink;
Water, water, everywhere,
Nor any drop to drink.

SAMUEL TAYLOR COLERIDGE

And this was all the Harvest that I reaped—
"I came like Water, and like Wind I go."

OMAR KHAYYÁM

But if it comes to slaughter
You will do your work on water,
An' you'll lick the bloomin' boots
of 'im that's got it.

RUDYARD KIPLING

Water is the only drink for a wise man.

HENRY DAVID THOREAU

[See also Abstinence, Drink]

WEAKNESS:

Never show your wounded finger.

BALTASAR GRACIÁN

There is a physical weakness which stems from mental ability, and a mental weakness which comes from physical ability.

JOSEPH JOUBERT

Credulity is the man's weakness, but the child's strength.

CHARLES LAMB

Throughout all past time, there has been a ceaseless devouring of the weak by the strong.

HERBERT SPENCER

He knows not how to wink at human frailty,
Or pardon weakness that he never felt.

JOSEPH ADDISON

WEALTH:

What a lot of things there are a man can do without.

SOCRATES

Although they possess enough, and more than enough, still they yearn for more.

OVID

Get place and wealth, if possible, with grace;
If not, by any means get wealth and place.

ALEXANDER POPE

Why are men like weasels? A weasel hoards and knows not for what purpose. So it is with men.

THE TALMUD

If a man owns land, the land owns him.

RALPH WALDO EMERSON

Corroding care, and thirst for more
Attends the still increasing store.

HORACE

He that's rich is wise.

DANIEL DEFOE

He does not own money whose money owns him.

ST. CYPRIAN

Wealth maketh many friends.

THE BIBLE

Well washed and combed domestic pets grow dull; they miss the stimulus of fleas.

SIR FRANCIS GALTON

A penny is a lot of money—if you haven't got a penny.

YIDDISH PROVERB

After a rich man gets rich, his next ambition is to get richer.

AMERICAN PROVERB

The best thing a man can do for his culture when he is rich is to endeavor to carry out those schemes which he entertained when he was poor.

HENRY DAVID THOREAU

Mere wealth can't bring us happiness;

Mere wealth can't make us glad;
But we'll always take a chance, I
guess,
At being rich, and sad.

Wealth after all is a relative thing
since he that has little and wants less
is richer than he that has much and
wants more.

C. C. COLTON

Increased means and increased
leisure are the two civilizers of men.

BENJAMIN DISRAELI

Few rich men own their property.
The property owns them.

ROBERT GREEN INGERSOLL

WEAPONS:

Among other evils which being
unarmed brings you, it causes you to
be despised.

NICOLÒ MACHIAVELLI

Never argue with a woman, a
winner, or a weapon.

FRANK DANE

WEATHER:

'Tis very warm weather when
one's in bed.

JONATHAN SWIFT

Don't knock the weather; nine
tenths of the people couldn't start a
conversation if it didn't change once
in a while.

KIN HUBBARD

Everybody talks about the
weather but nobody does anything
about it.

MARK TWAIN

Its warmth was not heat, and its
cool was not cold.

FIRDUSI OF PERSIA

Heat, ma'am! . . . it was so
dreadful here that I found there was
nothing left for it but to take off my
flesh and sit in my bones.

SYDNEY SMITH

For 'tis always fair weather
When good fellows get together
With a stein on the table and a
good song ringing clear.

RICHARD HOVEY

It was so cold the other day, I almost got married.

SHELLEY WINTERS

Perhaps from the 15th to the 23rd
of January it will be very cold
weather if it frese by the fire-side or
on the sunny side of a fense at noon.
—For April perhaps wet weather, if
it Rains; now fair weather if the sun-
shines; and windy or calm. If now
the weather do prove fair, People to
Cambridge do repair.

CLOUGH'S *Almanack,* 1702

WEDDING:

In olden times sacrifices were made at the altar—a custom which is still continued.

HELEN ROWLAND

The time approached; to church the parties went,
At once with carnal and devout intent.

ALEXANDER POPE

It is a woman's business to get married as soon as possible, and a man's to keep unmarried as long as he can.

GEORGE BERNARD SHAW

It is not bad luck to postpone a wedding—if you keep postponing it.

[See also Marriage]

WELFARE:

To receive a benefit is to sell your liberty.

LABERIUS

A government that robs Peter to pay Paul can always depend upon the support of Paul.

GEORGE BERNARD SHAW

[See also Charity, Government]

WEST:

Go West, young man, and grow up with the country.

HORACE GREELEY

The farther west he went the more he was convinced that the wise men came from the east.

HORACE RUSSELL

Out where the handclasp's a little stronger,
Out where the smile dwells a little longer,
That's where the West begins.

ARTHUR CHAPMAN

WHISKEY:

What whiskey will not cure, there is no cure for.

IRISH PROVERB

Women will be as pleasing to men as whiskey when they learn to improve as much with age.

[See also Drink, Scotch, Water]

WHISPER:

Some people will believe anything, if you whisper it.

Foul whisperings are abroad.

WILLIAM SHAKESPEARE

[See also Gossip]

WHY:

Every why hath a wherefore.
WILLIAM SHAKESPEARE

I keep six honest serving-men
(They taught me all I knew);
Their names are What and Why
and When
And How and Where and Who.
RUDYARD KIPLING

WICKED:

Give me the wicked over the
foolish. The wicked occasionally are
not wicked.
ALEXANDER DUMAS

All wickedness is but little to the
wickedness of a woman.
THE BIBLE

[*See also* Evil, Sin]

WIDOW:

The tragedy of Mormonism is, a
single death makes a dozen widows.
AMERICAN SAYING

Rich widows are the only secondhand goods that sell at first-class
prices.
BENJAMIN FRANKLIN

The rich widow cries with one eye
and laughs with the other.
MIGUEL DE CERVANTES

Who marries a widow and two
daughters marries three thieves.
GEORGE HERBERT

[*See also* Thrift]

WIDOWER:

Some widowers are bereaved;
others, relieved.
HELEN ROWLAND

Oh, 'tis a precious thing, when
wives are dead,
To find such numbers who will
serve instead. . . .
GEORGE CRABBE

WIFE:

When she had passed, it seemed
like the ceasing of exquisite music.
HENRY WADSWORTH LONGFELLOW

Wife: A former sweetheart.
H. L. MENCKEN

Here lies my wife; here let her lie!
Now she's at rest, and so am I.
JOHN DRYDEN

Helpmate: The wife, or bitter
half.
AMBROSE BIERCE

Whoso findeth a wife findeth a
good thing.
THE BIBLE

Wives may be merry and yet honest too.

WILLIAM SHAKESPEARE

. . . she's best married that dies married young.

WILLIAM SHAKESPEARE

It is slavery and a disgrace if a wife support her husband.

THE BIBLE

Who follows his wife in everything is an ignoramus.

THE TALMUD

All men are now henpecked.

THE TALMUD

Whether you wind up with a nest egg or a goose egg depends on the kind of chick you married.

WALL STREET JOURNAL

She is my goods, my chattels; she
  is my house,
My household stuff, my field, my
  barn,
My horse, my ox, my ass, my
  anything.

WILLIAM SHAKESPEARE

All wives are unjustly slighted for the faults of a few.

TERENCE

Seek a wife in your own sphere.

LATIN PROVERB

I am thinking of taking a fifth wife. Why not? Solomon had a thousand wives and he is a synonym for wisdom.

JOHN BARRYMORE

Everyone knows that the real business of a ball is either to look out for a wife, to look after a wife, or to look after somebody else's wife.

ROBERT SMITH SURTEES

If you think you have trouble supporting a wife, try not supporting her.

The man who says his wife can't take a joke forgets that she took him.

[See also Adultery, Husband, Man, Marriage, Sex, Woman, Women's Lib]

WILL:

Where there's a will there's a lawsuit.

ADDISON MIZNER

A man left the bulk of his fortune to his lawyers. If everybody did this a lot of time would be saved.

LONDON OPINION

The will of the dead actor requested that his body be cremated and ten per cent of his ashes thrown in his agent's face.

I owe much. I have nothing. The rest I leave to the poor.

FRANÇOIS RABELAIS, his last will

[See also Heir, Inheritance]

WIND:

For they have sown the wind, and they shall reap the whirlwind.

THE BIBLE

Blow, blow, thou Winter wind,
Thou art not so unkind
As man's ingratitude.

WILLIAM SHAKESPEARE

[See also Weather]

WINE:

Let schoolmasters puzzle their brain,
With grammar, and nonsense, and learning;
Good liquor, I stoutly maintain,
Gives genius a better discerning.

OLIVER GOLDSMITH

I often wonder what the Vintners buy
One half so precious as the stuff they sell.

OMAR KHAYYÁM

And if the Wine you drink, the Lip you press,
End in what All begins and ends in—Yes.

OMAR KHAYYÁM

These traitorous thieves, accursèd and unfair,
The vintners that put water in our wine.

FRANÇOIS VILLON

So heed me, fellow peasants,
For that is what we are,
It's best to die the winer's death
Than fiddle for the Czar.

TRADITIONAL RUSSIAN DRINKING SONG

[See also Drink, Water, Whiskey]

WINNING:

Life is strange. Every so often a good man wins.

FRANK DANE

Nothing can seem foul to those that win.

WILLIAM SHAKESPEARE

I hate a sore winner.

OSCAR LEVANT

If you want a track team to win the high jump you find one person who can jump seven feet, not seven people who can jump one foot.

[See also Loser, Victory]

WINTER:

If Winter comes, can Spring be far behind?

PERCY BYSSHE SHELLEY

A sad tale's best for winter. I have
one
Of sprites and goblins.

WILLIAM SHAKESPEARE

[See also Wind]

WISDOM:

The older I grow the more I distrust the familiar doctrine that age brings wisdom.

H. L. MENCKEN

Though Wisdom cannot be gotten for gold, still less can be gotten without it.

SAMUEL BUTLER

Wisdom is not wisdom when it is derived from books alone.

HORACE

In youth and beauty wisdom is rare.

HOMER

Old Marley was as dead as a doornail . . . the wisdom of our ancestors is in the simile.

CHARLES DICKENS

In wisdom is much grief.

THE BIBLE

Wisdom has been extolled from the house-tops but her practical advice seems to have been kept secret.

JOSEPH JACOBS

It [love] is the wisdom of the fool, and the folly of the wise.

SAMUEL JOHNSON

When you have got an elephant by the hind legs and he is trying to run away, it's best to let him run.

ABRAHAM LINCOLN

Everything I know I learned after I was thirty.

GEORGES CLEMENCEAU

Even in wise men there is more folly than wisdom.

SÉBASTIEN CHAMFORT

The first step to wisdom is to avoid the common fallacy which considers everything profound that is obscure.

[See also Age, Knowledge, Wise]

WISE:

Many persons are both wise and handsome—but they would probably be still wiser were they less handsome.

THE TALMUD

The wise people are in New York because the foolish went there first. That's the way wise men make a living.

FINLEY PETER DUNNE

Wise is the young man who is always thinking of taking a wife, but never takes one.

PIETRO ARETINO

The foolish sayings of a rich man pass for wise ones.

SPANISH PROVERB

Wise men learn more from fools than fools from wise men.

CATO

I don't think much of a man who is not wiser today than he was yesterday.

ABRAHAM LINCOLN, when charged with having changed his mind

It's a wise man who lives with money in the bank, it's a fool who dies that way.

FRENCH PROVERB

Anyone who follows a middle course is called a sage.

MAIMONIDES

A wise man sees as much as he ought, not as much as he can.

MICHEL DE MONTAIGNE

The ant is knowing and wise, but he doesn't know enough to take a vacation.

CLARENCE DAY

The wits of the wise the brew may beguile
And make the sage frolic,
And make the sad smile.

HOMER

[See also Wisdom]

WISH:

If man could have half his wishes he would double his troubles.

BENJAMIN FRANKLIN

If mankind had wished for what is right, they might have had it long ago.

WILLIAM HAZLITT

Always leave something to wish for; otherwise you will be miserable from your very happiness.

BALTASAR GRACIÁN

I wish I loved the Human Race;
I wish I loved its silly face;
I wish I liked the way it walks;
I wish I liked the way it talks;
And when I'm introduced to one
I wish I thought, *What Jolly Fun!*

SIR WALTER ALEXANDER RALEIGH

Wishing cannot alter facts—but lying can.

YIRME VERBENIKOV

WIT:

The salt with which the American humorist spoils his intellectual cookery by leaving it out.

AMBROSE BIERCE

All human race would fain be wits,   .

WOMAN

And millions miss for one that hits.

JONATHAN SWIFT

The well of true wit is truth itself.

GEORGE MEREDITH

A witty woman is a treasure; a witty beauty is a power.

GEORGE MEREDITH

Wit sometimes enables us to act rudely with impunity.

FRANÇOISE DE LA ROCHEFOUCAULD

A man likes his wife to be just clever enough to understand his cleverness and just stupid enough to admire it.

ISRAEL ZANGWILL

One of the bad things about our literature is that our scholars have little wit and our men of wit are not scholars.

JOSEPH JOUBERT

Brevity is the soul of wit.

WILLIAM SHAKESPEARE

A man of wit would often be embarrassed without the company of fools.

FRANÇOIS DE LA ROCHEFOUCAULD

[See also Humor, Joke, Politics]

WITNESS:

One witness, one liar; more witnesses, all liars.

GREEK PROVERB

As to the juror or the witness, bribe both.

LATIN PROVERB

[See also Justice]

WOE:

The stone fell on the pitcher; woe to the pitcher. The pitcher fell on the stone; woe to the pitcher.

THE TALMUD

In all the woes that curse our race
There is a lady in the case.

W. S. GILBERT

Woe unto you when all men speak well of you.

THE BIBLE

WOMAN:

Woman is unrestrainable, unguidable, intractable, undrawable, unleadable, harsh, bitter, austere and implacable.

MENANDER

Women have got to make the world safe for men since men have made it so darned unsafe for women.

LADY ASTOR

She who hesitates—is extinct.

GERALD BARZAN

Women are made to be loved, not understood.

OSCAR WILDE

Even if you understood women—you'd never believe it.

FRANK DANE

There are two ways to handle a woman, and nobody knows either of them.

KIN HUBBARD

When a woman is openly bad she is then at her best.

LATIN PROVERB

A woman either loves or hates. There is no intermediate course with her.

PUBLILIUS SYRUS

Age cannot wither her, nor custom stale
Her infinite variety.

WILLIAM SHAKESPEARE

Woman is a calamity, but every house must have its curse.

ARABIAN PROVERB

Woman is like the reed, which bends to every breeze, but breaks not in the tempest.

RICHARD WHATELY

Women have the understanding of the heart, which is better than that of the head.

SAMUEL ROGERS

Anatomy is destiny.

SIGMUND FREUD

A woman is really only a man in petticoats, or, if you like that a man is a woman without petticoats.

GEORGE BERNARD SHAW

Women exist in the main solely for the propagation of the species.

ARTHUR SCHOPENHAUER

Life of woman is like milk, butter and cheese. A girl is like milk, a woman like butter, and an old woman like cheese. All three may be excellent in their kind.

TEUTONIC PROVERB

Asses are made to bear and so are you.

WILLIAM SHAKESPEARE

The great question which I have not yet been able to answer despite my thirty years of research into the feminine soul is: What does a woman want?

SIGMUND FREUD

Most virtuous women are like hid-den treasures, safe only because they are not sought after.

FRANÇOIS DE LA ROCHEFOUCAULD

Here's to woman! Would that we could fall into her arms without falling into her hands.

AMBROSE BIERCE

You are not permitted to kill a woman who has wronged you, but nothing forbids you to reflect that she is growing older every minute. You are avenged 1440 times a day.

AMBROSE BIERCE

The ladies looked one another over with microscopic carelessness.

ARTHUR "BUGS" BAER

Woman is unrivaled as a wet nurse.

MARK TWAIN

When women go wrong, men go right after them.

MAE WEST

A woman will always sacrifice herself if you give her the opportunity. It is her favorite form of self-indulgence.

SOMERSET MAUGHAM

I'm glad I am not a man, for if I were I would be obligated to marry a woman.

MADAME DE STAËL

Woman is always a fickle, unstable thing.

VIRGIL

Of all calamities that befall mortal

man, nothing is worse, or ever will be worse, than woman.

SOPHOCLES

Being a woman is a terribly difficult trade, since it consists principally of dealing with men.

JOSEPH CONRAD

A woman's mind is cleaner than a man's; she changes it more often.

OLIVER HERFORD

I should like to know what is the proper function of women, if it is not to make reasons for husbands to stay at home, and still stronger reasons for bachelors to go out.

GEORGE ELIOT

The woman resembles the Venus de Milo in many ways. Like her, she is extraordinarily old, has no teeth, and has white spots on the yellow surface of her body.

HEINRICH HEINE

Woman has this in common with angels, that suffering beings belong especially to her.

HONORÉ DE BALZAC

Women are never stronger than when they arm themselves with their weaknesses.

MARQUISE DU DEFFAND

She was torn between love and booty.

FAITH BALDWIN

Tongue in the mouth of woman is one of God's less agreeable blunders.

THE TALMUD

A capacity for self-pity is one of the last things that any woman surrenders.

IRVIN S. COBB

The female of the species is more deadly than the male.

RUDYARD KIPLING

Woman . . . one of nature's agreeable blunders.

HANNAH COWLEY

A woman is like a teabag. You don't know her strength until she is in hot water.

NANCY REAGAN

If you don't think women are explosive, drop one.

The women of Greece counted their age from their marriage, not from their birth.

HOMER

I'm not denyin' the women are foolish; God almighty made 'em to match the men.

GEORGE ELIOT

Women deserve to have more than twelve years between the ages of twenty-eight and forty.

JAMES THURBER

Nothing upsets a woman like somebody getting married she didn't even know had a beau.

KIN HUBBARD

There are three kinds of women. Those one cannot live without, those one cannot live with—and those one lives with.

My only books,
Were woman's looks,
    And folly's all they've taught
    me.

THOMAS MOORE

Woman's body is the woman.

AMBROSE BIERCE

[See also Adultery, Age, Beauty, Chastity, Cosmetics, Husband, Jealousy, Love, Man, Marriage, Temptation, Virgin, Virtue, Widow, Wife]

WOMEN'S LIB:

Teach not thy lips such scorn; for they were made
For kissing, lady, not for such contempt.

WILLIAM SHAKESPEARE

Anyone who knows anything of history knows that great social changes are impossible without the feminine upheaval. Social progress can be measured exactly by the social position of the fair sex; the ugly ones included.

KARL MARX

If we have come to think that the nursery and the kitchen are the natural sphere of a woman, we have done exactly as English children come to think that a cage is the natural sphere of a parrot because they have never seen one anywhere else.

GEORGE BERNARD SHAW

Miss: A title with which we brand unmarried women to indicate that they are in the market. Miss, Missis (Mrs.) and Mister (Mr.) are the three most distinctly disagreeable words in the language, in sound and sense. Two are corruptions of Mistress, the other of Master. In the general abolition of social titles in this our country they miraculously escaped to plague us. If we must have them let us be consistent and give one to the unmarried man. I venture to suggest Mush, abbreviated Mh.

AMBROSE BIERCE

What frenzy rules your mind?
To increase the craft of womankind?
Teach them new wiles and arts? You may
As well teach snakes to bite, or wolves to prey.

OVID

Once made equal to man, woman becomes his superior.

SOCRATES

Men are vain; but they won't mind women working so long as they get smaller wages for the same job.

IRVIN S. COBB

I wanted to be the first woman to burn her bra, but it would have taken the fire department four days to put it out.

DOLLY PARTON

I like women's lib. Because of it nobody can ever call me a son-of-a-bitch again. I am now a person-of-a-bitch.

BILLY BOY FRANKLIN

A woman who moralizes is invariably plain.

OSCAR WILDE

My advice to the women's clubs of America is to raise more hell and fewer dahlias.

WILLIAM ALLEN WHITE

Women now insist on having all the prerogatives of the oak and the perquisites of the clinging vine.

IRVIN S. COBB

A woman impudent and mannish grown is not more loathed than an effeminate man in time of action.

WILLIAM SHAKESPEARE

If God wanted us to think with our wombs why did he give us a brain?

CLARE BOOTHE LUCE

Were there not an identity in the substance, men and women might join, but they could never identify.
SAMUEL TAYLOR COLERIDGE

Men now monopolize the upper levels . . . depriving women of their rightful share of opportunities for incompetence.
LAURENCE PETER

Will there be sex after liberation?

Some of us are becoming the men we wanted to marry.
GLORIA STEINEM

The sum of the matter is that unless Woman repudiates her Womanliness, her duty to her husband, to her children, to society, to the law, and to everyone but herself, she cannot emancipate herself.
GEORGE BERNARD SHAW

Now of all the idealist abominations that make society pestiferous I doubt if there be any so mean as that of forcing self-sacrifice on a woman under the pretence that she likes it.
GEORGE BERNARD SHAW

Everything in woman hath a solution—it is called pregnancy.
FRIEDRICH NIETZSCHE

I'm all for ERA. I want to see women equal to men—not so damn superior like they've been.
NIPSEY RUSSELL

Many women do not recognize themselves as discriminated against. No better proof could be found of the totality of their conditioning.
KATE MILLETT

Women do not find it difficult nowadays to behave like men, but they often find it extremely difficult to behave like gentlemen!

An occupation that has no basis in sex-determined gifts can now recruit its ranks from twice as many potential artists.
MARGARET MEAD

Male supremacy has kept woman down. It has not knocked her out.
CLARE BOOTHE LUCE

[See also Woman]

WORD:

The difference between the right word and the almost right word is the difference between lightning and the lightning bug.
MARK TWAIN

I never write *metropolis* for seven cents, because I can get the same price for *city*. I never write *policeman* because I can get the same money for *cop*.
MARK TWAIN

Words are always bolder than deeds.

JOHANN [CHRISTOPH] FRIEDRICH VON SCHILLER

Articulate words are a harsh clamor and dissonance. When man arrives at his highest perfection, he will again be dumb.

NATHANIEL HAWTHORNE

The saddest words that clog my head,
Begin like this: "I should'a said."

GERALD BARZAN

[See also Speech, Writing]

WORK:

Work is the curse of the drinking class.

OSCAR WILDE

There is no more fatal blunderer than he who consumes the greater part of his life getting his living.

HENRY DAVID THOREAU

When you see what some girls marry you realize how they must hate to work for a living.

HELEN ROWLAND

A champion of the workingman has never yet been known to die of overwork.

ROBERT FROST

Let us be grateful to Adam: he cut us out of the blessing of idleness and won for us the curse of labor.

MARK TWAIN

No labor, however humble, is dishonoring.

THE TALMUD

The sharp employ the sharp.

DOUGLAS JERROLD

He worked like hell in the country so he could live in the city, where he worked like hell so he could live in the country.

DON MARQUIS

So much of what we call management consists in making it difficult for people to work.

PETER DRUCKER

I go on working for the same reason that a hen goes on laying eggs.

H. L. MENCKEN

Work expands so as to fill the time available for its completion.

PARKINSON'S LAW

Early to rise and early to bed makes a male healthy and wealthy and dead.

JAMES THURBER

Work: The thing that interferes with golf.

FRANK DANE

The darkest hour in any man's life is when he sits down to plan how to get money without earning it.

HORACE GREELEY

I am a friend of the workingman, and I would rather be his friend, than be one.

CLARENCE DARROW

What's the good of being a genius if you can't use it as an excuse for being unemployed?

GERALD BARZAN

Some do the sowing, others the reaping.

ITALIAN PROVERB

[See also Employment, Occupation, Progress, Salary, Union, Wages]

WORLD:

Give me a lever long enough, and a fulcrum strong enough, and single-handed I can move the world.

ARCHIMEDES

We are told that when Jehovah created the world He saw that it was good: What would He say now?

GEORGE BERNARD SHAW

It would be a swell world if everybody was as pleasant as the fellow who's trying to skin you.

KIN HUBBARD

All the world's a stage, and all the clergymen critics.

GREGORY NUNN

The world is a stage, but the play is badly cast.

OSCAR WILDE

The world is like a big orchestra conducted by God, and everybody plays second fiddle.

YIRME VERBENIKOV

The world's mine oyster,
Which I with sword will open.

WILLIAM SHAKESPEARE

The world is a bowl of cherries, and we are all fruitcake.

FRANK DANE

[See also History, Life, Man]

WORRY:

Worry is interest paid on trouble before it falls due.

WILLIAM RALPH INGE

The reason why worry kills more people than work is that more people worry than work.

ROBERT FROST

[See also Fear]

WORSHIP:

The moral flabbiness born of the exclusive worship of the bitch-goddess *success*. That . . . is our national disease.

WILLIAM JAMES

Wives worship the ground their husbands have coming to them.

MODERN AMERICAN SAYING

[*See also* Money]

WRITER:

The best way to become a successful writer is to read good writing, remember it, and then forget where you remember it from.

GENE FOWLER

In picture-making the writer is the most important clog in the wheel.

SAM GOLDWYN

No man but a blockhead ever wrote except for money.

SAMUEL JOHNSON

A writer is a person who has solutions for which there are no riddles.

GREGORY NUNN

He dresses more entertainingly than he writes.
H. L. MENCKEN, of Richard Harding Davis

You can never correct your work well until you have forgotten it.

VOLTAIRE

Those poets do well who seek a subject for their verse at home.

HORACE

Most writers regard truth as their most valuable possession, and therefore are most economical in its use.

MARK TWAIN

Who'er writ it writes a hand like a foot.

JONATHAN SWIFT

There is something to me repugnant at any time in written hand. The test never seems determinate. Print settles it.

CHARLES LAMB

You must not suppose, because I am a man of letters, that I never tried to earn an honest living.

GEORGE BERNARD SHAW

Practically everybody in New York has half a mind to write a book—and does.

GROUCHO MARX

A writer never relaxes. Even his love affairs are a kind of research—but they're not tax deductible.

GENE FOWLER

A writer is always admired most, not by those who have read, but by

those who have merely heard of
him.

H. L. MENCKEN

What no wife of a writer can ever
understand is that a writer is working when he's staring out the window.

BURTON RASCOE

An author is a fool who, not content with boring his contemporaries,
insists on boring future generations.
BARON DE LA BRÈDE ET DE
MONTESQUIEU

Until he starts to sell a writer is a
bum to his family, a lazy lout to his
friends, and a self-deluding parasite
to his neighbors. When he becomes
known he is "one helluva neighbor"
to his neighbors, a genius to his
friends, and a favorite cousin to his
family. But none of them buy his
books.

CLIFFORD WELLES

[See also Author, Publishing,
Writing]

WRITING:

Unprovided with original learning, unformed in the habits of thinking, unskilled in the arts of composi-
tion, I resolved to write a book.

EDWARD GIBBON

Someday I hope to write a book

where the royalties will pay for the
copies I give away.

CLARENCE DARROW

It took me fifteen years to discover I had no talent for writing, but
I couldn't give it up, because by that
time I was too famous.

ROBERT BENCHLEY

With sixty staring me in the face,
I have developed inflammation of
the sentence structure and definite
hardening of the paragraphs.

JAMES THURBER

There are three things that every
man fancies he can do: farm a small
property, drive a gig, and write an
article for a review.

SYDNEY SMITH

When I had got my notes all written out I thought I'd polish it off in
two summers, but it took me twenty-
seven years.

ARNOLD TOYNBEE

Amuse the reader at the same
time that you instruct him.

HORACE

I wouldn't write any kind of book
without a contract and an advance.
You can't invest that amount of time
and effort without one.

HARRISON E. SALISBURY

You start with a general idea of
what you want. Beginning with one
subject, you read one book to give

you more ideas. The first thing you know you are going in all kinds of directions and wonder if it will ever come out right. Sometimes it does, sometimes it doesn't.

HARRISON E. SALISBURY

I have the conviction that excessive literary production is a social offense.

GEORGE ELIOT

In composing, as a general rule, run your pen through every other word you have written; you have no idea what vigor it will give your style.

SYDNEY SMITH

A dirty book gathers no dust.

MODERN AMERICANA

If you want to get rich from writing, write the sort of thing that's read by persons who move their lips when they're reading to themselves.

DON MARQUIS

The biggest obstacle to professional writing today is the necessity for changing a typewriter ribbon.

ROBERT BENCHLEY

People do not deserve good writing, they are so pleased with bad.

RALPH WALDO EMERSON

Your manuscript is both good and original; but the part that is good is not original, and the part that is original is not good.

SAMUEL JOHNSON

Only a mediocre writer is always at his best.

SOMERSET MAUGHAM

If all novels told the truth, there would never be a happy ending.

CLIFFORD WELLES

Write out of love, write out of instinct, write out of reason. But always for money.

LOUIS UNTERMEYER

I couldn't write the things they publish now, with no beginning and no end, and a little incest in the middle.

IRVIN S. COBB

As to the adjective, when in doubt, strike it out.

MARK TWAIN

How I wish I had never learned to write.

NERO

[See also Writer]

WRONG:

What youths, editors, and corporate vice-presidents are sure they are not.

FRANK DANE

The best way to convince a fool he is wrong is to let him have his way.

JOSH BILLINGS

It is better to suffer wrong than to do it, and happier to be sometimes cheated than not to trust.

SAMUEL JOHNSON

The wrong way always seems the more reasonable.

GEORGE MOORE

YESTERDAY:

Oh, call back yesterday; bid time return.

WILLIAM SHAKESPEARE

Think then you are To-day what Yesterday you were—Tomorrow you shall not be less.

OMAR KHAYYÁM

I do today from memory what yesterday I did in passion.

GERALD BARZAN

[*See also* History, Past]

YOUTH:

Even the youngest of us may be wrong sometimes.

GEORGE BERNARD SHAW

O ye, who teach the ingenious youth of nations,
Holland, France, England, Germany or Spain,
I pray ye flog them upon all occasions,

It mends their morals, never mind the pain.

LORD BYRON

You're only young once, and if you work it right, once is enough.

JOE E. LEWIS

Young men have a passion for regarding their elders as senile.

HENRY ADAMS

Except for an occasional heart attack I feel as young as I ever did.

ROBERT BENCHLEY

Young men think old men are fools; but old men know young men are fools.

GEORGE CHAPMAN

But I was one-and-twenty,
No use to talk to me.

ALFRED EDWARD HOUSMAN

Youth is always too serious, and just now it is too serious about frivolity.

G. K. CHESTERTON

To me it seems that youth is like spring, an over-praised season.

SAMUEL BUTLER

I am not young enough to know everything.

JAMES M. BARRIE

Nature makes boys and girls lovely to look upon so they can be

285

ZOO

tolerated until they acquire some sense.

WILLIAM LYON PHELPS

Youth is the best time to be rich; and the best time to be poor.

EURIPIDES

Youth is a wonderful thing. What a crime to waste it on children.

GEORGE BERNARD SHAW

The youth of a nation are the masters of posterity.

BENJAMIN DISRAELI

A youth with his first cigar makes himself sick; a youth with his first girl makes everybody sick.

MARY LITTLE

The old believe everything; the middle-aged suspect everything; the young know everything.

OSCAR WILDE

Yet ah, that Spring should vanish with the Rose!
That Youth's sweet-scented manuscript should close!

OMAR KHAYYÁM

[See also Age, Wisdom]

ZEAL:

A certain nervous disorder afflicting the young and inexperienced.

AMBROSE BIERCE

Had I but served my God with half the zeal
I served my king, He would not in mine age
Have left me naked to mine enemies.

WILLIAM SHAKESPEARE

My zeal hath consumed me.

THE BIBLE

It is false zeal to keep truth while wounding charity.

BLAISE PASCAL

[See also Moderation]

ZOO:

A zoo is a place of refuge where savage beasts are protected from people.

GERALD F. LIEBERMAN